P9-DWV-718

D0020271

PRAISE FOR *RO*

"After reading [*Role Models*], you feel that [Waters's] fascination with those on society's periphery is accompanied by real empathy, a generosity of spirit that most of us cannot fathom ... The book is surprisingly charming and riotously funny."

—ANDREA APPLETON, *Baltimore City Paper*

"*Role Models* is charming and chatty; ... it also reveals the making of a unique American artist through his influences. When [Waters] calls for people to make him a cult leader of filth—having left trash behind for becoming too acceptable—it's hard for any outsider not to want to follow along."

—CAROLYN KELLOGG, *Los Angeles Times*

"Waters is a greater National Treasure than 90 percent of the people who are given 'Kennedy Center Honors' each December. Unlike those gray eminences of the show-business establishment, Waters doesn't kowtow to the received wisdom, he flips it the bird ... [Waters] has the ability to show humanity at its most ridiculous and make that funny rather than repellent. To quote his linear ancestor W. C. Fields: It's a gift."

—JONATHAN YARDLEY, *The Washington Post Book World*

"How did somebody from a quiet Baltimore neighborhood grow up to become the outlandish, brilliant, and insane John Waters? Two words: *Johnny Mathis.*"

—AUGUSTEN BURROUGHS, author of *Running with Scissors*

"A delirious descent into Waters World, *Role Models* is a true-life confessional from one of America's greatest ironists. John Waters is a man always ready and willing to say the unsayable. He is the dark mirror of contemporary culture. From haute couture to low culture, from literary outsiders to lapsed actors, he delivers razor-sharp pen portraits of the women and men who have perverted and inspired him by turns. And yet Waters's warped imagination is always humane, his judgments insightful. *Role Models* is as much a philosophical manifesto as it is an utterly hilarious and shamelessly entertaining read."

—PHILIP HOARE, author of *The Whale*

"Waters may not be a gloater, but there is a delightful lunatic glee that pulses through the book. It combusts in the final chapter, titled 'Cult Leader,' which exhorts readers to rise up against the 'tyranny of good taste,' wear their belts off-center, and infiltrate living crèches. Happily, for all the reflective and tender moments, Waters never suppresses his radiant pervert self."

—LIZ BROWN, *Bookforum*

"Glory-hole-lujah. Amen."

—HEATHER McCORMACK, *Library Journal*

"[*Role Models* is] an impressive, heartfelt collection by a true American iconoclast."   —*Kirkus Reviews* (starred review)

"This man who never sought respectability may have become the most affectionate and radical humanist in American letters."

—CHARLES TAYLOR, *Barnes & Noble Review*

© Greg Gorman

JOHN WATERS

ROLE MODELS

John Waters is an American filmmaker, actor, writer, and visual artist best known for his cult films, including *Hairspray*, *Pink Flamingos*, and *Cecil B. DeMented*. He lives in Baltimore, Maryland.

ALSO BY JOHN WATERS

Crackpot: The Obsessions of John Waters
Shock Value: A Tasteful Book About Bad Taste
Art—A Sex Book (with Bruce Hainley)
Pink Flamingos and Other Filth
Hairspray, Female Trouble, and Multiple Maniacs

ROLE MODELS

John Waters

Role Models

FARRAR, STRAUS AND GIROUX
NEW YORK

FARRAR, STRAUS AND GIROUX
18 West 18th Street, New York 10011

Copyright © 2010 by John Waters
All rights reserved

Printed in the United States of America
Published in 2010 by Farrar, Straus and Giroux
First paperback edition, 2011

Some of these essays originally appeared, in slightly different form and with different titles, in the following publications and webzines: "The Kindness of Strangers" as the introduction to the New Directions reissue of Tennessee Williams's *Memoirs* (2006); "Leslie" in *The Huffington Post*; and "Little Richard, Happy at Last" in *Playboy*.

Illustration credits: pp. 2, 182, and 200: photographs by John Waters; pp. 34, 44, and 272: from the collection of John Waters; p. 94: photograph by Vincent Fecteau; p. 128: photographs courtesy of Eileen Murche; p. 240: courtesy of Peres Projects; pp. 248, 249, 250, and 251: courtesy of Cy Twombly; p. 162: photograph by Mathew Bainbridge.

The Library of Congress has cataloged the hardcover edition as follows:
Waters, John, 1946–
    Role models / John Waters. — 1st ed.
    p.   cm.
    ISBN 978-0-374-25147-5 (alk. paper)
    1. Waters, John, 1946—Sources.   2. Influence (Literary, artistic, etc.).   3. Motion picture producers and directors—United States—Biography.   4. Screenwriters—United States—Biography.   5. Artists—United States—Biography.   I. Title.

PN1998.3.W38A3   2010
791.43'0233'092—dc22
[B]

                                                    2009042211

Paperback ISBN: 978-0-374-53286-4

Designed by Abby Kagan

www.fsgbooks.com

10

Frontispiece: The young author, 1961, courtesy of Patricia Waters

IN MEMORY OF VAN SMITH

(AUGUST 17, 1945—DECEMBER 5, 2006)

CONTENTS

ILLUSTRATIONS

JOHNNY AND ME

I wish I were Johnny Mathis. So mainstream. So popular. So unironic, yet perfect. Effortlessly boyish at over seventy years old, with a voice that still makes all of America want to make out. Heavenly, warm. Yes, I'll say it out loud—wonderful, wonderful. I saw Johnny Mathis in real life once, but he didn't see me—the best way to glimpse a role model. I had just pulled into the parking lot of Tower Video, off Sunset Boulevard in West Hollywood, with my good friend the photographer Greg Gorman. "Oh my God," said Greg, who is never impressed with celebrities, having shot them for billboards, movie posters, and album covers for thirty years, "don't look up, but Johnny Mathis just pulled in next to us." And there he was. In a sports car with the top down and a cashmere sweater tied around his shoulders. Good Lord. Johnny Mathis himself. The legend you never hear about, never see on the red carpet, never read about in gossip columns. Highly successful but nearly invisible. Smooth for ever and ever. As my favorite girl group of the sixties, the Shangri-Las, might have said about how I felt that day, "That's called impressed."

I never got over seeing Johnny Mathis in the parking lot. I'd secretly think about those thirty seconds at odd moments, like when the Acela train between Baltimore and New York would have to stop so inspectors could examine the corpses of suicide victims who threw themselves on the tracks. Or waiting in line at the Department of Motor Vehicles to renew my driver's license. Or sometimes right when I woke up—bam!—for no apparent reason, there he'd be: Johnny Mathis in that car with that sweater. Is it because Johnny Mathis is the polar opposite of me? A man whose *Greatest Hits* album was on the *Billboard* charts for 490 consecutive weeks. Versus me, a cult filmmaker whose core audience, no matter how much I've crossed over, consists of minorities who can't even fit in with their *own* minorities.

Do we secretly idolize our imagined opposites, yearning to become the role models for others we know we could never be for ourselves? When I taught filmmaking at a jail in Maryland in the 1980s, I always got my class to loosen up by doing improv and asking them to play "the exact opposite of yourself." If Freud described psychotherapy as "transforming hysterical misery into common unhappiness," I figured this might be a revealing way to rehabilitate. Bikers wound up playing girls, blacks chose characters with wealth and power, whites became docile maids or butlers, and child molesters became tough guys. But did I need my own prison counselor because I kept reliving that Johnny Mathis "opposite" moment? Why would the mere sight of a performer so far outside the standard boundaries of my hero worship launch me into such a blissful, rapturous obsession? At this point in my career, could my misplaced idolatry become a road map to ruin? Was I in danger of becoming a

Johnny Mathis stalker? I figured I'd better try to meet him in a more legitimate way before I got in trouble.

It's not like I wanted to be Johnny Mathis as a kid. His music, however, *did* become the sound track for the end of my 1950s childhood innocence. Our thirteen-year-old babysitter, who lived across the street at the time, had a record hop, and because she wanted to borrow my 45 rpm records to play, she had to invite eleven-year-old me. Little did I imagine that the gathering would turn into a red-hot "necking" party! While her innocent parents (who were good friends of my mom and dad) were upstairs happily laying out refreshments, all the kids downstairs were grinding and French-kissing to Johnny Mathis's music, and I knew then that not only did I want to be a teenager— I wanted to be an *exaggeration* of a teenager.

But I had always felt nuts, not romantic. Too angry to be smooth. Too happily guilty to yearn for virtue. Before Johnny Mathis, Clarabell, the psychotic clown on *The Howdy Doody Show*, whose makeup later inspired Divine's, had been my role model. The man I saw in person in the early fifties at the height of *Howdy Doody*'s success, when I was just a child and my parents somehow got me on the show. The scary freak I watched from the Peanut Gallery who never spoke but communicated his hostility by honking twin bicycle horns or by squirting you in the face from a seltzer bottle. The same TV character parents complained about for getting their children too "excited" before dinner. Excited? I was apoplectic. Especially every time Clarabell got near Princess Summerfall Winterspring, the goody-goody but sexy Indian maiden nonpuppet star of the show. If only he could have burst out of his glorious "muteness" to say her name out loud—the best name ever! The only other name I wish were mine today (except for Lord or Lady Haw-Haw, which I can't use because they were Nazis). Matter of fact, readers of this book, if you see me on the street and call me Prince Summerfall Winterspring in a nice tone of voice, I will probably respond.

I followed the careers of Clarabell and Princess Summerfall Winterspring forever, hoping that I, too, could someday have an extreme career in show business. I mourned the fact that I was unable (and uninvited) to attend the 1957 funeral of Judy Tyler (the actress who played Summerfall Winterspring) after her tragic death in a car accident right before the release of the Elvis movie she had costarred in, *Jailhouse Rock*. All "Doodyville" was there that day in Hartsdale, New York, and I bet Bob Keeshan was sobbing out loud. Yes, that's the real name of the first Clarabell the Clown, who went even further in television career lunacy and became Captain Kangaroo for thirty years after. Imagine his life, his schizophrenia. Am I Clarabell? Or Captain Kangaroo? Why are those children staring at me? Who am I? Claraboo? Captain Kangabell? God, what a life! What a career! Bob Keeshan, I wish I were you, too!

But would Johnny Mathis understand all this? Luckily we both were represented by the same talent agency, so I called Steve Rabineau, my film agent, and he called Johnny's people, who suggested I write a letter to Mr. Mathis explaining why I wanted to talk to him. Hmmmmmm . . . "explain." Explain what? A role model? Someone who has led a life even more explosive than mine, a person whose exaggerated fame or notoriety has made him or her somehow smarter and more glamorous than I could ever be? A personality frozen in an unruly, blown-out-of-proportion position in society who earns my unmitigated respect for his or her other turbulent, ferocious will to survive frightening success or failure? Maybe Johnny Mathis *could* understand, but I'd better leave out the Princess Summerfall Winterspring part of my explanation. So I wrote a personal letter telling Mr. Mathis who I was (I still don't know if he had ever heard of me) and described the Tower Video parking lot imagery and how this book was an attempt to pay tribute to "amazing people who have inspired me." I added that I was not coming to him with any agenda (sexual, racial, ageist, or political), and I really wasn't. My Johnny Mathis lunacy was way beyond that anyway, but I tried to sound . . . well, reasonable.

Then I was told to get in touch with his legal representation, which, naturally, scared me, but at least I had passed the first audition. The lawyer was lovely on the phone and just what I expected; old-school Hollywood, incredibly loyal and protective of Mr. Mathis's career and, rightfully, suspicious of me. I explained my book idea as normally as I could and he asked if Mr. Mathis could approve what I wrote. I explained the journalistic mortal sin of his request and he said he'd get back to me. Lo and behold, a few days later an assistant to Mr. Mathis called to set up the meeting at 9:30 a.m. at Mr. Mathis's West Hollywood home. I felt like Prince Summerfall Winterspring. Until the night before, when I got an e-mail casually mentioning that the lawyer would also be present. Great.

Hoping for the best anyway, and arriving on time at Mr. Mathis's lovely, unostentatious thirty-year home overlooking Los Angeles from the hills above Sunset Boulevard, I ring the bell. Here goes. "The King of Puke" meets "Mr. Wild Is the Wind." Opposites attract? We'll just see. An Asian housekeeper who has clearly worked here for decades lets me in and leads me to a cozy corner off the living room, and there he is with a handsome smile and an outstretched hand to shake. *And* the lawyer. "What? Did you Google me?" I joke, and the lawyer is caught off guard by my question but then laughs and admits, "Yes." I set up my tape recorder and the goddamn thing doesn't work even though I had tested it that morning! I'm sweating, losing my cool. Mr. Mathis offers me his own recorder, but I give up and take notes. Johnny is called John by all his real friends, I begin to notice (I'm Johnny only to two people—my mother, who can never switch from my childhood name, and a certain friend in prison you'll meet in a later chapter). Mr. Mathis is dressed just as I had hoped—all in white: white shirt, unbuttoned three buttons to reveal hairless gym-bodied chest; white pants; white thick socks, no shoes. Just like Johnny Mathis should look, like he always has. Effortless. Twenty or seventy. Johnny Mathis is beyond fame itself—something I will never be.

We start off at the beginning—how he was "singing in white bars in the Tenderloin section of San Francisco" with his parents' permission, "doing great" right from the beginning and "feeling no racial prejudice." "Never?" I ask. "Not really," he says with understated charm. Amazingly, my own mother said to me after hearing I was going to meet him, "Johnny Mathis is black?" How could a beautiful black man who sang romantic love songs that white girls responded to not feel racism in the fifties? Maybe he's beyond race, too.

If Johnny Mathis has any regrets, it's that he listened to an early manager who advised him, "Don't mention jazz. There's no money in it." "I wanted to be Miles Davis," Johnny remembers. "Jazz legends. That's what I wanted to be. They were artists." He was "embarrassed around jazz people to be known for romantic music," "trivialized." When I mention that Johnny was a millionaire at twenty years old, he almost doesn't hear. "That had nothing to do with what I was about. I never wanted to be anything but a good singer."

God, who I wanted to be when I was six years old was Dagmar, the 5'11" supposed dumb blonde I watched on early black-and-white TV. Too young to stay up to see her on the show that came on at eleven p.m. and made her famous, *Broadway Open House*, hosted by Jerry Lester, I had to make do by catching her guest appearances on *The Milton Berle Show*. Predating Cher or Madonna, Dagmar was the first single-name bombshell, and I always knew she was smart. She hung out with Bob Hope and Joey Bishop when I was just an obsessive toddler in Lutherville, Maryland, and I daydreamed about her all day in grade school, hoping to become a caricature of myself the way she was. But for a child to form a fan club for his idol, he needs more than himself in the audience, and I could never find another kid who knew who she was. I finally met Dagmar herself, the older version, when I tracked her down in 1979. She was long retired and living as a guest on an amazingly plush horse farm in Southbury, Connecticut, and I tried to talk her into playing Divine's character's mother in *Polyester*. This great lady may have turned me down, but joked when she heard I'd come from Provincetown, Massachusetts, that beautiful beach town on the very tip of Cape Cod so popular with gay people: "Oh, yes, I was there; I was queen of the fairies." Would Johnny Mathis understand?

Of course he would. Like myself, Johnny realized some of his heroes "would be odd." He "loved" Liberace because "he used his money." I bring up another of my role models, the hypochondriac and germ-freak pianist Glenn Gould. "Oh, yes," Johnny recalls, "when I shook his hand he gasped, 'Are you trying to kill me?!' " He knew them all—every single deliriously original musician whose vocation seemed to be "going to extremes." "Johnnie Ray?" I dare mention, only hoping Mr. Mathis had met the white guy heartthrob singer who was deaf, handsome, skinny, gay, and immensely popular for a short time right before rock and roll was invented. The sexy one who wore a giant hearing aid and was called "the first great white soul singer." The crooner Frank Sinatra hated, who cried, sobbed, and made emotional breakdowns part of his song delivery. The guy who survived two "morals charges," arrested once in a bar and once in a men's room, and later had an intense love affair with the married, famously chinless crime columnist Dorothy Kilgallen. "Oh, yes," Johnny Mathis easily responds. "I visited him when he was dying [of liver failure]." "The Twelfth of Never," I silently title this beautiful imaginary hospital paparazzi photograph in my mind before realizing, hell, no—the two of them together in this situation could only be "The Thirteenth of Always."

Johnny Mathis's role model? "Lena Horne," he chuckles. "Some reviewer even said I stole everything but her gown." I know what he means; I have been copying Margaret Hamilton my whole life, and I am proud to admit it. The Wicked Witch of the West, the *jolie laide* heroine of every bad little boy's and girl's dream of notoriety and style, whose twelve minutes of screen time in *The Wizard of Oz* can never be topped. And her outfit! The Wicked Witch inspired my lifetime obsession with wearing weirdly striped socks (Tim Burton does, too). My God, this great character actress even worked later with William Castle in *13 Ghosts*, and appeared in *Gunsmoke*, *The Addams Family*, and *The Paul Lynde Halloween Special*! I never did get to meet Margaret Hamilton before she died, but she did send me a personally autographed Wicked Witch of the West photo, and the monogram "WWW" followed her signature. What an iconic monogram! Did her towels have "WWW" on them? Her sheets? If only I could have visited her at her summer house on a private island in Southport, off Boothbay Harbor, in Maine. So what if it didn't have electricity or phone service? More quality time with a *real* movie star!

I ask Johnny if he's a recluse, since I never see him at award ceremonies, parties, or nightclubs. "No, I'm not a recluse," he explains, "but I don't like social functions and I don't feel that newsworthy. It gets in the way." "Of what?" I wonder, remembering the art dealer Matthew Marks once saying to me, "You have the best kind of fame: only the people you'd want to recognize you do." What does Johnny hate about celebrity? Free travel? Free clothes? Gift bags? I never mind. I fondly recall whispering to Jeanne Moreau, "More free food!" every time we had to attend black-tie dinners when we served together on the jury of the Cannes Film Festival in 1995. Johnny Mathis admits he does go to private events, and we both recall happily those wonderfully insane dinner party salons that the late Roddy Mc-Dowell used to give for the most bizarrely mixed guest list ever. "He included everybody," Johnny says, laughing, and boy, did he! I remember being lucky enough to be invited there and meeting George Axelrod, and how happy I was to gush to him in person about the brilliance of his screenplay and his direction of the movie *Lord Love a Duck*. Then I turned around and there was an elderly couple dressed in full fringed cowboy outfits with holsters and guns. "Oh, John," Roddy asked casually, "do you know Roy Rogers and Dale Evans?" "No," I stammered, almost speechless. How could I? I live in Baltimore!

Johnny Mathis understands a lot about me. I can tell. He's a gentleman who lives alone and he's from another era. "Who wants people to know everything?" Johnny asks shyly. "A lot of life is putting things in perspective." How right he is! One thing I learned early was that if you're in any way famous, guaranteeing yourself a private life is very important for your mental health. Fans can't be friends; neither can the press. And even if certain critics have been supportive, there will always be a future project of yours they might *not* like, so palling around with reviewers can be awkward. The ultimate level of celebrity accomplishment is convincing the press and public that they know everything about your personal life without really revealing anything. Mr. Mathis only once responded to sexual preference questions from the press, in 1982, and he answered in a lovely way. His preference was "a way of life one's grown accustomed to." I had promised "no agenda" but I bring up this quote and compliment him on it, and he smiles and says, "It's a normal everyday part of my life."

I've always been pretty up-front about my sexuality (even though Mink Stole today says she didn't even know I was gay for a long time), but I understand Hollywood royalty's reticence about revealing anything personal, hetero *or* homo. Gus Van Sant and I always joke about the press saying we are "openly" gay. What's that supposed to mean? It sounds like we're arriving at a premiere shrieking, "Hey, Mary! Got any Judy Garland records?" When I read about any celebrity baring his or her soul to a journalist, I just figure the star doesn't have anyone else to confide in. "As the public started to mature," Johnny explains unapologetically, "I had to wait until the rest of the world caught up to celebrities being human beings." His fans? "Some of them," he chuckles kindly, "think they are Mrs. Johnny Mathis."

What do I know about *anyone's* sexuality? I always thought, and still do, that Tom Cruise is straight. When John Travolta got cast as Edna in the Hollywood remake of my film and the Broadway musical *Hairspray*, one wrongheaded gay militant reporter, an army of one, actually protested that John Travolta was a Scientologist and that this "religion" tried to "cure" people of their gay sexual preference. Well, first, if John Travolta were in any way homophobic, he'd be dead after filming that movie. Dancing in drag, dealing with the demands of the almost exclusively gay creative team—he would have had a heart attack. Implying Travolta was gay seemed wrong to me—he had a lovely wife and children, and how does the journalist *know* whom he sleeps with? And what do I care about the cast's religious beliefs, as long as they don't try to proselytize? Travolta never mentioned Scientology to me. And when a friend included in his Christmas card the funniest line Hallmark could never come up with—"A generous donation has been made in your name to the Church of Scientology"—I didn't repeat the joke to John Travolta, either. Am I supposed to police the religions of everyone who is cast in future projects? Should I never consider Nicole Kidman (whom I love as an actress) because she's a Catholic? I mean, *there's* a religion where I can show you homophobic dogma, but I've never actually seen proof that Scientology says being gay is wrong. And even if Travolta *did* experiment sexually sometime in his life, what business is it of mine? Let's even say for the sake of argument that Scientology (even though the church denies this) does claim it *can* make gay people turn straight. If someone is *that* miserable being gay, why would my team want them? It's not a numbers game! "Go on," I'd tell them, "let Scientology have you! Go back in the closet where you're happy—we don't want you anyway!"

As a kid, I'm not sure the term "closet" had been invented, and who knows if my other hero in entertainment at the time felt trapped? His name was Cyril Ritchard and he played Captain Hook in that Mary Martin–starring version of *Peter Pan*, first produced on Broadway and then filmed for television and broadcast in the fifties. If Margaret Hamilton was my showbiz "mother" in my ten-year-old mind, then Cyril Ritchard was definitely my "father." All I knew then was that I was a budding clotheshorse, and *here* was a character who knew how to dress— a real fashion plate! I didn't yet understand the word "fop," but

I sure wanted to be one, even if I had to cut off one of my own hands to look this dashing. As an adult I rewatched Cyril's villainous performance and was immediately struck by the character's jeweled fingers, ruffled shirt, and tight pants. Captain Hook now was over the top in a way that seemed much closer to *The Boys in the Band* than Never-Never Land, but he was still my favorite hambone actor and no learned gaydar could ever take that away from me.

Then again, maybe I'm wrong about his sexual preference. Despite being labeled "queer as a coot" by Noël Coward, Cyril was, as described by associates, happily married to Madge Elliott for thirty-five years, and together they were glamorous stars of the popular stage, first in Australia and then in London. Cyril claimed they were "never separated" from the day they were married until she died of bone cancer in 1955, while he was playing Captain Hook on the Broadway stage. They sure seemed to love each other no matter what they did or didn't do in bed. Maybe they just didn't care for sex. It *is* messy. Or maybe they agreed with the writer Paul Bowles, who supposedly tried sex with a man *and* a woman and found both unappealing. Cyril remained a man of contradictions and theatrical affectations, a "devout" Catholic who loved his poodle, named Trim, and once commented, "My background may be common but I have specialized in elegance." He's buried in Saint Mary's Cemetery in Ridgefield, Connecticut. I went there recently to pay my respects, and even though I was thrilled to see that his headstone actually says "Captain Hook," I hope mine doesn't end up reading "The Duke of Dirt."

Johnny Mathis is impossible to parody today; no one makes

fun of him. No drag kings ever "do" Johnny Mathis. "I saw a kid on the Johnny Carson show once who did an impersonation of me," he vaguely remembers. Whenever they have John Waters look-alike contests at the colleges where I appear, lesbians win! But what about his music? Am I serious when I say I really love it? Mr. Mathis invites me to his touring Christmas show, and I go when he plays Baltimore at the Lyric Opera House. I have a Christmas compilation album out that includes everything from the horrifying "Happy Birthday Jesus" by Little Cindy to the anticapitalist "Here Comes Fatty Clause (With His Sack of Shit)." I also tour every year or so with a spoken-word Christmas show and thought, gee, both Johnny Mathis and I have Christmas programs; what would happen if we switched tours and did each other's acts? Imagine his audience's surprise at me singing "O Holy Night," and picture the shock of my audience at seeing Johnny come out and talk about how Santa Claus could be erotic if you were a "chubby chaser." Johnny and I are like drag queens on Halloween: if it's Christmas, we'll be working!

Johnny Mathis Christmas had no prepublicity in the Baltimore press, but all 2,564 seats were sold. His appeal is broad and wide, something I could never achieve and he can never escape. Was watching this concert torture, or was it perfect? I'm still trying to decide. The greeting-card-snow-scene backdrops couldn't be more middle-of-the-road, but, like the phony mug shot of myself wearing a Santa hat that I use as my stage setting, it is perfect for the intended audience. No one ever introduces Johnny Mathis. He just moseys onstage and starts singing as the thirty-five-piece orchestra plays his holiday cheer spectacularly. Wearing that same old winter-white look he was painted in by Ralph Cowan in 1969 for the cover of his album *Heavenly* (the painting still hangs in his living room), Johnny breaks into medley after medley of Christmas songs that are beyond the valley of normal. But God, the man can sing every bit as beautifully as when I first heard him on the radio fifty-three years ago. Believe me, this is no oldies-but-goodies act. When he finally sings "Chances Are," I admit my blood starts racing and I have to refrain from joining all the middle-aged-or-older ladies in the audience, many wearing festive holiday jogging suits or Christmas corsages, in sighing unashamedly and loudly. When Johnny really concentrates and does "It's Not for Me to Say," I am confused, ecstatic, awestruck, and oddly aroused, yet slightly embarrassed to think of his yuletide act in the same breath as mine.

But those same songs, over and over! Is singing "When Sunny Gets Blue" hellish for Johnny Mathis, I wonder? As he hears the first notes of "Gina" onstage and knows he must sing the exact same song for the umpteen-thousandth time, does he feel like I do every time a well-meaning fan asks, "Did Divine really eat dog shit?" *Is* there a new way to interpret either? "Of course doing old songs can be torture," Johnny says, laughing good-naturedly. His secret is that before you go onstage, "you have to learn to be the audience! That way it will always seem new."

"What perfect advice," agrees the other top role model from my deep dark past, Patty McCormack. The nine-year-old actress who played Rhoda Penmark, the murderous little blond pigtailed girl in the smocked dress in *The Bad Seed*, first in the 1954

Broadway stage play and then again at age eleven in the movie that became a classic. Patty McCormack has long been my obsession. I wanted to be feared like Rhoda when I was a child. I wanted to yell out the movie's ad campaign, "*The Bad Seed* is the Big Shocker!" to my clueless grade school classmates. When Leroy, the hateful janitor in the movie, tells little Rhoda she'll be electrocuted in "that little pink electric chair" they got "for little girls," I wanted to hop right in her lap as they strapped her in and then feel the sizzle *with* her. I was consumed by Patty McCormack's celluloid evil.

Meeting your idols is always a thrill (despite what you'll read in one chapter later in this book). When Patty McCormack and I finally got together last year for lunch at the Beverly Hills Hotel, I realized that, like Johnny Mathis, Patty McCormack knows a thing or two herself about the "torture" of a greatest hit. At one point in her career, "a sad time," she remembers, she got sick of reminiscing about her role in *The Bad Seed* to cult followers like myself. "I didn't encourage talking about it," she says. "If you don't have as good a dish on the shelf," she remembers thinking, "it makes you feel bad about yourself." "But most actresses don't get even *one* role that is remembered like this," I argue, and she agrees. "Yes, that's what my nephew said. I embraced Rhoda way late in my career, really really late. It was healthy for me to do. I 'grew' her up."

Can a child become a healthy adult after playing such a famous murderess? Today Patty McCormack is a trim, beautiful, un-face-lifted sixty-eight-year-old woman with a twinkle in her eye about her villainous childhood creation. But did anybody explain to young Patty the psychology of Rhoda's character? "That horribly chilly place where we all can go?" as Patty remembers it now. "No," she admits with a shrug. "As long as it wasn't sex. *That* was bad," she adds, laughing. Like in today's Motion Picture Association of America rulings, murder was okay. "I'm a Catholic girl, so I used to worry I was 'an occasion of sin.' That was the expression if your clothes were too short and someone had lusting thoughts about you—you were 'an occasion of sin.'" I always worried as a little boy (and still do) that I *wasn't* "an occasion of sin." Will I ever, in my lifetime, be worthy of such a compliment, such a desired reverse state of grace?

Was it torture for a child to be a working actress, playing Rhoda through those years? "No," she laughs. "I remember having a lot of energy, big feelings, and doing the part gave me strength, courage. One thing I learned doing the play was that Rhoda was *always* right." "What about the endless bleaching of your hair so early in life?" I suggest. "It just seemed like that was part of the deal," says the still-blond Patty, hardly feeling traumatized by her early beauty treatments. "But," I argue, "the studio made you wear an outfit almost exactly like Rhoda's party dress to the Oscars the year you lost Best Supporting Actress to another (God, it never ends) role model, Dorothy Malone," the actress who always wore her collar turned up, on *and* off the screen. Dorothy Malone, the Douglas Sirk heroine who when I finally met her for lunch in Texas in the nineties *wasn't* wearing her collar up but shrugged and turned it up once I voiced my disappointment. They didn't make Dorothy Malone wear her *Written on the Wind* costume to the Oscars, did they?! Suppose the distributor made Charlize Theron go dressed as her real-life *Monster* character, the lesbian killer Aileen Wuornos! Imagine that acceptance speech!

Today, would the character Rhoda be put on Ritalin? When she reached puberty, would she have turned into a trench-coat-wearing, school-massacre-type teen? Patty doubts it. "Rhoda was clever, more tasteful than that. She wouldn't have gotten *caught!*" When I bring up the real Bad Seed, the child killer Mary Bell, Patty seems mildly interested but, like most Americans, has never heard of her. In 1968, when she was just eleven years old, Mary Bell strangled two small children in Newcastle, an industrial city 275 miles north of London. She pretended to help her victims' family search for the bodies and left notes saying "I murder so that I may come back" and "Fuck off. We murder. Watch out . . ." I started ranting to Patty about the two great books written about Mary Bell—*The Case of Mary Bell* (1972), which ended after her manslaughter conviction and life imprisonment sentence, and *Cries Unheard* (1998), which picks up after Mary was released from custody after serving twelve years. Both books are by the brilliant Gitta Sereny (who also expertly deconstructs Nazis in other books), and I am her full-time groupie, even though we have never met. Ms. Sereny always argued the exact opposite of the "bad seed" theory when the tabloid press wrote about Mary Bell. But what caused a real uproar was the fact that once Mary Bell was free and of legal age, she had a little girl of her own. And when Ms. Sereny's latest and very fair book about the case was released, detailing Mary's childhood abuse, which had not come out at the initial trial, the U.K. tabloids went into full attack mode. Mary Bell's then fourteen-year-old daughter didn't know her mother was the infamous child killer Mary Bell, and one can only imagine that frantic mother-daughter chat while journalists and news teams were banging on their front door. How exciting! My mother never told me *any* secrets about her past, much less involved me in any hysterical media event. Patty McCormack heard my whole tale of Mary Bell, but I doubt she ran home and ordered the books. If you once *were* Rhoda Penmark, I guess you've had enough of this type of thing.

Patty will stick up for Rhoda and protect her memory, but she's not loony about it the way I am. She thinks the many campy drag queen versions of *The Bad Seed* that have popped up on the West Coast are funny. I don't. I think the creators should be in movie prison. *The Bad Seed* isn't camp; it's terrific. Patty McCormack didn't save any props or costumes from the movie (not even the penmanship medal she killed for, her amazing dress, or those great sunglasses she wore), because no one had any idea the movie was destined to become a classic. I have copies of the original handwritten notes of William March, the author upon whose novel the play and the movie are based, which a wonderful fan sent me from the Special Collections Library of the University of Alabama, but Patty McCormack has no *Bad Seed* poster on her wall in her apartment. I lived with one in my living room for decades. For Patty, *The Bad Seed* was a role; for me, it was a lifestyle.

With a career as long as Johnny Mathis's (she's acted with everyone from Orson Welles to Fabian, been in movies as varied as *The Adventures of Huckleberry Finn* and *The Mini-Skirt Mob*, sung in a rock band and been in many television series, from *I Remember Mama* to *The Sopranos*), Patty has learned to be gracious and pretend to care about the same old questions from the same old fans idealizing a character she played fifty years ago. Johnny Mathis can still sing his greatest hits amazingly, but Patty can't exactly play Rhoda again.

Is there one possible undiscovered detail about being the bad seed that I can drag out of her? Is there one second of the film that hasn't been analyzed or deconstructed? I thought I was the only one who had noticed that bad "tooth continuity" in *The Bad Seed*. At some time during production of the movie, Patty had lost a baby tooth on the side of her mouth, and when they cut back and forth between the interior and exterior of the apartment building when Rhoda threatens Leroy the janitor, her tooth disappears and reappears. But no; Charles Busch (another Rhoda cultist) brings it up on the commentary track of *The Bad Seed* DVD when he interviews Patty. We *both* knew about that missing tooth (I even did an art piece about it), but Patty has no memory of it. Okay, how about her childhood obsession with the serial bank robber Willie Sutton, "the gentleman bandit" who wore a "trademark pencil-thin moustache"(!). "Oh, yes," she remembers enthusiastically, "he was big news. I drew newspapers about him when I was eight or nine years old." God! The Bad Seed's Willie Sutton artwork! There's a piece of memorabilia for the history books. But I can't be sure this is a real scoop. Patty can't remember if she ever talked to a journalist about this, but adds, "I can't really imagine that I'd volunteer that information to just anybody."

Suddenly Patty *does* remember something "new," something that hasn't ever come out about her in all the years of graciously grinning and bearing yet another *Bad Seed* interview. "I once took a college ethics class with Susan Atkins." WHAT?! The Bad Seed and the Manson Family in one classroom?!? "Yes," Patty reminisces, "I went back to college and took a class through Antioch College when they offered a psychology course in ethics and it met in prison, something about mixing together non-inmates with inmates." No one in the class, including the teacher, knew she was the Bad Seed but "everyone knew who Susan was. It was fun." "Fun"? It was crime showbiz history. Scary? Nothing could top the fact that Patty McCormack played Pat Nixon in Ron Howard's Oscar-nominated film *Frost/Nixon*. Now *that's* scary. She was wonderful in it, too.

Is it agony for all performers to have a "greatest hit"? Johnny Mathis has hundreds. I wish I had one. Even if it is the only one you *ever* had, like another singing role model, Bobby "Boris" Pickett. He crooned his Halloween novelty record, "The Monster Mash," for thirty-eight years without complaining and hit the *Billboard* Top 100 chart *three* separate times with the song he cowrote in a half hour and recorded in one take in 1962. Bobby sang the question that four generations have never been able to answer: "Whatever happened to the Transylvania Twist?" Mr. Pickett made me no longer care about the careers of Boris Karloff and Bela Lugosi, whose voices he totally appropriated. I only cared about the man who's been called "the Guy Lombardo of Halloween"—Mr. Bobby "Boris" Pickett himself.

Yes, Bobby "did the Mash." *I* "did the Mash," too, and many nights in the privacy of my own home I danced alone, or with real monsters I had brought home from my favorite redneck bars, and we blurted out, "It was a graveyard smash!" while sniffing poppers. I could play that song ten times in a row and never get sick of it. I've been listening to "The Monster Mash" forever and it *still* puts me in a good mood.

What would it be like to actually *be* Bobby "Boris" Pickett? To get up every day and know that you, and you alone, *were* "The Monster Mash"? Wouldn't it be easier than being Johnny Mathis on a bad day or me on a good one? To just concentrate on one thing—what freedom! Not having to "THIMK" (as the office sign parodying the IBM slogan "THINK" used to read in the late 1950s)? Not being forced to come up with new ideas every fucking month to keep your career new and reinvented? To just stop and do the same ridiculous and sublime song over and over again for eternity?

Some days when I'm touring colleges or rock-and-roll clubs with my spoken-word acts I feel like I *have* become Bobby "Boris" Pickett. Reading his obituaries, I get paranoid and wonder if I will end up like him, still "in demand" at Halloween and continuing to perform "The Monster Mash" at "small venues" until six months before he died. Think of that bittersweet last performance. It could happen in my career, but never in Johnny Mathis's. A psychiatrist once told me early in treatment, "Stop trying to make me like you," and what a sobering and welcome smack in the face that statement was. Yet somehow, every day of my life is *still* a campaign for popularity, or better yet, a crowded funeral. Johnny Mathis would never admit it, but at this point in show business he is basically beyond caring *what* you think of his act. Unlike Bobby "Boris" Pickett or myself, Johnny Mathis is incapable of trying too hard: the very definition of failure itself.

Backstage after his Christmas concert, Johnny sits alone in his dressing room until eventually a lone assistant comes in to check about packing up. All dressing rooms are basically the same, no matter how fancy or low-rent punk rock. A generic food spread, enough bottled water to quench the thirst of a small town in the desert, and the silent adrenaline drain of finishing your act. I've been in them. So has Bobby "Boris" Pickett. And so has Johnny Mathis. But he is as lovely and cheerful and seemingly unguarded as he was the day I visited his house. My friend Pat Moran, a rabid Johnny Mathis fan if there ever was one, had accompanied me to the show and later told me, "Meeting Johnny Mathis was as much fun as going with you to the Cannes Film Festival premieres of your movies," which even *I* thought might be pushing it. Pat was treated like royalty by Johnny and I struggled to think if there *ever* was any real dirt about Johnny Mathis. Remembering a favorite "scandal," which I *did* have the nerve to bring up to him when we first met, I had mentioned that I had read Johnny was in rehab for "champagne abuse." Talk about a perfect album concept! *Bubbly—Johnny Mathis Live from Rehab*. He didn't really comment then when I suggested the title, but I did see him chuckle.

For me, there is some "shock value" in the Johnny Mathis story. He's a Republican. A big one. Unashamed. I knew it but sort of hoped it wasn't true. When I snooped around Johnny's living room as he took an important phone call in the den, I saw nearby a proudly displayed photo of Johnny Mathis and President George H. W. Bush. I was . . . well, as the dialogue goes in one of my old films, "shocked silly but said nothing." Nixon's hardback book *Six Crises* is proudly displayed, too, and while I didn't open it, I'm sure it's personally dedicated and signed. I've also read that Nancy Reagan comes over and Johnny plays the piano and they sing together.

I don't mention any of this and neither does he. I'm always shocked when *anyone* says he or she is a Republican, but I've learned to not run screaming from the room. Imagine my surprise when I discovered one of my longtime assistants (and she does a *great* job of spreading my filth) is a Republican! *And* she was frontally nude in my last movie!! Tab Hunter is a Republican, too, and I remember how startled I was when he told me he was for Reagan when we were shooting *Polyester.* The same day he did a love scene with Divine! Members of my immediate family have certainly voted Republican, too. But not me: I'm a bleeding-heart liberal, a onetime Yippie sympathizer and full-time Weatherman hag. I'm one of the few who voted for Obama because he *was* a friend of Bill Ayers.

That doesn't mean I don't support the U.S. troops. When a major in the army wrote to me in 2004 and asked me to send a "care package" of swag from my films to our boys fighting in Iraq, I was stupefied at first and then patriotic. "I feel like Bob Hope," I told him after I gathered together Divine T-shirts, film posters, insane Christmas decorations I had designed, sound tracks, books, and DVDs of *Pink Flamingos* and *Female Trouble,* and sent them off to the U.S. embassy in Baghdad as I had been instructed to do. Imagine my happiness and delight when the major wrote to tell me the soldiers had received my package: "Right now, you are more popular in Iraq than Bob Hope. With the average age of a soldier being nineteen, they don't even know who Bob Hope is. They love the stuff you sent . . . When I was in Iraq all I got was baby wipes and Bibles . . . I understand the [plastic] dead cockroach in the Christmas ornament and the [ballpoint] pen with your picture in it were particular items they were fighting over." The major also got a call telling him "that when soldiers were watching one of John's movies, it was interrupted by a mortar attack." I was so moved I didn't know what to say. If I knew all the words of "The Star-Spangled Banner," I'd sing it all by myself. And mean it.

Who's the real extremist, Johnny Mathis or myself? I think of that great country-western hymn "If Jesus Came to Your House (I Wonder What You'd Do)." The follow-up lyrics are what make the song so unintentionally bizarre: "But when you saw him coming, would you meet him at the door?" or would you "hide some magazines and put the Bible where they'd been?" Suppose Johnny Mathis were snooping around *my* house; what would he see? Would he be appalled at the crucifix cigarette lighter on my living room coffee table? The brass knuckles I keep beside *my* bed just in case? The leather-bound Baader-Meinhof Gang wanted-poster kit, carried by all German police at the height of these hippie radicals' reign of terror, that I show proudly to all my visitors? Would he gasp at the Alberto García Alix photo *Nacho y Michelle* that hangs blatantly on the wall of my top floor? Would he understand the happiness of Michelle as she wraps her legs around her head, totally nude, showing her absolutely perfect vagina and asshole as Nacho, also nude except for a pair of white gym socks, holds her legs in porn arrogance and dignity? Johnny should; I mean, I tried with all my might when

27

Mr. Mathis proudly showed me some familiar-looking primitive paintings framed and displayed in his house that I assumed were by Grandma Moses. "No," he explained, unembarrassed, "they're copies . . . an antiques dealer arranged it." Shocked silly again, I *did* say something. "Isn't that illegal?" I stammered. "No," he answered casually and with a complete lack of guilt, just the way I would if Johnny had questioned why I had the artist Gregory Green install a full site-specific bomb-room art project on the top floor of my house. Mine's not illegal either, even though the pipe bombs and book bombs the fictitious mad bomber is planning on using to blow up Camden Yards, the beloved sports stadium in Baltimore, contain all the legal ingredients he'd need to do it except gunpowder.

Would the hideous books I keep displayed around my house stop Johnny in his tracks the way Nixon's did mine? *Jackal: The Complete Story of the Legendary Terrorist, Carlos the Jackal* isn't inscribed to me by the subject, but how I wish it were! Maybe I could write Carlos's recent jailhouse wife, the fifty-two-year-old Isabelle Coutant-Peyre, a wealthy left-wing lawyer who defended him in court and then married him in jail in 2001 after he was sentenced to life imprisonment for hijacking and other terrorist attacks in the seventies and eighties. If I chatted her up, do you think she might sneak my copy of the book inside prison and get him to autograph it? Would the noncollectible paperbacks *I Am a Teenage Dope Addict*, *I Was a Negro Playboy Bunny*, *Freak—Inside the Twisted World of Michael Jackson*, or *Roughhouse Rimmer*, which I have on my bedroom bookshelves, make Johnny Mathis run for the door? Or worse yet, the textbook a friend of mine gave me for Christmas that I keep in my guest bedroom, *Surgery of the Anus, Rectum and Colon?* I mean, who knows if Johnny would get the joke? I'm certainly accepting of *his* politics, so wouldn't he do the same for me? I admit I don't have any pictures of me with a president, but I do have a hideous set of wooden Bin Laden "nesting dolls" that a friend gave me after he had the nerve to smuggle them through U.S. Customs from Budapest not long after 9/11. When I'm feeling especially confrontational, I put them out to horrify myself (yes, you, too, can be your own role model). I imagine Johnny Mathis hates Bin Laden just as much as I do, but could Johnny agree Bin Laden had a better speechwriter than Bush? "Axis of Evil"? Come on. "A swimmer in the ocean does not fear the rain" is much more powerful propaganda. Poetic, even. And maybe no First Ladies have ever come over to my house to sing, but Patricia Hearst (my onetime demigoddess and now good friend) has been here countless times, and we once plotted her upcoming courtroom outfits and change of hair color when she was subpoenaed to be a witness against the S.L.A. in yet another bank robbery–related case. In my world, that's just as impressive.

I hate to think about it—what will happen when Johnny Mathis and I die? Who will guard my humble tawdry belongings? Will Johnny have to worry about the posthumous exploitation of his signature songs? Will his estate deny the commercial use of his hits the way Johnny Cash's did when Preparation H tried to license "Ring of Fire" for a hemorrhoid commercial? Or will they exploit his publishing copyright the way Elvis's heirs did when they allowed "Viva Las Vegas" to be resung as "Viva Viagra" for a TV commercial?

As far as I know, Johnny Mathis is single. Me, too. We've had great lives as single men. When I went to Elton John's sixtieth birthday party alone, I got seated right next to Yoko Ono! At another event—Joan Kennedy. Just think where they'd put Johnny in the VIP seating chart if he would ever show up stag at these kinds of events. Next to whom? Madame Chiang Kai-shek? I know she recently died at the age of 106 years and I never met her, but there's a conservative I'm fascinated by. She used to live with a huge staff in a giant apartment in the same building as a wonderful New York friend of mine, and every time I'd visit, I'd try to get the doormen to gossip ("Does Madame Chiang Kai-shek order takeout pu-pu platters?"), but they'd never talk.

Bobby "Boris" Pickett succumbed to leukemia in 2007 with his daughter by his side, but who will surround us single men on our deathbeds? I've long accepted the fact that unless some hideous disease gets me first and I have to make forced small talk with dedicated caregivers, I will die alone. And that's fine as long as I have my moustache drawn on straight. Hopefully it will be a quick death. Maybe onstage. I already have my final destination—the last piece of real estate—a condo burial spot I've picked out in the same graveyard as Divine's in Towson, Maryland. Pat Moran and her husband, Chuck Yeaton, bought plots right next to me, and Mink Stole and my great longtime friend the film critic Dennis Dermody are nearby. I'm trying to talk Mary Vivian Pearce and other comrades into joining us while there's still room. Cult Graveyard! Just like the People's Temple final resting spot in California. Come on down!

But how about Johnny Mathis: how does he want to go? Courageously private and elegantly unaccompanied, as I imagine? Alone but not lonely, like me? I guess it would have been "too familiar" to ask. I only met him twice.

THE KINDNESS OF
STRANGERS

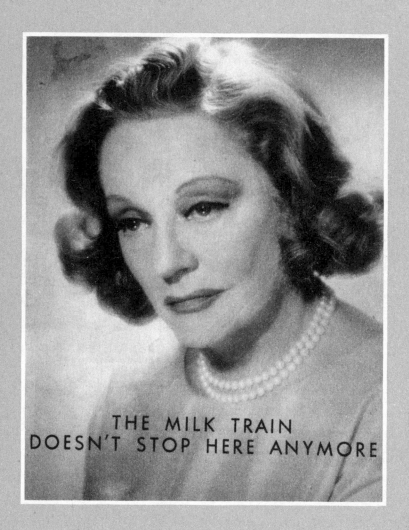

THE MILK TRAIN
DOESN'T STOP HERE ANYMORE

Tennessee Williams saved my life. As a twelve-year-old boy in suburban Baltimore, I would look up his name in the card catalog at the library, and it would read "See Librarian." I wanted these "See Librarian" books—and I wanted them now—but in the late fifties (and sadly even today), there was no way that a warped adolescent like myself could get his hands on one. I soon figured out that the "See Librarian" books were on a special shelf behind the counter, so when the kindly librarian was helping the "normal" kids with their book reports, I snuck behind the checkout desk and stole the first book I wanted on my own. *One Arm*, read the forbidden cover—a short-story collection by Tennessee Williams that I later found out had been only available in an expensive limited edition, sold under the counter in "special" bookshops before New Directions released the hardback version in 1954. And now it was mine.

Of course, I knew who Tennessee Williams was. He was a bad man because the nuns in Catholic Sunday school had told us we'd go to hell if we saw that movie he wrote, *Baby Doll*—the one with the great ad campaign, with Carroll Baker in the crib sucking her thumb, that made Cardinal Spellman have a nationwide hissy fit. I cut out that ad from *The Baltimore Sun* countless times and pasted it in my secret scrapbook. Hoping to one day own a dirty movie theater, I planned to show *Baby Doll* for the rest of my life, attracting the wrath of the Pope and causing a scandal in my parents' neighborhood.

Yes, Tennessee Williams was my childhood friend. I yearned for a bad influence and Tennessee was one in the best sense of the word: joyous, alarming, sexually confusing, and dangerously funny. I didn't quite "get" "Desire and the Black Masseur" when I read it in *One Arm*, but I hoped I would one day. The thing I did know after finishing the book was that I didn't have to listen to the lies the teachers told us about society's rules. I didn't have to worry about fitting in with a crowd I didn't want to hang out with in the first place. No, there was another world that Tennessee Williams knew about, a universe filled with special people who didn't want to be a part of this dreary conformist life that I was told I had to join.

Years later, Tennessee Williams saved my life again. The first time I went to a gay bar I was seventeen years old. It was called the Hut and it was in Washington, D.C. Some referred to it as the "Chicken Hut" and it was filled with early-1960s gay men in fluffy sweaters who cruised one another by calling table-to-table on phones provided by the bar. "I may be queer but I ain't this," I remember thinking. Still reading everything Tennessee Williams wrote, I knew he would understand my dilemma. Tennessee never seemed to fit the gay stereotype even then, and sexual ambiguity and turmoil were always made appealing and exciting in his work. "My type doesn't know who I am," he stated according to legend, and even if the sex lives of his characters weren't always healthy, they certainly seemed hearty. Tennessee Williams wasn't a gay cliché, so I had the confidence to try to not be one myself. Gay was not enough.

It *was* a good start, however. "I was late coming out but when I did it was with one hell of a bang," Tennessee wrote in 1972 in *Memoirs*, the same year my film *Pink Flamingos* was world-premiering in Baltimore. While I was just getting my first national notoriety, Tennessee was struggling to finish the final version of *The Milk Train Doesn't Stop Here Anymore* and horrifying theater purists by appearing in his new play *Small Craft Warnings* onstage and answering questions from the off-Broadway audience afterward to keep the show running. I never once thought this was unbecoming behavior on my hero's part and tried to follow his example by introducing, in person, my star Divine at midnight screenings of our filth epic. "I never had any choice but to be a writer," Tennessee remembered at the time, and he remained my patron saint. I followed his career like a hawk.

Maybe I like "bad" Tennessee Williams just as much as "good." Naturally his better-known classic plays are important to me but I must confess I'm drawn more to his supposedly "second-rate" work. Sorry, I also like Alvin and the Chipmunks better than the Beatles, Jayne Mansfield more than Marilyn Monroe, and, for me, the Three Stooges are way funnier than Charlie Chaplin. And while I knew there really was a streetcar that ran for years in New Orleans toward the neighborhood of Desire and that destination was printed above the exterior front windshield, I get more of a kick today riding the city *bus* named Desire (there really *is* one!) now that the streetcar itself has been retired.

In 2006 a boxed set of Tennessee Williams DVDs was released with all his best-reviewed movie titles: *Cat on a Hot Tin Roof, Sweet Bird of Youth, The Night of the Iguana, The Roman Spring of Mrs. Stone,* but I want the "bad" Tennessee Williams boxed set. *Boom!* (the greatest failed art film ever), directed by Joseph Losey and starring Elizabeth Taylor as Sissy Goforth, the richest woman in the world, and Richard Burton as "the Angel of Death"; *Last of the Mobile Hot Shots* (the film version of *The Seven Descents of Myrtle*); *This Property Is Condemned* with Natalie Wood; even *Noir et Blanc,* the 1986 Claire Devers film version of "Desire and the Black Masseur." "Bad" Tennessee Williams is better than most of the "good" contemporaries of Tennessee.

Was Tennessee Williams nuts to reveal everything about his personal life as he got older, or was he just high? Would his longtime agent, Audrey Wood (with whom he sadly broke in 1971), have put her foot down and stopped him from baring his soul in print if she had still been in charge of his career? "Since 1955 I have written usually under artificial stimulants," Tennessee admits in *Memoirs,* before adding, "aside from the true stimulant of my deep-rooted need to write." Did Tennessee ever really get over the 1960s, which he called "my stoned age"? "To know me is not to love me," he concedes, remembering the "seven year depression" he went into after the death by lung cancer of his longtime boyfriend, Frank Merlo. "I'm about to fall down," Tennessee announced to whoever was present in those years, "and almost nobody, nobody ever caught me."

When Tennessee suddenly is levelheaded, it can come as a surprise. "I have never doubted the existence of God," he writes soberly before later confessing a "disbelief in an after-existence." His guarded optimism always seems to save the day. "Mornings, I love you so much," he enthuses, celebrating "their triumph over night." Self-pity? Never. "I've had a wonderful and terrible life and wouldn't cry for myself: would you?" Hardly.

"Is it possible to be a dirty old man in your middle thirties?" Tennessee wonders, remembering his very active sex life— a kind of sex life that we are much more used to reading about in memoirs today than we were then. "Baby, this one's for you," he tells himself whenever Mr. Right Now appears, but he seems to be realistic about safe sex with strangers even before the on-slaught of AIDS, recommending that "penetration be avoided" with hustlers "as they are most probably all infected with clap in their ass." He may be the only Pulitzer Prize winner to write about A200, a product used to rid your body hair of crab lice. He has standards, too. "The way I feel tonight I could fuck a snake," a young sailor confides to Tennessee one night in a gay bar, "and I am proud to say that I told him to go snake-hunting," Tennessee writes.

Tennessee falls in love a lot, too. "I have a funny heart. Some-times it thrives on punishment," he concedes. What other mem-oir, besides his, has "loneliness" listed in the index? He also loved Provincetown just as much as I do. Not only did he meet two of his best boyfriends there (and Tallulah Bankhead), he wrote the line "I have always depended on the kindness of strangers" while holed up in a cabin before the summer season began. I hitchhiked to Provincetown in 1964 just because somebody told me, "It's a weird place," and God, were they right. A very gay place, too, but a different kind of gay. "I may be queer, but I *am* this," I remember thinking. I've gone back to Province-town for forty-six summers and every time I pass Captain Jack's Wharf or the "little bar" at the A-House, two places Tennessee got lucky in love, I mentally genuflect in respect.

Tennessee knew how to have fun with fame, too, and it seems he met many of my past role models. Jean Marais, James Purdy, Yukio Mishima. So what if Jean-Paul Sartre once stood Tennes-see up—I bet Sartre was a bum date anyway. Tennessee helped William Inge, the great playwright who lived in Tennessee's shadow, through alcoholism (the blind leading the blind?) and tried to understand the "folie de grandeur" of his best friend Lady Maria St. Just, one of the most difficult women who ever lived. Even Truman Capote was written about sympathetically by Tennessee. But unlike Truman, Tennessee never took the up-per class seriously. He hung around with street queens in New Orleans and prostitutes in Key West, and later in life, the War-hol superstar Candy Darling became a best friend. He isolated himself far away from New York and Los Angeles to write, and whenever he panicked, travel seemed to be the answer. "My place in society," Tennessee remembers, "then and possibly al-ways since, has been bohemia."

Suppose Tennessee Williams had lived? What if he hadn't choked on that prescription drug bottle cap that he supposedly used as a launching pad for his meds? Would he have had a sec-ond wind in his career like Edward Albee? Or would he have despaired and crumbled further when the AIDS epidemic hit and wiped out many of his new younger friends? Surely he would be appalled at the end of "trade" as he knew it, but would he be like some of the older gay men I see in onetime hustler bars in Baltimore now, who wait for these tough guys even knowing they will never come? Would Tennessee have teamed up with Paul Morrissey? "I would like him to make a film of one of my short stories," Tennessee had written, and who knows— maybe these two mavericks could have reinvented each other as a pair in the same way Douglas Sirk and Fassbinder did. Most important, could Tennessee have ever really hit "bottom" and gotten sober once and for all? On the wagon, would he have been able to continue to think up the best titles in the history of theater the way he always had? Even with all the substance abuse, Tennessee seemed to age well and remained cheerfully handsome, but if he had reached his late seventies, would he have ruined it all by getting a face-lift? Could anyone have saved Tennessee? Critics? Fans? Tricks? We, his readers? One thing is for sure: flattery would have gotten us nowhere. "When people have spoken to me of 'genius,'" he writes with a wink, "I have felt an inside pocket to make sure my wallet's still there."

I never met Tennessee Williams, but I saw him once at the Pier House restaurant in Key West, surrounded by admirers, looking a little woozy, and decided maybe this wasn't the time for us to be introduced. Nobody has to meet Tennessee Williams; all you have to do is reread his work. Listening to what he has to say could save your life, too.

LESLIE

I have a really good friend who was convicted of killing two innocent people when she was nineteen years old on a horrible night of 1969 cult madness. Her name is Leslie Van Houten and I think you would like her as much as I do. She was one of those notorious "Manson girls" who shaved their heads, carved X's in their foreheads, and laughed, joked, and sang their way through the courthouse straight to death row without the slightest trace of remorse forty years ago. Leslie is hardly a Manson girl today. Sixty years old, she looks back from prison on her involvement in the LaBianca murders (the night after the Tate massacre) in utter horror, shame, and guilt and takes full responsibility for her part in the crimes. I think it's time to parole her.

I am guilty, too. Guilty of using the Manson murders in a jokey, smart-ass way in my earlier films without the slightest feeling for the victims' families or the lives of the brainwashed Manson killer kids who were also victims in this sad and terrible case. I became obsessed by the Sharon Tate murders from the day I read about them on the front page of *The New York Times* in 1969 as I worked behind the counter of the Provincetown Bookshop. Later, when the cops finally caught the hippie killers and I actually saw their photos (ARREST WEIRDO IN TATE MURDERS, screamed the New York *Daily News* headline), I almost went into cardiac arrest. God! The Manson Family looked just like my friends at the time! Charles "Tex" Watson, a deranged but handsome preppy "head" who reminded me of Jimmy, the frat-boy-gone-bad pot dealer I had the hots for in Catholic high school, the guy who sold me my first joint. There was Susan Atkins, aka "Sadie Mae Glutz," devil go-go girl, with an LSD sense of humor just like Mink Stole's sister Mary (nickname: "Sick"), whom I lived with at the time in Provincetown, in a tree-fort commune. And look at Patricia Krenwinkel, aka "Katie," a flower-child earth mother just like Flo-Ann, who squatted with us that wonderful summer on Cape Cod. And, of course, my favorite, Leslie Van Houten, aka "Lulu," "the pretty one." The homecoming princess from suburbia who gave up her title for acid. The all-American girl who went beyond insanity to unhinged criminal glamour just like Mona, my last girlfriend, who took LSD and shoplifted and starred in my underground movies all under *my* influence. Until, that is, the day she caught me in bed with a man (who looked kind of like Steve "Clem" Grogan, another Manson fanatic) and dumped the contents of an entire garbage can on us as we lay sleeping.

The Manson Family members were the hippies all our parents were scared we'd turn into if we didn't stop taking drugs. The "slippies," as Manson later called his followers, the insane ones who didn't understand the humor in Yippie Abbie Hoffman's fiery speeches on his college lecture tours when he told the stoned, revolutionary-for-the-hell-of-it students to "kill their parents." Yes, Charlie's posse were the *real* anarchists who went beyond the radical Students for a Democratic Society's call to "Bring the War Home." Beyond blowing up their parents' townhouses, draft boards, even the Capitol in Washington, D.C. Sure, my friends went to riots every weekend in different cities in the sixties to get laid or get high, just like kids went to "raves" decades later. But, God, this was a cultural war, not a real one, and the survivors of this time now realize we were in a "play" revolution, no matter what we spouted. But the Manson Family! Yikes! Here was the real thing—"punk" a decade too early. Dare I say it? Yes, the filthiest people alive.

Even before the Manson Family had been caught, "the Dreamlanders," my gang of actors, took credit for the Tate/LaBianca crimes in a $5,000-budgeted movie entitled *Multiple Maniacs*, which I wrote, directed, and shot in Baltimore in the fall of 1969. Divine's character tortures David Lochary's with knowledge of the murders. "How about Sharon Tate?" she threatens. "How about THAT?!" "I told you never to mention that again!" David pleads, but Divine won't let it go. "Had yourself a real ball that night, didn't you?!" she chortles. "Who's Sharon Tate?" Divine's dim-witted but studly teenage bodyguard, Ricky, asks. "It doesn't matter, darling," Divine coos lecherously, dismissing his nosiness; "go fix yourself a sandwich."

Later, after Manson was arrested, I drove across the country for the first time in my life to Los Angeles for the California premiere of *Multiple Maniacs*, and the next day began attending the insane LSD media-circus Manson trial, which I've never really gotten over. After Manson and the three girls were convicted of the Tate/LaBianca murders and sentenced to death, my rabid following of the subsequent but much lesser known Manson-related trials never ceased. I needed to know more. How had these kids, from backgrounds so similar to mine, committed in real life the awful crimes against peace and love that we were acting out for comedy in our films?

In late 1971, still free, second-tier Manson Family members robbed the Western Surplus store in the suburbs of Los Angeles and stole fourteen guns (supposedly to break Manson out of jail), and a shoot-out with the police occurred. All six robbers were arrested. At their trial, many members of Manson royalty, now awaiting the promised Helter Skelter end of the world from death row, were called as witnesses by the robber defendants so they could have a courtroom reunion of sorts. The nervous trial judge called the proceedings "the biggest collection of murderers in Los Angeles County at one time." There were only two court spectators the day I went to a pretrial hearing: myself and a lower-echelon Manson groupie with a shaved head and a fresh X carved in her forehead who was furiously writing what looked like a thirty-page letter to one of her "brothers." When about fifteen of the Manson Family were brought into court, handcuffed and chained together, women on one side and men on the other, many with their heads shaved, the atmosphere was electric with twisted evil beauty. Not having seen one another in about a year, the cultists started chanting, jerkily gesturing, and speaking to one another in a nonsensical language that only the Family could understand. Sexy, scary, brain-dead, and dangerous, this gang of hippie lunatics gave new meaning to *folie à famille*, group madness and insanity that lasts as long as the same people are together and united. It was an amazing thing to see in person. Heavily influenced, and actually jealous of their notoriety, I went back to Baltimore and made *Pink Flamingos*, which I wrote, directed, and dedicated to the Manson girls, "Sadie, Katie and Les."

Then I went deeper into the Manson flame and started visiting Charles "Tex" Watson in prison. "What on earth were you thinking?" you may wonder, and today it is a question I have to ask myself. In Los Angeles I had met his post-conviction girlfriend, Lu, a German hippie girl with an obvious off-kilter sensibility who had come to America speaking little English and accidentally met some of the still-free Manson girls as the initial trial was taking place. "God, kids sure are wild in the United States," she told me she remembered thinking, not understanding how different these hippies were from the American "love-children" she had read about back in Munich and hoped to hook up with when she came to our shores. But Lu would only go so far. Refusing the demands to shave her skull, she broke away from the unincarcerated B-list Family members to the relative safety of a "jailhouse" love affair with Tex, a convicted killer who was still clearly out of his mind and had almost no chance of ever being paroled.

Charles "Tex" Watson was perhaps Manson's best piece of work; a high school football star who turned hippie and came to L.A. like thousands of other kids to find sixties grooviness. Instead he met Manson and was turned into a killer zombie in just ten LSD-and-belladonna-drenched months. Tex personally stabbed or shot all nine Tate/LaBianca victims. Lu and I would hitchhike to the California Men's Colony in San Luis Obispo from either L.A or San Francisco to visit him and I wrote about our times, rather inappropriately and with little insight, in my book *Shock Value*.

At that time, Charles Watson was no longer Tex, but he was definitely still coming out of his Manson indoctrination. You could tell by the toy wooden helicopter he made me in jail, decorated with words like "Game is Blame," "Tweak," and "Fear." I used it in the credits of my next movie, *Female Trouble*, a fictitious biopic of a woman who is brainwashed into believing "crime is beauty." The film was also dedicated to Charles "Tex" Watson, and a few critics—quite correctly, I guess—were appalled by my flippant disregard for the terrible aftermath of these crimes. Maybe I had taken too much acid myself? How could these villainous murders seem so abstractly "transgressive" to me? Could a movie ever be as influential as these monstrous crimes?

Was Manson's dress rehearsal for homicide, known as "creepy crawling," some kind of humorous terrorism that might have been fun? Breaking silently into the homes of middle-class "pigs" with your friends while you are tripping on LSD and gathering around the sleeping residents in their beds, not to harm them but to watch them sleep (the way Warhol did in that movie), and "experiencing the fear"? It *does* sound like it could have been a mind-bending adventure. When the Mansonites went further and moved the furniture around before they left, just to fuck with the waking homeowners' perception of reality, was this beautiful or evil? Could the Manson Family's actions also be some kind of freakish "art"?

When Charles Watson left behind his Tex persona for good, found Jesus Christ, and became saved, he and Lu broke up, and

I slowly drifted away from the visiting room. While I understood his need to find comfort and forgiveness, I wasn't a born-again believer and I sometimes made insanely sacrilegious movies, so we now had little in common. He then got married to a fellow Christian on the outside, started a ministry, and through conjugal visits fathered three children (who have turned out fine), much to the horror of Sharon Tate's family and the citizens of California. Lu went back to Germany and had an un-Manson child of her own, and we stayed in touch right up to her sad death from emphysema a few years ago. I remember once staying in some fancy hotel in Munich on a studio promotional tour for *Cry-Baby*, where I invited Lu over for a visit, not having seen her in person for many years. The concierge called up to my room and said, "We're not sure if it's a man or a woman, but there's somebody here who claims you told them to come over and we're sure it's a mistake." "Is her name Lu?" I asked. "Well . . . yes," he stammered. "Send her up!" I bellowed. Lu had cut off most of her hair (I'm not sure whether for politics or fashion) and was now obsessed with Sarajevo refugees, and I loved hearing her rant about jumping out of military helicopters (in her mind?) to spread the word for her new cause. Charles Watson is, to no one's surprise, still in prison, and once or twice a year we correspond politely and he always sends kind words.

In 1985, ten years or so after Charles Watson and I had last seen each other, I was doing some journalistic pieces for *Rolling Stone* and they asked me to interview Manson. I had little curiosity about a man who had reminded me of someone you'd move away from in a bar in Baltimore, and was still much more interested in the followers who had come to their senses and were

now definitely ex-followers. Leslie Van Houten always seemed
the one who could have somehow ended up making movies with
us instead of running with the killer dune-buggy crowd. She
was pretty, out of her mind, rebellious, with fashion daring, a
good haircut, and a taste for LSD—just like the girls in my movies. Instead of being a "good soldier" for Charlie and participating in the murders of Leno and Rosemary LaBianca, which she
certainly believed was the right thing to do at the time, I wish
she had been with us in Baltimore on location for *Pink Flamingos* the day Divine ate dog shit for real (*our* own cultural Tate/
LaBianca). Maybe she would have enjoyed cinematic antisocial
glee and movie anarchy just as much as a misguided race war
entitled Helter Skelter and designed by a criminal megaloma-
niac who believed the Beatles were speaking directly to him. If
Leslie had met me instead of Charlie, could she have gone to
the Cannes Film Festival instead of the California Institute for
Women? Actually, I think if Leslie hadn't met either of us she
might have ended up as a studio executive in the movie business
in Los Angeles. A good one, too.

So I pleaded with Jann Wenner, the editor of *Rolling Stone*,
to let me interview Leslie, "the only one who has a chance of
ever getting out," the one I could tell from press reports had
broken from Manson's control and was beginning to see that the
apocalyptical scenario Manson had preached was complete bullshit.
What a painful, horrible realization that must have been!

In 1972, Leslie's death sentence (and those of her codefendants) had been abolished by the California State Supreme
Court and, like that of all death-penalty prisoners at the time,
her sentence had been changed to life in prison. *Not* life without

parole. The two other female death-penalty cases at the time besides the three Manson girls, also murderesses with very serious cases, were paroled eight or nine years later with little fanfare or outrage.

In 1976, Leslie's original conviction was thrown out due to "ineffectual counsel" (her original lawyer drowned in the middle of her trial and was replaced), and she was given a new trial in 1977. This time, she was all by herself as a defendant in the courtroom. Remorse had started to creep in soon after she was imprisoned away from Manson. Locked away forever, Leslie, Susan, and Patricia were of no further use to Charlie and he dropped them quickly. The outsider voices of reason from the prison social workers started to seep in and Leslie began to see the holes in Manson's brainwashing. "When I'd be questioned," she later told the author Karlene Faith for her very insightful and intelligent but little-known book *The Long Prison Journey of Leslie Van Houten*, "I'd go blank and become frustrated like when a machine jams and just sits there making noise. In my head nothing was functioning. I was trying to understand, breaking down stiff little slogans that had been drilled into me." When two other Manson girls, Mary Brunner and Catherine Share, aka "Gypsy," were sent to jail and placed with Leslie, Susan, and Patricia, Leslie grew tired of listening to their Manson talk and confided to Patricia, "I've changed. I'm not into this." "It took three years to understand and five or six years of therapy to 'take responsibility'" for the terrible crime she had helped commit.

Leslie finally had a good lawyer for her second trial. Taking the witness stand truthfully for the first time, she tried to explain her state of mind through the Manson madness and his control techniques. And the jury listened, too. After about twenty-five days of deliberation, there was a hung jury; seven voted guilty of first-degree murder, and five manslaughter due to her cult domination and uncertain mental health at the time of the crime.

Refusing to offer a plea bargain, the prosecutor took her to trial for a third time in 1978 and added a felony robbery motive (clothes, a wallet, and a few coins had been taken from the LaBianca home), a crime that now couldn't legally be excused by state of mind. But this time Leslie made bail, was released from prison, and found employment as a law clerk while living in the Echo Park area of Los Angeles. She was free for six months and lived quietly, unnoticed by the press. When a few of her new neighbors found out who she really was, after they already thought they knew her, all were "supportive" and "protective" of her anonymity.

When Leslie's third trial finally began, she came to court every day on her own. Long gone was the shaved head, and the X on her forehead was covered by bangs. No more trippy little satin riot-on-Sunset-Strip miniskirt outfits either, like the ones she and her female codefendants had worn to the first trial. This time she was dressed tastefully and looked lovely, something that obviously didn't sit well with Stephen Kay, the prosecutor who had inherited all the Manson-related cases from Vincent Bugliosi. "All dolled up," Mr. Kay cracked to the press, giving Leslie one of her first, but definitely not last, opinionated fashion reviews. When she was finally convicted of first-degree murder at the end of the trial, life imprisonment suddenly became very real.

Rolling Stone gave me the go-ahead to pursue the Leslie Van Houten interview, so, in 1985, seven years after her final conviction, I wrote to "The Friends of Leslie," a now-disbanded loose-knit support group made up of Leslie's real family (Mom, Dad, brothers, sisters—all glad to have her back from Manson even if it *was* in prison) and her jailhouse teachers and counselors, who had seen how this teenage girl had been completely dominated by one of the most notorious madmen of our time during the 1960s, a decade that may never be surpassed in misguided revolutionary lunacy. Susan Talbot, one of the organizers, who met Leslie via classes offered in prison through Antioch College (the same ones Patty McCormack attended!), wrote me back and told me that Leslie was not interested in being in *Rolling Stone* or any other magazine at the time, but recommended I write Leslie to see if there was any rapport. In other words, Susan (who *did* know who I was, whereas Leslie did not) was intrigued and slightly puzzled by my offer of support but mistrustful of my intentions. Who could blame her?

By now I certainly knew that what Leslie had done was anything but "art." Her participation in the LaBianca murders was a very real atrocity that she could never make go away like a bad hairdo or a dose of the hippie clap. This was no youthful recklessness that today some baby boomer might turn into a nostalgic tattoo. No, this was fucking awful. I used to joke that "we've all had bad nights"; well, Leslie really had a horrible one! But of course the LaBiancas' night was much, much worse.

I wrote to Leslie to let her know I sympathized about the terrible predicament she must be in now that she realized that the ludicrous truth she once believed in was a complete sham. Leslie was left holding a bag so terrible that few of us could imagine the weight. I hoped in some tiny way to help her carry it by imagining it myself.

Leslie wrote back guardedly. She didn't know my films, of course; she had been on death row when *Pink Flamingos* had been released, and even I knew my trash epics were certainly not shown in prison during those years. She admitted my letter did not "put her off" as I had worried, but added she was "not certain of my intentions." "But if you are in a hurry," she warned, our friendship could never happen.

So I took it slowly. I wrote to her of my frustration in trying to get the sequel to *Pink Flamingos* made and she wrote me back about what else? Prison. Living in a cell "the size of an average bathroom with another person." Leslie never complained but called jail "a big tragedy. All those broken souls desperately seeking a way to leave themselves." What I soon realized was that Leslie was trying to do the exact opposite—seeking a way to get back to who she would have been if she had never met Manson. I knew that jailhouse manners dictated that the prisoner, not the visitor, is allowed to bring up the crime, and if it is mentioned ("Manson is a pathetic, disgusting, worthless old man"), you are allowed maybe one or two follow-up questions. When Leslie finally wrote, "I'd enjoy meeting you," I still hoped to interview her and hopped on a plane.

I have now visited Leslie in the same visiting room in the California Institute for Women in Frontera, California (without freeway traffic problems about an hour's drive east of Hollywood), for the last twenty-four years. The only real change in the cafeteria-style space is the cheesily cheerful photo backdrop you can pose in front of with your convict friend. This "green screen" of prison happiness has been altered through time—first it was a yellow-tinged country scene, then a blue floral motif, and finally a green and blue skyline. When friends look at the Polaroid pictures of Leslie and me that I have displayed privately on my office bulletin board, they are often confused. Not knowing that an in-house prison photographer snapped these shots through the years for five dollars each, they wonder who the woman standing next to me in front of the misleading generic tableau is. "Your sister?" many ask. "High school reunion?" others assume. When I trust someone enough to tell the truth, they are shocked at "how nice she looks." How "like one of our friends" she appears.

On our first visit, Leslie, who looked then, and still does, very much like the actress Hilary Swank, explained that she had no interest in being in *Rolling Stone* because of what she had done. She was ashamed of it, not proud, and hoped that one day the terrible notoriety would fade. Little did either of us know that this wretched infamy would not only never fade away, it would become stronger through the years as Manson became the great American tabloid bogeyman.

Leslie and I continued to correspond and I was flattered that she grew to trust me. After several more visits, she wrote in 1987, "I feel good about you because I do not believe you would harm me. You make me feel good about myself . . . I need that . . . not to feel like a freak. I'd like to propose that this year we become

closer friends. You inspire me to do something with myself."
Leslie inspired me, too. Inspired me to believe that if you wait
long enough and work hard enough on your damaged psyche,
you can eventually come out of it with some kind of self-respect
and mental health. I never again asked Leslie to be interviewed
until I began to write this book in 2007, and by then she knew I
wanted to write about her recovery, something she could finally
feel good about.

Will there ever be a "fair" answer to how Leslie should pay
for these crimes? Can you ever recover from being called "a human mutant" or a "monster" by the government, especially
when you know that they were *right* at one time in your life?
How can you feel optimistic about your own rehabilitation when
you see yourself reproduced as a bald-headed dummy with an
X carved in your head in Madame Tussauds Wax Museum?
How do you begin to deal with the pain of the victims' relatives
when the world has turned your former image into a Halloween
costume?

With patience. God knows, Leslie Van Houten has patience.
Patience to not find religious fanaticism that would forgive her
instantly and take away her responsibilities for her actions. Patience to know and accept that she can't take back the defiant
and deluded things she was programmed to say at her first trial:
"Sorry is only a five-letter word. It can't bring back anything."
Or her rantings to the jury on hearing all the defendants, including herself, being sentenced to death: "You blind stupid
people. Your own children will turn against you." Or the terrible
thoughts she admitted to prison psychologists at the time, about
how she "felt kind of bad" she didn't get to go the first night

(when Sharon Tate, her unborn baby, and four other victims were brutally murdered). Or how she was "hoping if we did it again, I would get to go." Or worse. After Tex Watson stabbed both Leno and Rosemary LaBianca, he told Leslie to "do something," and "feeling like a shark" or "a primitive animal, a wildcat who had just caught a deer," Leslie remembered, she stabbed Mrs. LaBianca sixteen times with a knife in the lower back.

Decades later, when a parole officer had reviewed eleven different favorable psychiatric reports, all concluding that Leslie was suitable for parole and no longer a danger to the community, he listened to her sadly try to explain her addled thought process at the time of the murders and her shame for "the girl I was at nineteen. The best way to show remorse is to be the best person I can be today." He told her sympathetically but unforgivingly, "You've dug yourself quite a hole and it's going to take a little time to get out of it." It sure has.

Can you ever dig your way out of that hole by trying to explain LSD to a parole board whose members have never taken a trip? Could they understand Leslie's plea that at the time of the murders "it was a constant exercise to try and not come down," as she remembered in Connie Turner's excellent but as yet unpublished Van Houten book, tentatively titled *Talk About Leslie*? "We spoke to each other in the nonsensical space the drug induces," Leslie struggled to explain. "I became saturated in acid and had no sense of where those who were not part of the psychedelic reality came from. I had no perspective or sense that I was no longer in control of my mind." Could a parole board ever fathom that Leslie actually believed she was an elf "three inches high" who would "grow fairy wings" at the time of Helter Skelter, as she later told Michael Farquhar in *The Washington Post* in 1994? Apparently she was not a lone elf. The Family women "would try to find elves hiding up in the trees and sitting quietly, so they might show themselves." Leslie's dad backs her up, too, remembering in Connie's book how he visited Leslie "in county jail right after they had been picked up. Leslie told me she didn't know if she should cut holes in the back of her blouse to hold her wings or to put little pockets." Great. What does society do with a killer elf who decades later is now all better? Who *could* understand?

I could. I took a lot of LSD myself when I was young. From 1964 to about 1969, I took acid many, many times and never once had a bad trip. LSD quickly gave me confidence in my lunacy. "Don't tell young people that!" my mother always begs; but it's true. I remember tripping my brains out and dangerously crawling around the roof of the Marlborough Apartments in Baltimore after an LSD party and suddenly realizing I *could* make these crazy movies I had been dreaming up. My friends and I cemented our relationship with LSD, and became a parody of a movie studio, and together our celluloid madness began to strengthen and grow. We had a "family," too.

But as nuts and angry as we were, would we have committed the atrocious crimes of my movies in real life if we hadn't had the outlet of underground filmmaking? Well, who knows? We certainly never met one of the most notorious con men of the century, Charles Manson. And we were *never* looking for a spiritual leader the way Leslie was. I guess *I* was our gang's leader. My parents never blamed the crowd I ran with; they knew I was the bad egg. "We're not your puppets!" David Lochary used to yell at me when I went overboard on directing or thinking up stunts to film, like Divine shooting up liquid eyeliner for real. My "family" knew how to say no to me. Why couldn't Leslie do the same in her distorted world?

Could I have gone off the deep end with my cinematic "orders"? I had planned a raid on the Maryland State Board of Censors in which the actors from *Desperate Living* would "home invade" the offices, chain themselves to the furniture, and refuse to leave until the anticipated cuts from our film were restored. Some of the actors (including three-hundred-pound Jean Hill) had actually agreed to this photo op if I'd pay the bail, but luckily I didn't have to test their dedication to movie cult-madness, because right before our Board of Censors screening Governor Harry Hughes took office and disbanded the board in his first days of power. And even though Divine's character in *Female Trouble* asks his audience, "Who wants to die for art?" and then shoots a fan who yells, "Yes!" (played by Vincent Peranio, my longtime friend and production designer), I don't think any of my movie gang would have killed for cinema.

I never told Leslie this, but off camera I had killed somebody, too. Accidentally. *Completely* accidentally. In 1970 Mink Stole and I were driving up Broadway, a Baltimore thoroughfare that is divided by a safety island. It was early Sunday afternoon, we were not on drugs or liquor, and an elderly man, without looking, stepped off the curb right in front of my car. His body flipped up and landed on the hood with his face pressed toward mine through the driver-side windshield. This image so horrified me that I have used it over and over in my later films (Tab Hunter run over in *Polyester*, the schoolteacher killed by Kathleen

Turner in her car in *Serial Mom*, the "Fidget" character's near death as he falls off the drive-in marquee and lands on his parents' car windshield in *Cecil B. Demented*). As I pulled over to the side of the road in shock, the man's body slid off the hood of my car to the street, leaving indentation marks that reminded me of the snow angels you made as a child by lying down in snow drifts and waving your arms. "He's okay," Mink mumbled in hope. "No, he isn't," I said realistically as I heard his death rattle. A crowd gathered around the car and luckily, oh so luckily, a cop approached and said, "I saw it all happen and it wasn't your fault." What a miracle. I had long oily hair and was dressed in my usual thrift-shop-pimp-meets-hillbilly outfit and Mink was still in her "religious whore" period—wearing all black clothing with tons of rosaries around her neck *way* before Goth. We looked like complete lunatics. I called my dad to get our insurance information and he was immediately nervous. "Is anybody hurt?" he asked. "Well, yes . . . the man died," I had to admit. "Oh, my God!" I heard my poor father moan. "Now this!"

But did I feel guilty? Even when I heard the victim was the beloved "peanut man" from the nearby Broadway Market? I didn't know him, but some of my friends did. I felt no guilt because I knew the accident wasn't my fault, but I certainly felt horrified. When my grandmother called later that night, she said, "I'm praying for that man's soul." I honestly replied, "Can't you ask God why he picked my car to walk out in front of?"

If any deaths result from a car accident, you have to go to court, no matter whose fault it was. As my "manslaughter" trial began, my parents sat next to me in support, worried that, because of my hair and my already notorious cinematic reputation, I'd get convicted. It was a great relief to see that the deceased had no survivors, or at least none came to trial. The whole hearing was over in three minutes after the cop testified to seeing the unfortunate man just walk into oncoming traffic without looking. This awful experience will never leave me, but it hardly qualifies me as a murderer. I can't begin to imagine what Leslie feels today when it *was* her fault. All I could do was try to warn future jaywalkers of the dangers through dialogue in my movies. Patricia Hearst, playing a school crossing guard, tells Johnny Depp as he exits school in *Cry-Baby*, "Look left. Look right. *Then* walk!"

The attorney Paul Fitzgerald, after many years' involvement defending the Manson women at various trials, said to the *Los Angeles Times*, "If Leslie Van Houten had never existed, the LaBiancas still would be dead." But Leslie won't let herself off that easily. "I blame myself," she answered. "I'm part of what made him [Manson] a leader. If he didn't have followers, he wouldn't be a leader." She later told Karlene Faith, "A follower is as responsible [as a leader] for allowing a leader to lead them foully."

As much as the sex angle was built up in the press, the truth was surprising to some. Leslie slept with Manson "maybe three times," she testified in court, and only "in the first month" she was with the group. Leslie would never admit this, but she had better taste in Manson men. Bobby Beausoleil, aka "Cupid," was the most traditionally handsome of Charlie's boys—he had starred in Kenneth Anger's movie *Lucifer Rising*—and was Leslie's first boyfriend inside the Family. Even Charlie was a little in love with Bobby, and Leslie remembers being shocked at seeing Bobby orally service Charlie during one of their group sex evenings. "I didn't 'sleep with the devil,'" Leslie told Karlene Faith, "I slept with an ex-con who had an extensive record of pimping and abusing women. But I didn't know that." "The ranch," she remembered, according to Connie Turner, "was set up and run the same way as a stable of hookers, although none of us realized it at the time."

"Are you crazy enough to believe in me?" Charlie asked Leslie, and after months of LSD trips, isolation in the desert, and hours and hours of his continuous insane political rantings, Leslie, like most of the other girl converts, was. "'Bow like sheep,' Manson would order us," Leslie recalled in 1983. "We wore Bowie knives on belts around our waists and were only [dressed] in our underwear, I think, unless it got cold," she told Connie Turner. "We'd sit around on our feet and grunt . . . we were seeing how long we could go without drinking water . . . I was carrying a twenty-pound backpack filled with rice. We were building roads from nowhere to nowhere by moving rocks around . . . It was hard." Susan Atkins, Leslie's codefendant, said in one of her parole hearings that they "were three young women clearly not in our right minds who lived in slavish obedience to a madman." Catherine Share, an early Manson Family member who finally managed to break free after serving time for the gun robbery, remembers Manson "just stealing everyone's soul." "Thinking is stinking," he used to say. And while Gypsy never killed for Charlie, she understood the state of mind of the ones who did. "The killers couldn't even form a thought," she sadly remembered from her own experience. Tex Watson's psychologist's reports stated that Tex "had confusion as to who or what he was. Sometimes he 'felt like a monkey'! He actually believed that the victims were imaginary people." Tex told the shrink that he looked in the mirror at the Tate house, trying to figure out who he was. "I wasn't anyone," he remembered. "I wasn't Charles Watson, I was an animal. The end of the world was then. I was the living death . . ."

Seeing Leslie today in the visiting room, it's hard to imagine her with this past. The X on her forehead has almost faded away, and she looks like an upscale intelligent woman I could definitely come across in my life in New York or Los Angeles. She could be seated next to you at any dinner party of professional people and it would never dawn on you that this woman had been in prison for four decades. She even went to the Oscars with a female friend in 1978 when she was out on bail, and nobody recognized her! "But what did you talk about to the people you met that night?" I wondered, knowing she had been released not *that* long before from death row, not exactly a center of industry screenings or "For Your Consideration" Oscar campaigns. "If someone brought up one of the nominees," she said with a shrug, "I'd just say, 'No, I missed that one' or 'I was away when that was playing.'"

Leslie and I have gotten older together in that visiting room and I've seen the prison rules constantly change. I used to be able to buy her three packs of cigarettes to take back to her cell, but now it's illegal to smoke anywhere in jail in California. The cigarettes-as-money system that used to feel so old-school *Women Behind Bars* is gone forever. Now I get to buy her three cans of Pepsi! Stylistically, it's just not the same thing. Worse yet, about five years ago, suddenly none of the women in Leslie's jail were allowed to use any kind of hair coloring. Overnight the entire prison population aged ten years in appearance, and on my first visit since the ban, I knew something was wrong, but it took me several minutes to realize that everybody had two-inch gray roots. Talk about cruel and unusual punishment!

Leslie and I have shared good times and bad times. And yes, Leslie *does* have good times. She's taught illiterate women to read in prison classes, she's stitched a portion of the AIDS quilt, made bedding for the homeless, recorded books on tape for the blind. She has clerked for the administrators, the nurses, the associate warden, the head of education, the kitchen, and the priest. And it's not that she jumps from job to job—rules restrict inmates from working longer than two years in the same position. She can be lighthearted, too. She even sang "Santa Baby" at the prison Christmas show one year.

Yet somehow Leslie continues to live through the bad times without despair and inspires others to do the same. When Divine died suddenly in 1988, Leslie was one of the first to console me by letter. "I'm so sad and wish I could be closer for you. I know you loved him and enjoyed in the success of his life and helped him through his hard times . . . I am sorry I will not get to know him." She counseled me on a personal level, too. After a relationship of mine ended, Leslie was a good shoulder to lean on, and I hope I've given her good advice, too, when she's had crushes from prison on men in the outside world. I've met two of her longest-lasting roommates: Becky, the bank robber whom I adored and who is now free, and another inmate I called "Little Miss Manslaughter" because she was so bubbly and was an actual fan of my movies *before* she was sentenced.

Since no cable TV is available in jail, Leslie has seen few of my movies, but did finally get to see my version of *Hairspray*, and it was nice to get her good review. "I loved it," she wrote to me. "I was *really* into the public dances and all that. I lived to go to the Harmony Ballroom in Anaheim. I bought my shoes by how well they slid on the wood floor. I'm telling you, it was my life!" It *was* her life. From "Mashed Potato" to Manson's "Monster Mash" is just a few short years. Luckily for her, Leslie still has a sense of humor. She even joked about my role in *Hairspray* as an evil psychiatrist who uses a ridiculous optical medical tool to hypnotize a teenage white girl into never dating black boys. "I never had one of those spinning wheels flashed in front of my face," Leslie admitted, referring to decades of therapy. "Do you think it would help?"

I've always secretly wondered if Leslie ever felt "cool" when she was with the Manson gang and I finally got up the nerve to ask. She looked at me in confusion. "Cool? We had no concept by then of any such possible word!" she answered. And now the "celebrity" was even more unfathomable. "There's nothing sadder than to be asked for an autograph because of infamy," she once wrote to me. "I've had to explain I'm not proud of what I have done or why they [people] are aware of me. It's an awful feeling. The 'unwilling star.'" And when her autograph or letters are sold on murder memorabilia sites, it makes her feel worse because someone she has written to has betrayed her, and she's not sure who—"So creepy. All disgusting and distasteful."

We've always discussed current events, how paralyzed she was with sadness over the Waco tragedy and how similar David Koresh was to Manson—even more so than to Jim Jones. Or how she understands the mind-set of kamikaze suicide bombers because that was how she was trained by Manson to feel and act once. And when the riots broke out in L.A. in 1992, after the acquittal of the police in the Rodney King beating, an event Manson loyalists likened to Helter Skelter finally happening for real, Leslie was so far away from the Manson ideology that the comparison never even occurred to her. "This has been a really emotional time for me," she wrote that week. "First there was the first execution in nearly half a century in California"— Robert Alton Harris, who was strapped into the gas chamber for thirteen minutes, released due to appeals, and then put back in the same day and executed—"and then the days L.A. went mad. I sat watching on TV images usually seen in other countries. John, it was so frightening—to think of what is supposed to be safe as totally out of control."

I've tried to be Leslie's "agent" in the world of Hollywood. She agonized with me about whether to cooperate and be interviewed for the TV newsmagazine show *Turning Point*, but once she met Diane Sawyer, Leslie agreed this news correspondent was "a class act." After seeing the completed show, Leslie admitted she "had been treated better than I ever have." When the distressing news came in 2003 that CBS was remaking *Helter Skelter* as a new TV movie, I called the director, John Gray, whom I didn't know, at his home. Probably wondering why I was calling, or worse yet, thinking I was happy about the news, he took my call and listened quietly as I begged him to realize what a terrible unfair effect this project would have on Leslie's parole chances, how she was ashamed and horrified about the crimes, how further notoriety on the case would only please

Manson and hurt the privacy of victims' families. I think my
call may have worked a little, because when I saw the finished
project, Leslie's character was minimal and her part in the crime
was truthfully shown to have been ordered by a vengeful Manson. A year or two later, my hunch was proven correct. In Los
Angeles, in a restaurant to meet my agent and five minutes early,
I was shown to my table alone and the waitress approached me
with an odd expression. "Can I ask you something personal?"
she shyly requested. "Sure," I replied, realizing she recognized
me but never expecting what was coming next. "Are you the
head of that 'Friends of Leslie' organization?" "No, there is no
'head' and that group has been disbanded officially, but there
are many people who support her parole chances," I answered.
"Because I played Leslie in the newest *Helter Skelter*," she revealed. Only in L.A.! Her name was Catherine Wadkins, and I
suddenly felt bad, realizing I might have contributed to making
an actress's part smaller. "Yes, you did," she confided after I told
her the story of my call to her director, which she already knew
about. "That's okay." Catherine smiled. "I think Leslie *should*
get out and I tried to play the part in a way to show how brainwashed she was."

Leslie never asked me for money or material goods over the
years. I've sent her books I loved and together we've discussed
novels by James Purdy, Mary McGarry Morris, Michael Cunningham, and Anne Tyler. After maybe one too many of my
intense choices, Leslie started requesting her own titles, many
of which had to do with the history and plight of the Native
American Indian, and I was happy to oblige. The only reading
material I sent her that was rejected by the mailroom was, oddly

enough, an issue of *Paper* magazine that included a fashion shoot that must have contained a little too much nudity. Once I offered to buy Leslie a TV for her cell but she declined. My kind of gal.

I was lucky enough to meet some of Leslie's friends on the outside, too. She has a support group that is tireless and relentless. "I like that several people close to me are also now friends of yours," Leslie wrote me after years of visiting. The most dedicated is Linda Grippi, a friend of Leslie's since high school who began visiting her not long after she was convicted and has never stopped. Linda is practically a nun in the religion of Leslie's rehabilitation and the firmest believer that Leslie should be paroled. Linda has dedicated her life to the cause of Leslie's freedom. She is a kind but convincing levelheaded pit bull who goes after anyone who believes otherwise with a reasoned defense. If Linda could testify at Leslie's parole hearing as "support," the way the victims' families can, I think Leslie might have already received a release date.

But Leslie meeting *my* friends was more problematic, because of their East Coast locations and the strict rules about visiting high-profile prisoners like her. I am afraid I have betrayed Leslie, too. A long time ago she mentioned to me that she "hoped I never 'used' our friendship or her plight for freedom" as dinner party conversation in my travels around the world. And I am embarrassed to admit, in my enthusiasm for her rehabilitation and my pride in our friendship, I have. Leslie Van Houten is quite a name to drop, and famous people are eager to hear her story. When we were filming *Cry-Baby*, Johnny Depp heard my pleas concerning Leslie's parole and offered to visit her. Leslie, like everyone else in the world, had great respect for Johnny Depp and was moved that he, as my buddy, cared about her case. But we must have been nuts! Can you imagine the press if they found out? Think of the headlines—"Johnny Depp joins Manson Family." Luckily for all of us, Johnny's visiting form was turned down because of an "impending assault charge," probably a hotheaded reaction to paparazzi.

Initially both my mother and Leslie's were nervous about our friendship. "Does the Manson Family have to have our address?" my mother moaned when I once had a letter sent there. And in 1998, Leslie commented to *The Baltimore Sun* in a long profile of me that she "found it ironic" that her mother and supporters initially "were concerned" for Leslie, as if "knowing him could somehow hurt my reputation." But over the years our mothers softened and grew used to the idea. Leslie's mother went to see *Pecker* and my mother needlepointed me a pillow that says "Leslie." As our parents got older and poor health struck, Leslie and I commiserated on how lucky we were to have parents who had lived long enough so we both could make peace with them over our notorious pasts. "None of this" was her parents' fault, Leslie told a parole board. And when Mrs. Van Houten died in 2005, Leslie wrote her friends a great tribute, admitting it was "very hard for me not to be there for her at this terrible time (of her illness) just to fix her hair, read to her, just be near her. As it is, I cherish all the qualities of her that are alive in me. She lived a good life. She was a world-traveler, helped in unionizing the L.A. teachers, she was part of the Mothers Marching Against Vietnam and was very proud of that. Mama liked Hillary Clinton and wrote her support letters. So I share with you, my friends, the life of Jane Louise Edwards Van Houten. A woman who was a good mother who I loved dearly. We worked our way over very hard times and came through with sincere tenderness. She was pleased you were my friend. Take a moment to say, 'Hear, hear,' for a life that was well-lived."

But, yes, I know the LaBianca kids don't have a mother around anymore because of my friend Leslie. No matter how patient Leslie or her supporters are, we know this terrible fact will never change. But when, if ever, will there have been enough punishment? Vincent Bugliosi, the original and fairest Manson Family prosecutor and author of *Helter Skelter*, originally predicted in his book that the "girls" would serve "fifteen to twenty years" and called Leslie "the least committed to Manson," but later told the *National Enquirer*, "I want Leslie Van Houten to remain in prison for the rest of her life." He once admitted to Larry King after hearing Leslie speak on the show, "I was impressed by her. In defense of her I can say this, she seems to be a model prisoner and everyone seems to say she is very remorseful for the murders." But Stephen Kay, who prosecuted Leslie in her later trials and has argued against her parole many times since, seems even more confused on how much time she should serve. Admitting "I've always said she [Leslie] was the smartest and maybe the most normal of them all," he also commented in the *Los Angeles Times*, in 1980, that he didn't feel Leslie Van Houten should be locked up forever, but it was "too soon to release her now." He would rather "wait until she was at least forty years old." Sixteen years after that, a Court TV reporter asked him, "Will you always fight Leslie Van Houten's parole?" And he answered, "Always is a long time. I'm not say-

ing she will never be suitable for parole, I've not said 'never.' "
But when the old *National Enquirer* comes around, he encourages their readers to send in coupons against her release and claims, "Leslie Van Houten should never be paroled."

The parole board can be equally confusing when it comes to sending signals to Leslie about a possible release. After eighteen parole hearings, some members praised her—"You've come a long way," "You're much closer [than] you might realize"—while denying her a date, always citing "the enormity of the crime," the only thing she can never change. It is painful to watch Leslie sit there year after year, her face lined in sorrow in long Warholian close-ups on Court TV as she listens to the same gruesome details of her crime that the prosecutor read into the record at every hearing. No matter how much progress she's made or how good the psychiatric reports, she is forced to redescribe or come up with new details of that terrible night or be accused of "not opening up" to her part in the crime, and then is punished as the prosecutor takes her honest memory of the insane Manson reasoning and uses it against her in future hearings. As Christie Webb, Leslie's last parole defense attorney, so succinctly put it in 2004, "Deputy D.A. has proved that Leslie Van Houten was a danger in 1971 and, yes, she was. She was when she was with the Manson cult. She tried to explain her relationship to Manson— how she would die for him, how she would kill for him. She tried to explain that and told that to psychiatrists in 1970 and 1971 when she was still under the influence of cult indoctrination and then it's used against her 38 years later."

In 2002 a California Supreme Court judge realized that a rejection of her parole was made "without any explanation of reason" and ordered the parole board to get back to him in ninety days to show "some evidence" of why Leslie should not be released and what she must do to rehabilitate herself. In November of that same year Judge Bob Krug said of the parole board's ruling, "I cannot find any indication where Miss Van Houten has done anything wrong in prison. They can't keep using the crime forever and ever. That turns her sentence into life without parole. If I was Ms. Van Houten I wouldn't have a clue what to do at the next hearing."

"Unreasonable risk to the community" is another reason used to turn down Leslie year after year. "I don't want anyone to wake up and find Leslie Van Houten is the next-door neighbor," Stephen Kay argued in 1986, conveniently forgetting that Leslie *had* had next-door neighbors when she lived peacefully on parole between her second and third trial. An even more persuasive argument against this reasoning was the successful parole and release of Steve "Clem" Grogan, aka "Scramblehead," one of the most brainwashed men in the Manson Family. Grogan was convicted (along with two other defendants) in a separate trial for the murder of ranch hand Shorty Shea, carried out because Charlie thought Shea was a snitch. Sentenced to life in prison but released after serving fourteen years (maybe because there was at least a *reason* for this type of murder that someone could understand), Mr. Grogan commented to the parole board, "I still haven't got over the emotional part . . . the atrocity that I did." Grogan, who was certainly as committed to Manson's lunatic cause as Leslie was at the time of the crimes, has never been heard from by the law since. Away from Manson, he got his life back together, found employment, and now lives lawfully and quietly out of the eyes of the press, crime historians, or Manson groupies. Contrary to what Charlie preaches, sometimes sense *does* make sense.

"Not taking responsibility" is another charge thrown at Leslie each time she comes up for parole. Because she once said she stabbed Mrs. LaBianca after she was already dead, the D.A. always brings up the fact that Leslie doesn't "come clean" to details of her involvement. But Leslie has already stated that "earlier in my incarceration, in my sobriety, in my coming to terms with what I had done, I used to find a lot of relief in thinking she was dead. But really honestly looking at it, it is of no consequence whether she was or not. The action was reprehensible." "Each day I wake up," she told the board, "I know why I'm waking up where I am." "I feel a great responsibility for what I did to the world," she sadly stated at a 1991 hearing. "I carry this crime with me as if I was the only one," she said in 2000. "Each act we did in that house, I take responsibility for," she testified in 2004, adding, "I can't . . . place the blame on someone else. It was me."

Naturally, the victims' families' words and anger are incredibly strong and hard to argue against. What they say can actually *never* be wrong. If Leslie had killed my mother, could I forgive her? For many years the LaBianca children did not come to Leslie's parole hearings. "You may have wondered why I haven't attended," wrote Leno's oldest son in 2004; "let me tell you why. When confronted with the nightmare at the time, I decided to put my faith in the legal system. I tended to my wounds privately, knowing that if I let my parents' death define me the rest of my life, then those who killed them would have gotten me, too." But when it looked like Leslie had a real chance at parole in 2000, Stephen Kay encouraged LaBianca's nieces and nephews to attend, and their words were devastating. "How many times must we come?!" asked an indignant LaBianca nephew, frustrated at having to appear yet again, given what he thought was Leslie's ironclad life sentence. Seeing the family testify on TV, I kept thinking how they didn't want to *have* to be there. How they had to take off work. Drive to the prison. Pay for gas. Buy an outfit they knew they'd be photographed in. How painful an ordeal this intrusion on their attempt to come to terms with their tragedy. "We lost our privacy and suffered untold depression, frustration, anxiety, and financial ruin," a LaBianca relative testified, calling the hearing a "sacrilege to Leno's memory that the family has to be confronted with parole hearings of these individuals." A resentful LaBianca niece continued, "I don't personally support execution but I feel life in prison is an adequate punishment for what was done." Sometimes the family's words were so terrible they could have come from a horror movie: "The house was a family sanctuary . . . one of the murder weapons used was the carving fork that was used for our holiday festivities. I saw, as a youngster, my grandfather Leno and my father use these instruments of joy that were turned into tools of torture and death. We are stained for life." It doesn't matter that Leslie herself never touched this fork; it was her codefendant Patricia Krenwinkel who plunged it into Mr. LaBianca's neck after Tex had already stabbed him to death. But what awful details to keep straight! Who cares who did what? Leslie knew they weren't going trick-or-treating when they went into that house. And she has to pay for everything that happened. Every single gruesome detail.

Even I am sometimes still horrified. To me, almost more incomprehensible than the murders is the fact that my friend Leslie, after stabbing Mrs. LaBianca, changed into her clothes before hitching back to the Spahn ranch. "How *could* you?!" I once asked Leslie, who looked back at me stricken with disgust and humiliation. "I know," she mumbled. "Tex made me change my clothes and I told him I didn't have to." "Did you actually pick out one of her outfits?" I whispered, horrified to imagine fashion decisions in the time of such bloodshed. "No," she gasped as she lowered her eyes in shame that I would even *think* of such a thing, "I just grabbed the first thing I found!" What a terrible, terrible question to have to answer!

At the parole hearing, a LaBianca niece testified she was outraged to have "never heard from Leslie Van Houten, not by phone, email or letter. She should apologize to me," she added with anger. But Leslie wasn't even aware of these nieces and nephews until they came to parole hearings decades after the crimes. She knew about "two children" but not cousins. Leslie had earlier told a parole member that she had wrestled with writing a letter of apology because she thought "how I would feel if it had been my own mother and father—not sure I would have wanted the perpetrator to have contacted me." In 1994 Leslie told *The Washington Post* that she had written dozens of apologies and never mailed them because they would amount to a request for a favor.

When the LaBianca nieces and nephews first appeared at

Leslie's hearing, Leslie said, "I am relieved that family members came forward . . . it's really hard to live with the murders when no one was there. It was incomplete dealing with it." And she *had* apologized to the unseen LaBianca family many times at earlier parole hearings. "I feel great shame and remorse when I think of the LaBianca children and their family today . . . when I think back on the night of August 10th, all I think about is the horror these two very innocent human beings were subjected to. I'm so sorry. I'm so sorry."

Leslie has agreed to meet with the victims' relatives, but only if there is no tape of the meeting to be exploited by the media. "If the family works with the Institute I certainly would welcome a chance to apologize to them in a personal way." In other words, *not* on TV, not on videocassettes bought and sold online on Manson groupie websites, and not for the whole world to see. "A virtuoso performance," a commentator blurted on TV after seeing footage of Leslie baring her soul at a parole hearing. And this is exactly the kind of "entertainment" value she is trying to avoid.

"She cannot repay," a LaBianca nephew told the board before turning to Leslie and saying, "Therefore accept your punishment and pray for the good Lord's forgiveness in the hereafter." Worse yet, Debra Tate, sister of Sharon, who is not allowed to testify at Leslie's hearings because Leslie is not convicted of the Tate murders but is allowed to be there in "victim support," told the news media outside the hearing her feelings about all the convicted Manson Family members. "I have no animosity," she reasoned. "I want these people to flourish within the confines of these [prison] walls. I want them to be productive and have lives within the confines of these walls right here."

Yet forgiveness can seem insane, too. Susan Le Barge, the born-again Christian daughter of Leno and Rosemary LaBianca, outraged her family and Sharon Tate's mother by appearing at Charles "Tex" Watson's 1990 parole hearing and testifying that the man who stabbed to death both her mother and father should be released. "I believe twenty-one years of imprisonment and his having to live with the memory of what he did is punishment enough," she told a startled and disbelieving board. "It's my belief Charles could live in society peacefully and should be given a parole date," she concluded as Tex Watson sat there, seemingly stunned.

Knowing the schism Susan Le Barge's testimony must have caused with the LaBianca family, Leslie never tried to hop on board this almost ludicrously forgiving bandwagon, but I'm sure she felt some relief to hear one of the victims' family trying to get past her hatred of the perpetrators. Leslie must have been encouraged to read the words of the father of the murder victim Myrna Opshal, who was killed in a bank robbery committed by the Patty Hearst–kidnapping Symbionese Liberation Army. When one of its members, Kathleen Soliah, was about to be released on bail for taking part in this crime, he was angry but expressed hope, according to the *Los Angeles Times*, "that Soliah can emerge from jail to offer society some productive years. I hope she [Soliah] has learned something from this," he continued, "and can go out and be a good citizen and contribute to the community where she lives. And she'll have some life left to live."

Most likely Leslie would be inspired by the forgiveness the Amish community showed the gunman who insanely shot to death five schoolgirls and severely wounded five more before killing himself in a one-room schoolhouse in Pennsylvania. A year later a local historian gave a speech on the anniversary of this horrible event called "Why the Amish Forgave a Killer." "The Amish community believes forgiveness is about giving up," he said, "giving up your right to revenge. And giving up feelings of resentment, bitterness and hatred, replacing them with compassion toward the offender and treating the offender as a human being."

Could Leslie's expression of remorse remain "superficial," as was charged in her 2003 parole hearing? She has been saying she's sorry for so long and with such eloquence, it is hard to imagine these suspicions could be founded. "I was raised to be a decent human being," Leslie has pled. "I turned into a monster and I'm very ashamed." "If I had known what the word 'sorry' really meant, I wouldn't have made light of it the way I did [at her first trial]," she has admitted. "There have been times," she sadly remarks, "when I'm eating a meal and feel guilty I'm eating a meal." "I have spent these years going back to [being] a decent human being," she confessed. "I find it very difficult to live with myself a great deal of the time. If you look at my file, there's no violence. No violence. That one night. That one night has just tormented me. I am not a person that corrects problems through violence. I don't confront. And it has been really, really difficult to live with. And I hope that the family understands . . . I know that you loved them and I know they were wonderful people. They didn't deserve it and you didn't deserve it. Not a bit of it. All I can tell you is that I'm so sorry. I'm sorry."

Through the years the district attorneys have been very effective at keeping Leslie incarcerated. They can be brutal. When one psychiatrist talked of Leslie being "charming," Stephen Kay correctly wisecracked, "I'm sure Leno and Rosemary LaBianca didn't think she was so charming." But recently, the D.A.'s arguments for not granting Leslie parole seem almost desperate. One of the very few mixed psychiatric reports once stated that Leslie "possesses a degree of verbal acumen that is very convincing. The obvious question is whether this represents real change in reconstructing your personality or someone who is so smooth in their manipulation that they are barely perceptible . . . Under the control of evil, she *did* excel; now under the control of what could be called society's rules and regulations, she has excelled. She has attempted to please authority no matter if it is good or bad." In other words, damned if you do, damned if you don't.

Patrick Sequeira, the new D.A. who took over arguing against Leslie's parole after Stephen Kay's retirement, even contended at her last hearing that something seemed suspicious about Leslie going back to college behind bars to get her master's degree in philosophy. He described Antioch University, the struggling college that offered these courses, as a "hotbed of radicalization," and then went on to rail against the classes she would be taking, Theory of Justice, Problems of Men, Democracy in Education, Origins of Intelligence in Children, as if this curriculum were somehow connected to Leslie's future criminality. "Clearly the inmate has a fascination with philosophy just as she had a fascination with the concepts that the Manson Family embraced," he told the parole board accusingly. "If there was true educational intent in changing oneself," he went on to lecture a dumbfounded Leslie, who kept her head held high, "you'd think it would be beyond studying philosophy."

The parole board's advice to Leslie at the end of each denial was sometimes perplexing. "We look forward to seeing you in two years," one parole board member told her, as if her hearings were some sort of positive anniversary. In 2002, one board member encouraged her to "continue with classes" but then admitted that there were no more classes for her to attend. When Leslie was denied that year and told by the board she needed more counseling in prison, she replied politely, "I would like to say there is no more therapy available to me. So you just recommended something to me that they don't offer. But I'll do what I can. That's all I can do." At the end of her 2007 hearing, Leslie was advised that "this being prison, the panel understands that sometimes programs are not as available as we'd all like. Therefore we commend to you that—independent reading is available to you—that you can read books that you believe are appropriate for you, speak to your particular situation. Prepare a short report, two or three paragraphs indicating an understanding of what you've read and how it applies to your particular situation." Thirty-six years in prison and she is now sentenced to book reports! A flummoxed Leslie asked politely, "Do I send *you* these . . . these reports on the books?" "Yes," they said, "you do."

"Remember she is only one dose away from doing something like this again," warns a LaBianca relative. While one can understand his frustration, it seems very unlikely that Leslie, after three decades of successful therapy and NA and AA meetings, would have the slightest desire for one more LSD trip. Does Manson have to die before Leslie can ever be paroled? "Suppose Manson told her to kill again?" people who have not followed Leslie's progress sometimes ask. As if. She has had no voluntary contact with Manson for over thirty-five years, and if any concerned citizen who asks this question had ever seen Manson on TV recently, they would know better. A repellent old man with an unappealing pot belly and teeth rapidly becoming similar to Edith Massey's, he would have a hard time leading *any* cult today, believe me. He looks more like a homeless fool who forgot to take his meds. "It's coming down fast!" was a good recruiting line in the sixties, but interrupting a 1987 *Today* show interview and telling the female host, "I gotta take a shit, will you excuse me?" won't exactly get him many new followers. Manson is "just a creep," Leslie told a parole board in 1996.

How right she was. Manson watched on camera his despondent middle-aged codefendant Patricia Krenwinkel (who thought the first trial was a "play") tell Diane Sawyer, "Every day I wake up and I know that I am a destroyer of the most precious thing there is—life." His gentlemanly response? "She got old on me," he snorted. What a reward for the hippie girl who stupidly gave up her life for him when she was nineteen years old. A girl convicted of seven murders for the man she believed was God, a woman so defeated now that she doesn't even ask her outside friends or family to write letters of support to the parole board because she "doesn't believe a date will be given." What a tribute to the onetime flower child who is described now by Karlene Faith as "a good-hearted woman who suffers the anguished burden of interminable guilt." How kind Manson is to his now horrified ex-follower, who told a parole board in 1993, "It is very difficult to live with the fact that I could do something so horrible because that is not who I am, not what I believe in. On a day-to-day basis it is a terribly difficult thing to live with because I feel *terrible*. But no matter what I do, I can't change it," she sobbed. "I am paying for this as best as I can. There is nothing more I can do outside of being dead," she cried as the board members watched her nervously, "and I know this is what you wish, but I can't take my life. I'm sorry . . . ," she mumbled, looking down in complete defeat.

"What happens when the next con man comes along?" is a frequent argument by Stephen Kay against Leslie's release. One would think after all Leslie has been through she would be on guard, but one bad judgment she made in 1981 is still used aggressively against her at every parole hearing. Lonely, and facing a lifetime in prison, she began corresponding with Bill Cywin, a fellow convict, and when he was released he began to visit her and she eventually married him in a small prison ceremony and was allowed to have conjugal visits, something that must have seemed like a godsend to a young woman in jail forever. Completely unbeknownst to Leslie, her husband was evidently planning some harebrained prison break for her, and a prison matron's uniform was discovered by the police in his apartment. Leslie immediately cut off all contact with him, divorced him, and never saw or heard from him again. Not one of her prosecutors ever tried to say she was in on this plan in any way, and they admitted they knew she was innocent of any knowledge of her husband's attempt. But they never let her forget it. Her "bad judgment," her supposed "continued desire to be with 'bad men,'" is constantly brought up at every parole hearing to prove she is unsuitable. "Who *hasn't* had a bad boyfriend?" I wish her lawyer would ask the board.

Am I, too, a "bad man" in Leslie's life? The one year the parole board read my name as a supporter and it was broadcast on TV, I watched for Stephen Kay to somehow bring up my notoriety and use it against Leslie. Will they take this chapter of my book and use certain sentences out of context to hurt her chances? I told Leslie of my fears, but she urged me to stay firmly in her corner, pointing out I had taught in prisons, had been successfully making my movies for forty years, and could help her find employment if she were ever released. "I have stable relationships," Leslie tried to explain to the board in 1996. "Often relationships are measured in man/woman/marriage/romance. As a forty-six-year-old woman, I feel my most important and cherished relationships are my friends."

What would Leslie Van Houten do if she *did* get paroled? She has many offers of employment and housing, and a large support group of friends and family could usher her quietly back into society. "She'll never get out," some friends of mine have always said, and in the 1970s Leslie probably agreed. "I try to figure out, how do I live out the rest of my life in here and be able to say it wasn't a wasted life?" she has wondered in the past; but later, "naturally mourning my own life that has never been," Leslie began daring to hope. "If I am ever paroled I want to be anonymous and live a life as quietly as I can." She said much the same in 1978, imagining "a private and humble life." And finally, in the nineties, her lawyers began fighting against the perception that she had been sentenced to life without parole, because she was not. "The fact that she should realistically be considered [for parole]," her defense lawyer at the time, Dan Mrotek, argued to the board, "is not due to the fact she has done something exceptional in this institution—it is due to how your regulations are written. So we do not want just your subjective opinion about what should happen to her. We want justice in terms of the fair application of your regulations." Fifteen positive psychiatric reports have been read into the record over the years, and her lawyers could not understand why the board could not hear their message. "It is my opinion," a doctor in Leslie's jail wrote, "that she [Leslie] has continued this self-improvement, not as a motivation to parole but as a genuine interest in bettering herself. It is my opinion that the inmate would not be dangerous if she was released to the community."

In 1996 Leslie started to fight back, too, by arguing she should be paroled "because there is a system that says I can earn it. I have taken seriously what I have done. I have redesigned my life where I am a conscientious and caring individual. I am now who I would have been if I had not gone into a drug/Manson lifestyle." At her last hearing she could not have been more honest. Still "deeply ashamed," Leslie ignored the rule against looking at the victim's families and begged the LaBianca survivors, "I ask that I be shown the mercy I didn't give . . . and that is not easy in this [parole board] room but I'm going to ask for it. I am who I say I am."

Leslie Van Houten has served more time than any Nazi war criminal who was not sentenced to death at Nuremberg. She has served more time that *any* of the Nazi defendants who were sentenced to life in prison except for Hitler's deputy, Rudolf

Hess, who died in his fortieth year in prison (the exact amount of time Leslie has now served). She's served more time than Lieutenant William Calley, who was originally sentenced to life in prison for the My Lai massacre of hundreds of Vietnamese civilians. She has served longer than the surviving female members of the Baader-Meinhoff Gang, a German terrorist group who murdered thirty-four people in the name of left-wing "politics" and "revolution." This group began with the student protest movement in 1968, the same year Charles Manson was recruiting his hippie army of LSD soldiers. Brigitte Mohnhaupt was convicted of nine political murders and sentenced to five life sentences, but served just twenty-four years. Another member, Irmgard Möller, convicted of a 1972 bomb attack in Heidelberg that killed three American soldiers, was released in 1994 after serving twenty-four years. Courts ruled that "the decision for probation was reached based on the determination that no security risks exist today." And none of these radicals even said they were sorry!

But how sorry is sorry enough? Albert Speer, Hitler's architect and armaments minister, and one of the few Nazi defendants to take responsibility for Nazi war crimes, even though he denied knowing of the Holocaust, struggled with this question. When Gitta Sereny (here she is again!) interviewed him for her amazing book *Albert Speer: His Battle with Truth*, following his release after serving all twenty years of his sentence in Spandau Prison, she asked the same kind of question about responsibility for the crime that the parole board asks Leslie. While Leslie participated in a much tinier version of a fascist regime, there are definite similarities in the issue of degrees of guilt. Was there something "inherently evil" inside Leslie, as Stephen Kay has charged? Was there a "lack of morality" underneath Speer's initial attraction to "the cause," wondered Ms. Sereny? "If I just answer that question with a 'yes,'" a free Speer honestly responded after decades of reflection, "it would be too simple. For of course *now* I think it was immoral. But what does that mean? Nothing. How can it help our understanding of these terms which is what you and I are trying to do here, I presume, for me to say, 'Yes, yes mea culpa.' Yes, of course, mea culpa, but the whole point is that I *didn't* feel this and why didn't I? Was it Hitler, only Hitler, because of whom I don't understand? Or was it a deficiency in me? Or was it both?"

"How can a man admit more and go on living?" Gitta Sereny asked Speer, probing how deeply he could go inside himself to take in the full weight of his repression of the horror of Hitler's regime. The same incredulous response the prosecutors continue to have over the fact that Leslie knew there had been five killings the night before, yet chose to go along for the next night of mayhem fully aware of what would happen. "You knew all this," Ms. Sereny challenged Speer about Nazi slave labor, "yet you stayed, not only stayed but worked, planned with, and supported. How can you explain? How can you justify? How can you stand living with yourself?" His answers could have been Leslie's. "You cannot understand. You simply cannot understand what it is to live in a dictatorship and you can't understand the game of danger but above all you can't understand the fear on which the whole thing is based." Leslie, too, struggled to explain to a parole board in 2004 how her life was hijacked onto such a horrific track. "It didn't start out that way. It started off like a commune. And then the more he [Manson] measured how much we believed in him, the violence would become more acute until at the end it was very prevalent." "I wanted to leave," she remembered in sadness and frustration, "and I told him I was going to leave. And he took me to the edge of a cliff and he told me I may as well jump off because if I left I would die. Now, you know when you say something like this years and years and years later, and it seems so small. But at the time I believed him. I believed if I left him, the very same thing that happened to Leno and Rosemary LaBianca would happen to me. And now I carry the responsibility for that . . ."

While Speer admits "the intensity of the crime precludes any attempt at self-justification," he stated wearily something I don't think Leslie feels and, as much as I understand his statement, I don't think she ever will. "I awake with it," Speer says of his guilt, "spend my day with it and dream it. But my reply— I know it—has long been routine. I can no longer answer with emotion and people resent this."

One wonders if the Manson Family today were all in one room, would there be an evil spectacle of hippie-devil anarchy, like I saw in that courtroom in 1977, or a group of broken, sad, disillusioned ex-con baby boomers? "These children that came at you with knives," as Charlie once called his followers, are now senior citizens begging forgiveness. The other Manson girls are unrecognizable from the famous early newsreel footage that is still played ad nauseam every time a mention of the crime comes up. Susan Atkins, before having her leg amputated and dying in prison from brain cancer in 2009, wore a hearing aid and could have been mistaken for a suburban dental technician. Patricia

Krenwinkel looks like an elderly high school history teacher. The men, many bald now for *real*, have a sadness and embarrassment about them. How humiliating to have been taken for a ride by such an obvious con man as Charlie. All the repentant Family members cling to the hope they will be forgiven or—even better—forgotten. Albert Speer wondered with Rudolf Hess as they served their long sentence in Spandau Prison whether, if released, they would meet "and have a good bottle of wine and perhaps find it in us to laugh about some of the memories of Spandau." Rudolf Hess answered much in the same way as I believe Leslie would. "If we were ever all out, none of us would ever see each other again and most certainly we would not laugh."

There is an amazing press photo that was taken by Peter Phun for *The Press-Enterprise*, a newspaper in Riverside, California, which shows a beautiful but haunted Leslie Van Houten being walked before the press in 2002 on her way to a court hearing in hopes of overturning the board's rejection of her parole. Leslie is humiliated to still be handcuffed and chained after decades of nonviolence and she is sad that the press is still there to give the Manson brand another jolt of publicity. For security reasons the cops have made her wear her waist-length hair down, not in the dignified bun she usually wears. You can tell Leslie fears it will look "witchy," as Charlie used to order. She is embarrassed by the attention but firmly proud of who she has become. Leslie looks absolutely stunning in her clear-headed maturity. This is the woman I am friends with today.

But one of her prison guards looks over at her in the picture in almost cartoonish fear—he still sees her as a dangerous Manson girl, and one can imagine the excited story he can now tell his wife and kids over dinner that night. Leslie will never be able to overcome this notoriety. But if that same prison guard knew her the way I know her, he wouldn't be afraid anymore. He might even ask her to babysit his kids. Her crime was a long, long time ago and she has paid her dues to society. I hope Leslie Van Houten can be given a second chance. The best gift I can give her is a promise that she doesn't ever have to see me again once she is released. "I'm not trying to get away with anything," Leslie has told anyone who would listen. And she's not. She's really not.

REI KAWAKUBO

Fashion is very important to me. My "look" for the last twenty years or so has been "disaster at the dry cleaners." I shop in reverse. When I can afford to buy a new outfit, something has to be wrong with it. Purposely wrong. Comme des Garçons (like some boys) is my favorite line of clothing, designed by the genius fashion dictator Rei Kawakubo. She specializes in clothes that are torn, crooked, permanently wrinkled, ill-fitting, and expensive. What used to be called "seconds" (clothes that were on sale in bargain basements of department stores because of accidental irregularities) is now called "couture." Ms. Kawakubo is my god. The fashion historian Kazuko Koike has described Rei as "almost like the leader of a religious movement." I genuflect to Rei's destruction of the fashion rules. She is formidable, reclusive, intimidating, and has described her work as an "exercise in suffering."

Ms. Kawakubo's reviews have mostly been brilliant but the bad ones make me prouder to wear her clothes: "unwearable," "post-atomic," "that shrunken, hopeless look," "as threadbare and disheveled as Salvation Army rejects," and, best of all, "fashion is having a nervous breakdown." "I'm always more or less annoying," Kawakubo admitted to Judith Thurman in a revealing 2005 *New Yorker* profile. Wearing what Ms. Thurman describes as "Rei's favorite accessory—a dour expression," Kawakubo admitted that, between collections, she and her husband, Adrian Joffe (president of her company, who sees her once a month), "travel to Yemen or Romania" for . . . what? Fun? When asked by Thurman, "What makes Rei laugh?" she answered without a smile, "People falling down."

I had first heard of Comme des Garçons in 1983, when my friend Gina Koper, who was from Baltimore but now lives in New York, said to me, "You've got to see this new fashion place that opened in my neighborhood—you won't believe it!" Since I knew Gina understood radical fashion situations from working as a white teenage girl in 1969 in a Baltimore *Super Fly*–type men's store called the Purple Bone, I eagerly went with her. The first Comme des Garçons boutique in America was in SoHo, on Wooster Street, and it looked like a morgue. A few black rumpled pieces of clothing lay like wounded bodies on slabs. "Is that a hat or a coat?" nervous customers would ask the severely intimidating sales staff (or "co-combatants" as Rei later called them—"We are the Comme des Garçons army. 'Staff' is too boring a word"). I was amazed at the gall and the wit of the Japanese clothing designs. Many pieces looked fresh out of the sale bin at the Purple Heart thrift shop in Baltimore, but as *Vogue* later put it, "Destruction has its price and it's not cheap." I couldn't afford any of the men's clothes at the time but I hoped one day I could. Suddenly I felt like a drug addict who takes his first shot of heroin. I was about to become addicted to Comme des Garçons and maybe, if I worked hard, Rei Kawakubo could be my dealer. I left the store feeling like a king.

I always cared about clothes but I rebelled early against the preppy look my parents wished I'd wear. Even today the sight of a pair of khakis turns my stomach. As soon as I got out of the house and moved to downtown Baltimore I discovered thrift shops and, brother, did we have good ones. Still do. Where do you think all the vintage shops in New York get their stuff? It's just a three-and-a-half hour drive south to "Charm City," and even though today the most mutant thrift shop worker in the deepest ghetto knows what a Bakelite bracelet is, Baltimore is still cheaper than anywhere else. Our favorite fashion showroom in the sixties was the Carry On Shop, then located downtown on Howard Street. Most of the clothes were donated by rich people associated with Johns Hopkins Hospital, which ran the place. I remember "Fill Your Shopping Bag for a Dollar" day, when all the Dreamland-ers purchased their looks for the year. We bought so many clothes there for our early movies it felt like the wardrobe de-partment at MGM. And even on regular days, when the prices were a little higher, we got creative. Especially Divine and David Lochary. Outraged that any item might cost more than three dollars, they began bringing their own pricing equipment: cardboard that matched the existing price tags, a crayon the same color as used in the store, and a trusty little stapler. Rip-ping off the existing price tags, scribbling in the price *they* felt was fair, and stapling it back on the garment made stylish clothes available to even the poorest fashion fanatic.

Of course there were cheaper thrift stores, but you had to work hard to find good stuff at places like the Hadassah, a real dive that even homeless people snubbed. Maybe stuff was free; I can't remember. But you can see Divine shoplifting there in a scene in *Mondo Trasho* that was filmed while the shop was open, with real customers, and without permission. Divine, dressed in a gold lamé toreador outfit and a tousled blond wig, just walked in and started picking her way through the dresses, many crammed in so tight you could hardly move the hangers, while I just filmed away with my silent 16 mm movie camera. I guess somebody was working there that day, but with this clientele the clerk had seen it all and obviously didn't care *what* we were doing. The bins of clothes were even worse, filled with stained smelly garments that inmates of locked wards in the state mental institutions would reject. But if you picked through long enough and hard enough and didn't mind getting a skin rash, you might, *if* you were very lucky, find a stunning 1950s gown that nobody was wearing in the late sixties. It might have cost a nickel.

In those days, our parents' generation had just thrown away all their 1930s and '40s clothes, and since those were freshly *out* of fashion, our gang started dressing like we were in a low-budget Busby Berkeley movie. I soon grew tired of the Dick-Powell-on-amphetamines look and switched over to a style I developed that made even speed freaks nervous. I loved finding the most hideous cowboy shirts, ones with padded guitars on them, or shrunken heads, or my favorite—giant tarantulas (Stiv Bators later ripped off the sleeves and wore it in *Polyester*). I found a jacket that was a uniform for some sort of dog handler/watchdog company that featured a giant snarling German shepherd on the back and wore that for years (you can see me in it on the cover of the *A Date with John Waters* CD). Pointy-toe suede shoes were easily purchased pre-punk, and we called them "shit-kickers." With my pre-moustache skinny 6'1", 130-pound frame and my long stringy hair, I succeeded in horrifying even seasoned thrift shop enthusiasts.

Then, in 1970, in a misguided attempt to steal Little Richard's identity, I grew my pencil-thin moustache. At first it didn't work right. It's tough for a white man who isn't that hairy to grow one. Sure, I shaved with a razor on top and trimmed the bottom with cuticle scissors, just like I do every day now, but it still looked kind of pitiful. Then "Sick," the friend of mine from the Provincetown tree fort who had moved to Santa Barbara and changed her nickname to "Sique," gave me some fashion advice when I was staying with her. "Just use a little eyebrow pencil and it will work better," she advised, and then showed me how. Presto! An "iconic" look: a ridiculous fashion joke that I still wear forty years later. Surprised? Don't be! It *is* called a "pencil moustache," isn't it? And there is only *one* pencil that does the trick—Maybelline Expert Eyes in Velvet Black. My entire identity depends on this magic little wand of sleaze. It has to be sharpened *every* time it's applied, too—which in my case is twice a day or so. More if you've been making out. Believe me, I've tried expensive, smearproof eyebrow pencils, but they're too thick, too penetrating, too indelible. There's only one eyebrow pencil for me—and that's Maybelline!

I always carry one in my pocket, keep another in my car, and have backups in each of my homes. Once I was in the hospital after being mugged and I guess because of my concussion I had forgotten to bring my Maybelline. I was so panicked that I would limp over to the mirror and try to gouge it on with a regular number two lead pencil used for writing. It didn't work. Since I knew the only visitors I had scheduled that day were my parents, I decided to involve them. I didn't have much of a choice. We had certainly never discussed *how* I did my moustache. I just remember their vaguely nauseated expression when they saw it for the first time when I came back from California. We had so many issues at the time, the moustache had to get in line. I bit the bullet, called my mother, and said, "Don't ask any questions, just go to the drugstore, get me a Maybelline eyebrow pencil in Velvet Black, and bring it to me in the hospital." Silence on her end. "Okay," she finally muttered with mortified annoyance. When Mom and Dad came in the hospital room, she snuck the prized package behind her back and gave it to me without my father seeing. We never ever discussed it again.

I've forgotten to put on my moustache some days and I have to lurk around like Clark Kent looking for a phone booth until I find a car mirror on an uncrowded street (not easy in Manhattan!) or a public restroom where I can, unobserved, repair the damage to my image. I remember once starting out the day with a visit to Mary Boone's midtown art gallery. Mary came out of her office, took one look at me, and blurted in a horrified voice, "What happened to your moustache?!" Instantly feeling nude in public, I realized the problem, mumbled some excuse about the lighting, and left immediately. I raced home in the privacy of a cab, drew it in, blended it, and started the day all over again.

You, too, can have an iconic signature. It's not about money; it's about a look. Angela Davis, the beautiful black radical who helped free the Soledad Brothers in the sixties and ended up on the FBI's Ten Most Wanted list is, much to her chagrin, remembered today more for her amazing Afro hairdo than she is for her radicalism. "It is humiliating because it reduces the politics of liberation to a politics of fashion," she complained in a Baltimore speech, now wearing blond dreadlocks, which made it hard to feel much sympathy for her. But just because you are identifying yourself as a communist, as she is these days, doesn't mean you have to be dreary. You can be smart *and* be known as "The Hairdo," if you play it right. Think Mao—nobody refers to him as "The Jacket," maybe because he never complained about being labeled a fashion influence. Or Che, who may have known how to wear a beret but was a homophobe in real life who rallied against "longhairs" and homosexuals. He was a sexual reactionary, not a "friend of Dorothy," but cool people refuse to believe the truth because of his iconic look, which proves all ideology can be embraced if the leader dresses well. You can be a committed Marxist *and* a fashion enthusiast. Remember the Cockettes? Those bearded San Francisco drag queens from the late sixties who, high on LSD, read Lenin, put on their outlandish makeup, and actually believed "the revolution" was going to happen? They were influential *and* left-wing, and their amazing take on female impersonators liberated drag queens everywhere.

You don't need fashion designers when you are young. Have faith in your own bad taste. Buy the cheapest thing in your local thrift shop—the clothes that are freshly out of style with even the hippest people a few years older than you. Get on the fashion nerves of your peers, not your parents—that is the key to fashion leadership. Ill-fitting is always stylish. But be more creative—wear your clothes inside out, backward, upside down. Throw bleach in a load of colored laundry. Follow the exact opposite of the dry cleaning instructions inside the clothes that cost the most in your thrift shop. Don't wear jewelry—stick Band-Aids on your wrists or make a necklace out of them. Wear Scotch tape on the side of your face like a bad face-lift attempt. Mismatch your shoes. Best yet, do as Mink Stole used to do: go to the thrift store the day after Halloween, when the children's trick-or-treat costumes are on sale, buy one, and wear it as your uniform of defiance.

But past the age of forty you need all the help you can get. Now is the time for designers and, believe me, Rei Kawakubo has made it possible for older people to be as fashion daring as the young. "Too rich? Too nuts?" Yesiree, these are Rei's customers, and we are proud to be her cult members on "Planet Rei." Rei Kawakubo was "the first to make polyester cost more than silk," the model Linda Evangelista told me when I met her at a film festival in France. Rei is not a fashion designer; she's a magician.

All celebrities would look better dressed by Rei Kawakubo. Why do all female movie stars show their tits at the Oscars? Pamela Anderson, Traci Lords, Mariah Carey, even Jessica Rabbit would look so much sexier dressed in a Comme des Garçons creation, one that showed confidence in being smart by purposefully downplaying their curves and looking, as a *Washington Post* critic described them, as though "they had a bad night and gone to bed sweaty and smelling of smoke."

Even Aretha Franklin could benefit. She may be the "Best Soul Singer Ever," but she designs her own clothes and someone should intervene. Lady Soul even wore a black version of Divine's red fishtail gown from *Pink Flamingos* but forgot to bring the humor. Wouldn't it be great if Aretha surprised us all by showing up at her next gig wearing Rei Kawakubo's most notorious design—the "bump" dress, dubbed the "Quasimodo look" by the fashion press? "The ugliest dress of the year," as *Vogue* reported the reaction. The dress with built-in pads that "deformed the stomach, hips or shoulders," the very parts of the body most fashionable women go to the gym to eliminate. Not since Chanel introduced the "sack dress" in the fifties had a garment caused such a fury. Wouldn't Aretha shut up her severest fashion critics by wearing the Comme des Garçons "hunchback" look! Don't try to be sexy at three hundred pounds, Aretha; be cutting edge. Exaggerate the bulges in your body through fashion and nobody will see the real weight. Anybody that calls herself "the Queen" and hopes to get away with it has to have nerve.

I modeled for Rei Kawakubo once. In Paris. In those tents outside the Louvre where collections are unveiled every year. I was really surprised to be asked but leaped at the chance for a new job. Me? A model? I guess Rei had seen press photos of me wearing some of her outfits to openings, or maybe the salespeople told her what a fan I was. Before accepting, I begged that Comme des Garçons consider my age (forty-six at the time) and maybe let me wear some of her more conservative outfits, not the most ridiculous ones. I *loved* the most ridiculous, but, please, let the "real" models strut their stuff in them. However, I soon learned there were no "real models." Rei likes her menswear modeled by amateurs—boys off the European street—who are somehow rounded up to wear her amazingly ludicrous and beautiful clothes on the runway.

Arriving backstage for rehearsal the day before the show, I realized I was the fattest model among the scrawny, gorgeous, blasé street urchin skeletons who were trying on their outfits and pointing at each other and laughing good-naturedly at their Comme des Garçons makeovers. My first outfit was a relief— a black suit with flood-length trousers and a white shirt with an exaggerated shirttail partially worn outside and hanging halfway to the knees. But then I saw the crazy hat. No man looks more stupid in a hat than I do. Oh God, I wondered, could I talk Rei Kawakubo out of the hat? When I saw her enter, I trembled in my Comme des Garçons boots. There she was—dressed all in black with that Louise Brooks bob hairdo and looking like she had been locked in a cell for months meditating on the deconstruction of the concept of hemlines. Bald-headed girls, who I think were her assistants, hovered around her. When I was introduced, I just told her how proud I was to be there and then begged her to let me not wear a hat. She frowned deeper, then without a word, switched my hat to one a little less ridiculous. Suddenly I thought, What the hell! She flew you over here first class, is paying you, giving you some free clothes. So just shut up, wear a hat, and do what you are told.

The day of the show, I'm backstage with all the motley cool

pretend models who looked more like drug-addled janitors or concentration camp victims (Rei later got in trouble for designing pajama-type outfits that some misguided critics claimed were reminiscent of death camp uniforms) and I realized that here were the kind of boys I like best—my type if there ever was one. I could hear the buzz (or was it the venom-dripped whispers?) of the A-list fashion press on the other side of the curtain and suddenly I got up my nerve. *Until* I was told I had to go out first. Talk about terror. Right before I had to go on, I had to pass through the stylists and end up later under the hawk eye of Rei herself for a final inspection. She took in my entire look in one critical glance and suddenly grabbed the collar of my shirt and yanked it sideways so it hung clumsily. Whatever courage I had managed to work up vanished instantly, but she gave me a severe pat of confidence and shoved me through the curtain onto the runway.

Jesus Christ, I'm a model in Paris. Don Knotts meets *Mahogany*. Cover of *Spy* magazine, here I come. But be brave, I thought, hold your head high and look unafraid. I walked to the end of the runway, turned around, and people applauded, quietly and severely. Other models followed me. No one laughed. It started to feel kind of great. It's a long way from Lutherville, Maryland, to the runways of Paris. How did this ever happen?

Later that evening, after the show, there was some kind of party for the models, and boy could these Comme des Garçons recruits drink! Few could speak English, but who cared? Maybe it was their newfound fashion aggression, but they sure were friendly. I was in hog heaven. I can't remember much about what happened after the party except driving to the hotel in the backseat of my limo with a gang of crazy, young, drunk street models who were hanging their heads out the windows and howling at the moon before being dropped off. What a great Paris memory! Isn't fashion fun? And you know what? I didn't end up on the cover of *Spy* magazine but on the cover of *DNR*, the men's version of *Women's Wear Daily*, and I looked . . . well, not so bad.

So now, when I get dressed every day, I pretend I'm a model. Even in Baltimore, where people I love insult me daily over my fashion choices. "That's a shame about that coat," a big bruiser blithely told me, eyeing my meatball-brown, permanently wrinkled polyester sports jacket as I stood next to him on a Friday night in a favorite biker bar, the Holiday House. The jacket my old dry cleaner had tried to "fix," unaware it had been designed by Rei Kawakubo so it could not be ironed or pressed no matter how hard you tried. True, this great little coat had dry cleaning instructions inside more complicated than the ones for assembling the atomic bomb, but who could figure *them* out? Only I knew that this Value Village look-alike garment had actually cost a thousand dollars. "Thank you," I answered, as I ordered the biker a drink and caught him shaking his head at my pin-striped shirt, which was permanently stained with what looks like oil. Since I was in a blue-collar bar, I thought for sure I'd fit in better in this Comme des Garçons tribute to grease monkeys everywhere. If I was lucky, maybe somebody would rub more grease on my shirt after the bar closed. "It comes like that," I tried to explain before he noticed the Comme des Garçons Shirt

Line pants, the ones with panels sewn in the bottom of each leg in a different material and that seem to have been hastily altered because you had mysteriously grown in height. "I'll take a beer," he chuckled, mercifully not commenting on my Rei Kawakubo–designed brown oxfords that came with shoelace holes, but no laces, just elastic underneath the tongue that kept them magically on your feet and eventually was copied by every tennis shoe designer in the world.

The next day it's Saturday, so I go to visit my parents and I hesitate while choosing an outfit. They know about "that lady whose clothes you like," but I try not to start a fight by wearing Rei's most insane, like my gold lamé sports jacket similar to one Elvis wore on that album cover for *50,000,000 Elvis Fans Can't Be Wrong*. Well, Ten Fashion Casualties Can't Be Wrong either, but I decide to spare my parents this debate. Similarly rejecting my off-white shag rug favorite—the sports jacket that looks so much like a dirty bath mat that strangers always laugh in my face—I also pass by the blue shirt with the pink splotches all over it. "You *bought* that?!" my dad (who died in June 2008 at the age of ninety-one) had bellowed when he first saw it, and I must admit, a shirt that makes you look like a moving target for a paintball gun did have a certain fashion edge. Even *I* hesitated before leaving the house wearing it, but some days you just need fashion gall.

Today can't be that day. I lunge for and then reconsider my favorite CDG pants, the ones with the seams that have the threads hanging off, the trousers that literally unravel without falling apart as you wear them. "Don't worry, they get worse," the salesperson told me with a fashion wink as I signed the credit card slip. And I certainly knew better than to wear my pink leather pointy-toe Comme des Garçons tennis shoes, which I also have in bright orange. Matter of fact, I bought all six colors in the canvas style, too. I can't get enough of Rei's pointy-toe tennis shoes, and in the summer in Provincetown I line them all up on the floor like some kind of art installation, but today I'm dressing for the family so I'd better be careful. Pink shoes and Dad are a fight waiting to happen.

Trying to be conservative, and remembering my parents' hoot of derision when I showed them the press clipping of me being named to the Best Dressed Men list when it was written by the late Eleanor Lambert of *Women's Wear Daily*, I slip into my gray pinstripe jacket designed by Rei to look normal on the outside. Underneath was a whole different story, of course— coffinlike blue satin ruffles that made you both fat *and* ready for the undertaker give the jacket an inner lunacy that you could keep secret as long as the coat remained buttoned. Finally choosing my "inside-out" Comme des Garçons shirt with the pockets sewn inside, therefore making them impossible to use, I figured this "fashion theory" was too complicated to be noticed by fashion civilians like my parents. I took a chance and wore tennis shoes from the same inside-out line. I knew my mom and dad wouldn't notice the size and model number painted on the outside of the shoe and hoped they wouldn't pick up on the shoe tongue flapping in the wind over the laces. Being inside-out fashionwise is the best way to visit your parents if you can be stealthy about it and slip away before they get pissed off at the whole idea.

Now it's Saturday night and I'm headed to the Kitty Kat Bar, my favorite ska/punk-rock saloon, filled with non-racist skinheads and punk-rock boys, even angrier and cuter because they are too old to be in a band. If it's summer, I know I can get away with the jacket I wore to the new *Hairspray* movie musical premiere at the Kennedy Center, the one *The Washington Post* called "the ugliest sports jacket in the world." I might get beaten up if I wear this hideous Rei-designed Dunkin' Donuts–like patterned jacket on the street, but at this great dive bar nobody notices, because the boys here dress like IRA members at the height of the conflict. I remember a New Year's Eve at the Kitty Kat Bar when I was there in some ridiculous outfit—probably my green plaid Comme des Garçons jacket that was shrunken hideously by Rei throwing it into the washing machine instead of having it dry cleaned. With my favorite two-toned Comme des Garçons tie that featured bad stitching and pseudo rips, I felt all ready to ring in the New Year. Right at the stroke of midnight, all these kids suddenly wrapped scarves around their heads like terrorists, put on ski masks, zipped up their hoodies, and ran outside into the streets and set off the most frighteningly insane display of fireworks I've ever seen. Industrial-strength ones. All noise and no beauty. Bomblike explosions on a tiny street instead of a stadium. The neighbors flipped, the cops came, and everybody scattered in fashion terror. If Rei Kawakubo had been there that night, she would have been so inspired.

How far can you push fashion in blue-collar Baltimore? My onetime favorite bar, Kildaire's, is still there, but under a whole different management these days. For a very short while this watering hole held a special place in my vodka-soaked heart. I liked to go there alone. Then stuff can happen. Never bad stuff, because I dress appropriately. Comme des Garçons can be subtle, especially if danger is lurking. I have on one of Rei's jackets that looks sort of normal from a distance, but up close the blue material looks stained. Some might say with a semen-like pattern. Spurted. Glamorous "pecker tracks," if you will. The mostly all-male, heterosexual clientele, who are white, dress like Eminem, and dance feverishly and by themselves to gangster rap music, don't notice my sartorial detail. But I know I have on a killer jacket, and as I sit alone at the bar marveling at the scene before me (where are the girls?), I feel accepted. Sure, they know who I am, but they don't seem the slightest bit impressed. The DJ, the only black man in the house, honors my presence by playing Eminem's "Puke" every time I come in the door, but this small tribute hardly qualifies him as a star fucker. "Hey, John," a hopped-up but scarily cute redneck guy says as he makes eye contact, "watch this." Suddenly he slam-dances the table near the dance floor with all his might, splintering the wood in front of me. As he gets up off the floor and gives me a sheepish grin, I applaud his destructive dance steps and feel so happy to live in Baltimore, secretly dressed by Rei Kawakubo.

But wait, down some steps at the back of the entrance hall is a whole other bar. And guess who that's for? The Hells Angels! For real. The true fashion leaders of the universe. They've always been nice to me, no matter how unbutchly I was dressed. The Fat Boys, too—another local biker gang I've known for years from hanging around another bar up the street. I even went once to the Fat Boys' secret clubhouse that was *so Scorpio Rising*. One of the main Hells Angels, though, was a tougher nut to crack. It took him ten years to finally say hello to me, but after agreeing to appear in *A Dirty Shame* he was downright cordial. "Wanna come downstairs with me and have a drink?" I ask the cute slam-dancing "wigga" upstairs, marveling at the fact that this is a convertible bar—two in one! Downstairs: bikers; upstairs: white-boy gangstas. Could there possibly be a better setup?! But "Noooooo," the imitation African American answers in fear, "I'm not going down *there*. No way!"

What the hell. I go downstairs alone in full fashion confidence. I mean, bikers have the best possible look, but it is a style that is vanishing. Young bad boys don't want to be bikers anymore; they want to be black. Unfortunately, for the young these days, Hells Angel is a trick-or-treat outfit. It's a confusing look, too. In the one store in Baltimore that sells custom-made biker leathers, there are *two* very different breeds of shopper: the straight bikers and the gay sadomasochist crowd, and both are going through the same midlife crisis. S&M men are having a hard time recruiting, too! Young gay people don't feel guilty about being homosexual—they don't need to be paddled or whipped anymore. Still, the middle-aged enthusiasts of both biker and gay culture ended up wearing the exact same look with very different intentions. They have no choice but to shop side by side, avoiding all eye contact. No wonder the bikers didn't punch me out for wearing Comme des Garçons.

In some Baltimore drinking establishments, the patrons are so happily drunk you can model your most ridiculous Comme des Garçons outfit and no one will be sober enough to see it.

Dimitri's, at last call, is the perfect place to wear my ludicrous Burberry-like brown plaid sports jacket with a panel of the same material sewn on the bottom, making it too long. The plaids don't line up and this extra material added in by the designer gives the jacket the embarrassing suggestion of a skirt. Many nights I put it on before I go out, look in the mirror, and chicken out. But not tonight; it's late and what the hell, I need some new stories. After all, this *is* the tavern where I stupidly asked a guy, "What do you do for a living?" and he said, "Can I be frank?" When I answered, "Sure," he replied matter-of-factly, "I trade deer meat for crack." You can't make this shit up. Screenwriters are paid a fortune in Hollywood to come up with this kind of dialogue and I get it for free. The only problem is, in Dimitri's, many of the karaoke customers are so sloshed and have such Baltimore accents that when they try to have conversations, they can only yell at top volume in your face in a kind of excited gibberish that only a local (and I mean four-blocks-away local) could possibly understand. It really doesn't matter to me and I yell back, having no idea if my answer addresses their question. One thing I *do* know for sure—no one has noticed my ridiculous brown plaid Comme des Garçons coat that looks like a stupid skirt. *And* I'm sixty-three years old!

On the way out, a young tough-looking white kid who has his own ridiculous look—full-tilt ghetto baggy—follows me out and offers, "Hey! My dad used to know you from up BJ's." BJ's, a long-ago-torn-down legendary scary white bar up the street, was used as the location for the final scene in my movie *Pecker*. "Who is your dad?" I ask, remembering fondly the night when a friend and I went into the men's room to take a leak and came face-to-face with two junkies freebasing. "Beat it, Curley," one barked at my friend, and we turned in our tracks and fled. "He's dead now," the kid responded sadly, "but he told me he used to watch your back up at BJ's and I just want to tell you *I'll* watch your back from now on whenever you come in here." Now, *that's* what I call accepted. And safe. I was touched. Who knows, maybe next time I'll wear my gold lamé Comme des Garçons tennis shoes.

Wearing fashion in New York is a whole different story. "Dressed in his thrift shop finest," the press has written many times when I go to openings wearing Rei Kawakubo's newest reinvention of "bum wear." But here, I can model my "I, a Notebook" jacket, the one made out of material exactly like the black-and-white cover of every schoolkid's composition book, and no one will bat an eye. Sometimes strangers ask, "Is that Comme des Garçons?" I can slip into my hideous gold-and-copper fake-snakeskin-patterned Beatle boots that Mary Boone bought from Comme des Garçons and gave to me for my sixtieth birthday, and a few will recognize that they didn't come from the sale bin at the Flagg Brothers shoe store. Even if I go out to my favorite New York restaurant, Prune, and wear my snappy little fall jacket that zips up crookedly and hangs on me in an unflattering way, no one will sneer. New Yorkers understand that sometimes everybody needs to dress crookedly.

Only in Manhattan do I dare wear a fragrance. And that's Odeur 53, Rei Kawakubo's scent that to me smells exactly like Off! insect repellant. The best thing about Odeur 53 is that the smell doesn't last very long. "Rei doesn't really like perfume for men," a salesperson needlessly tried to explain. I love the idea of a perfume that disappears—you don't need to convince me! Designed to "confront the nose"—the press release's copy for this "anti-perfume" was art in itself—"a memory of smell . . . entering the world of abstraction by way of a feeling . . . the future, the space, the air." With astonishing seriousness Rei listed the *in*organic ingredients: "the freshness of oxygen, wash drying in the wind, nail polish, burnt rubber and the mineral intensity of carbon." That's exactly what I want to smell like! How did she know?!

You have to be careful about fashion at the beach. And Rei Kawakubo refuses to acknowledge the seasons, often showing air-suffocating polyester or wool for summer or skimpy little jackets with mesh seams cut in that make the hawklike winds of New York City even more shocking to your skinny body. In Provincetown, I try to blend in. I'm always on my bicycle, so I can't wear any of Rei's suave little orange suede loafers that might slip on the pedals or her black "fashion stunt wear" pants with the strings hanging off that could get caught in the spokes. And since I love minorities and Provincetown is a gay fishing village, I hang out in the two straight bars. My first stop is always downstairs at the Bradford, which is a little-known large bar beneath a popular Commercial Street drag karaoke tourist hangout. The grouchy stock boys who work in the local supermarket and refuse to make eye contact with you in the aisles, the handymen around town who don't show up for their jobs renovating all the expensive new condo conversions, and the hetero townies who grew up in a gay town and have a certain wariness about the homo majority without being homophobic make up the customers. There's a pool table and a DJ who plays all rap music. It reminds me of that Jodie Foster movie *The Accused*, where her character gets raped on a pinball machine by a gang of New Bedford–type morons. I usually wear my brown CDG sports coat that Rei Kawakubo hastily spray-painted black right before putting it out on the rack. You can tell because, if you turn up the collar, you can see she forgot or, better yet, *chose* not to spray underneath. It's a really ugly jacket but it makes me feel . . . well . . . of the people. So many of the customers here could just go home and spray-paint their daywear uniforms and presto—they'd be right in fashion, but I wisely decide to keep that information to myself.

If that place is dead I go across the street to the Old Colony, which used to be a fisherman bar but now is a nice place for budding alcoholics. It looks like the set of a whaling movie, and there is some vomiting at the height of the season. Since people knock into you a lot, I like to wear a blue coat that, if you look really closely, you realize, no, it doesn't need to be cleaned; those coffee stains are part of the fabric. This way if a drunken fisherman spills a drink on you, you've turned him into a fashion designer and he's none the wiser.

My real passion is hitchhiking and I do it a lot in Provincetown. I have a sign that reads LONGNOOK BEACH on one side and PROVINCETOWN on the other. Very Depression-era, just like today. But it works. Cars pick me up immediately; it's like hailing a cab. I try to look very hobo-like, yet not scary. If it's chilly I'll even wear a sports jacket—Rei's very conservative green number that looks completely normal except for one hideous, large clownlike button on the front. But when the temperature soars I go for her lightweight pajama-type jacket, so preppy yet so *Titicut Follies*–mental institution. Rei has never done a men's bathing suit as far as I know and I tremble to think what she could come up with—drawstrings that hang to the knees? Shorts with faux beet-red suntan lines? A reason to live.

I have a place in San Francisco, too. My filth empire keeps expanding and I'm so happy to once again spend time in the first city where my films caught on outside of Baltimore, way before New York. I live in a great apartment on Nob Hill, just five blocks from where I used to pull over and sleep in my car in 1970. I don't feel that different. I still dress like I'm homeless. The weather is so perfect for fashion here—always a slight chill, so I'm free to wear year-round the jacket from Comme des Garçons I wear most. It's a beautifully cut traditional three-button black sports coat, but Rei must have had a fashion vision the day she was finished, because she angrily tore off the entire collar. It's now ragged, and dirt gets caught in the tears, but "la mode destroy" never looked so beautiful. Of all my CDG jackets, this is the one the dry cleaners hate the most. "No! No! No! Don't repair it!" I always have to yell when they look at the jacket with a dumbfounded expression. To make matters worse, I like to pair it alongside her all-white dress shirt buttoned up to the top (I copied David Lynch, who invented this look) with one half of the front collar in black, which always gives a cockeyed optical illusion when worn with a black tie.

I'm obsessed with taking public transportation in San Francisco so I can feel like a real local. I read about someone in L.A.

who rides the buses just to pick up people. A "transfer queen"? I wouldn't be very good at this because when I get on a bus, people in the Bay Area start laughing. Not meanly. And I don't think at what I'm wearing—a lightweight four-button black sports coat with the fabric around the shoulders dyed gray in a dripping motif paired with a CDG white shirt that has a random mismatched piece of green material sewn awkwardly on the front for no apparent reason. No, it's just because they don't expect to see me. "What are you doing on a bus?!" they ask, as if they expect me to have my own personal filthmobile and driver. What can I say? I'm just a model-about-town and the bus routes are my runway.

The Comme des Garçons boutique on West 22nd Street in New York is my favorite of all Rei's stores. When you walk in, it feels architecturally like you just entered the Tilt-A-Whirl. Tomoko is my favorite salesperson . . . no, excuse me, fashion warrior. Even though she, I *think*, has a good sense of humor, she is quite serious about her customers. Once she called me at ten p.m. in Provincetown, and since it was kind of late for a "school night" (weekday nights before the next day's writing hours in the morning), I didn't pick up, but heard her voice on the answering machine. "We got them in!" she breathlessly announced. Stumbling from my bed where I had been reading, I picked up the phone, worried she was in some kind of trouble. "Got *what* in?" I asked, mystified. "The new line!" she responded without the slightest suggestion of a joke. "Is this some sort of fashion emergency?" I asked half in jest. "Well . . . yes," she declared like a proud drug dealer. "I thought you'd want to know we got everything through customs." She was calling from the *airport*?! God, how great! "Of course I want to know, Tomoko! Thank you for calling, and I'll be in to see the new stuff the first day I get to New York." "Good night," she said, and hung up. Fashion bulletins! I slept easier that night knowing Tomoko was looking out for me in the fashion trenches.

I've only been to the Tokyo flagship store twice: the old one in Aoyama once and later the new one in Minamiaoya, Minato-Ku, that opened in 1998. The very best thing about shopping here is the woman who seems to be the manager, although that title hardly seems appropriate. She is, quite simply, the ultimate Comme des Garçons woman and has worked there for years. Her name is Ms. Keiko Mimoto and she is of undetermined age, wears such fierce CDG outfits that I'm not even sure they are for sale, and looks exactly like a witch. A stunning, stylish witch like the one in *Snow White* with the crooked teeth. Imperious, yet flawed in a brand-new way, she is hardly who you'd expect to greet you as you enter a high-end fashion boutique. I am actually scared of her chicness. No one would ever laugh at her "look," no matter how Kawakubo'd-out she may appear. She is not a fashion casualty; she is fashion authority itself. You almost expect her to offer you a poison apple. I'd eat it. I bow down to her fashion divinity.

Rei Kawakubo's Dover Street Market store in London is one of her newest experiments: an actual Comme des Garçons department store that also sells other designers whom Rei deigns to anoint. You have to see it to believe it. Six floors, thirteen thousand square feet of fashion lunacy. Or, as Rei puts it, "an ongoing atmosphere of strong and beautiful chaos." In other words, "DARE TO SHOP HERE!!" You walk in past off-putting freakish taxidermy displays, and if you decide to try something on, there are porta-potties instead of dressing rooms, and if you purchase your item, you pay in Mortville-style checkout huts that bring back images of Tent City, U.S.A. It truly is the deconstruction of the department store you may remember from your youth. There are beautiful velvet drapes, but they are torn and tattered and have holes in them that bring to mind a hungry moth attack. To further alienate the traditional shopper, rap music or obscure speed-metal fills the air instead of Muzak. There is a bookstore stocked with obscure vintage art books. And yes, there is a lunchroom, but here it is called an "organic café." It is so sparse that any kind of appetite is mocked. Lunch specials? Parsnips, the day I was there. Yummy! I'll have two orders, please. On the basement level is an actual CD shop, and I was amazed to see that I had not heard of one of the musicians for sale. In the back is my favorite section. You have to bend down to kind of semicrawl through an opening leading to an entire section of "elf wear": tiny, shrunken, amazing little outfits that are designed to be too small for the skinniest, most severe Japanese male fashion radicals.

I've never been to Rei Kawakubo's Guerrilla Stores, but I want to open one in Baltimore similar to the kind she began showcasing in 2005 in remote, ungentrified areas in cities of Europe. Like Dogme 95 movies, Comme des Garçons has a strict series of guidelines for their shops that are explained in *Guerrillazine— Extracts of a Corporate Nightmare*, a combination shopping guide—instruction manual whose cover is riddled with bullet holes. One can picture Rei Kawakubo nailing her "guerrilla rules" to the door of the Gap or Banana Republic like a fashion-obsessed Martin Luther.

"Rule Number One—The Guerrilla Store will last no more than one year in any given location." Heresy for Baltimore, a town where the word "trendy" seems almost preposterous. Ideal, however, for the ten shoppers here who might actually like to be CDG customers.

"Rule Number Two—The concept for the interior design will be largely equal to the existing space." Perfect! And I know just the spot for the one I'm going to manage in Baltimore. Armistead Gardens, a neighborhood originally built as public housing for the influx of people coming to work in factories during World War II. It has been called a "white ghetto" of "row-ranchers," surprising in their "now outdated modernity." There is an amazing graveyard nearby where the star of my early movie *Eat Your Makeup*, Maelcum Soul, is buried. No one *ever* shops in Armistead Gardens.

"Rule Number Three—The location will be chosen according to the atmosphere, historic connection, geographical situation away from established commercial areas or some other interesting feature." Well, I remember seeing the perfect house. A tiny little home surrounded by vinyl siding, concrete block exteriors, and Formstone motifs. Where, driving by, spying on a location for a movie script I was writing, I saw an amazing Russ Meyer–type woman walk out her front door with her little baby nestled in her giant silicone bosoms, which couldn't be hidden even under a winter coat. She looked so bold, so exaggerated, that I kept making up fictitious biographies of her in my mind.

There she goes—an obvious exotic dancer who happens to be a single mother in Armistead Gardens. Trying to make ends meet, just like everybody else, on her way to work, first dropping off her kid at day care before showing up to lap dance her way to the mortgage payment. Her apartment is the perfect place for a hidden Comme des Garçons–John Waters boutique.

"Rule Number Four—The merchandise will be a mix of all seasons, new and old clothing and accessories . . ." I can just picture the shop now! You walk through her front door under a ladder for bad luck and see the most radical Comme des Garçons women's lines displayed on plastic-covered furniture stamped "March of Dimes," the sweaters with purposely stitched holes or the pants with a bonus leg that my buddy Dennis Dermody once described as "fashion formerly owned by onetime Siamese twins." The few misfires, the CDG lines I *didn't* like, would definitely be carried here, too. The Rolling Stones' *Sticky Fingers* tongue–patterned men's wear and *anything* with a cartoon character in its design, especially Oswald the Rabbit. I'd put them all in the bizarre female urinal in the bathroom, the one we'd borrow from the ladies' room of the nearby Bengies Drive-In Theatre. This actual working toilet, made and then abandoned in the 1940s, was for women to urinate in standing up. Don't believe me? Go look for yourself. Just enter the ladies' room at the drive-in (the same one we shot the final scene of *Cecil B. Demented* in) and there it is, on the right-hand wall, lonely, just begging to be used.

Inside the living room would be the main shopping area of our little Guerrilla Store. We'd have shelves that collapsed if you touched the "Hiroshima chic" classics, but a helpful salesperson from the Man Alive program, high on methadone, would wait on you and assist in picking up stuff. In the tiny kitchen our stripper muse would have left out some old pit beef to nibble on, and if it was humid outside there would be some rusty ice shavers and a few bottles of the most obscure syrupy flavorings, like Egg Custard, and you could cool off by making yourself a snowball. But don't get *too* comfortable. As soon as you even try to sit down, short high school dropouts from the neighborhood, hiding beneath the cushions of the furniture, will push up and "reject" you just like the couch did in *Pink Flamingos* after Divine had licked it. And payment? Well, we *do* accept food stamps.

"Rule Number Five—The partners will take responsibility for the lease and Comme des Garçons will support the store with the merchandise on a sale or return basis." "Sale?" Yes, they have sales at Comme des Garçons, but what about the stuff that doesn't sell even then? I had always heard of the great Comme des Garçons fire, but I'm not sure it's not just a fashion myth. Supposedly, on the final day, after the final sale, in a secret location, the remaining stock, the stuff absolutely no one in the world wanted even reduced in price by 80 percent, is burned in a giant bonfire so as to not end up in some common outlet shop. Even if this tale isn't true, couldn't we have the fire for the first time for real at my Baltimore shop? Think of the amazing photograph! Couldn't Rei light the first match herself? Think of the polyester-and-rayon-polluted smoke drifting over the Armistead Gardens neighborhood and the magic spell it could possibly cast on the unsuspecting neighbors. The ecstasy of rejection, the raptures of unavailability, and the open-sesame of Rei's vision could turn this beautiful downscale section of Baltimore into an international fashion mecca.

Rei, I have a wish list for you. I know you're busy. I realize you don't take "notes" (the new n-word for all film directors), but I just have some ideas for future outfits that I would happily pay you too much money for. I hate weddings; I've never had fun at one in my life. I know you've designed a black wedding dress with a white veil, and it was so cutting-edge *Modern Bride*. But how about something for *me* to wear to a wedding to take my mind off the romance pressure I feel pulsating around me? Something secret, because I'm not a rude person and you never want your outfit to upstage the bride's or groom's. How about an elegant black wool Vincent Price–type suit: on the outside so seemingly conservative and beautifully tailored, but inside lined with the fur of the mice who were living and nesting under the hood of my car in my garage, nibbling away at the engine's wiring harness and causing about a thousand dollars' worth of damage? Wearing fur coats always makes one look like an old person, but poisoned or trapped mouse-fur lining seems politically correct to me, especially when the same little fuckers had friends who were setting up house inside the exterior air-conditioning compressor of my Baltimore home and chewing on the wiring. If we hadn't discovered these little *Ben* and *Willard* movie-type wannabes and had turned on the cooling system the first hot day, these unwelcome squatters would have been ground up by the motor fan blades and their death fumes would have been

piped into my home in all their decomposed glory. So what better purpose could their deaths have than to be recycled as fashion? Even their little heads could be designed as buttons for the
inside pockets!

Let's talk about the suit pants. Couldn't they have faux
"scraped knees"? You like to see people fall down—here's the
perfect reminder for your customer of the one thing that gives
you pleasure. You've already done shirts with triple collars, but
how about one with an extra arm that hangs in the back under
the coat that nobody but me would see or know about? Of course
the tie, an item of clothing I love and you seem to rarely design,
should be covered with clever soup stains. We know how hard
and expensive it is to properly clean a tie, so you can now charge
double the price and it will still be a deal, because you'd never
have to take it to the dry cleaners.

My dream socks that you would create only for me would be
mismatched and stretched out with holes where the big toe
sticks through ("summer socks," we used to call these castaways).
Your belts would go around me twice and would be tested for
possible autoerotic strangulation use. It would be too vulgar to
ask you to design faux "skidmark" underwear, so how about
white boxers stained from purposely washing them with a load
of brightly colored laundry?

But, Rei, my final wish is a pair of creepily sophisticated
faux Pic 'N Pay shoes that I hope you'll design for me to wear
inside my closed (as my will demands) coffin. Like the ones the
Moe Howard look-alike, the "shoe bomber," wore that day on
the airplane. Scruffy, ugly oxfords whose hideousness has been
negated by your "relentless sobriety," as the critics have written.

Shoes with wires and fuses hanging off them. And real dyna-mite inside. Scary and aggressive footwear—the perfect acces-sory to my final outfit. The worms go in, the worms go out; the worms play pinochle on my snout. Now I'll be ready to blast off into Comme des Garçons heaven.

BALTIMORE HEROES

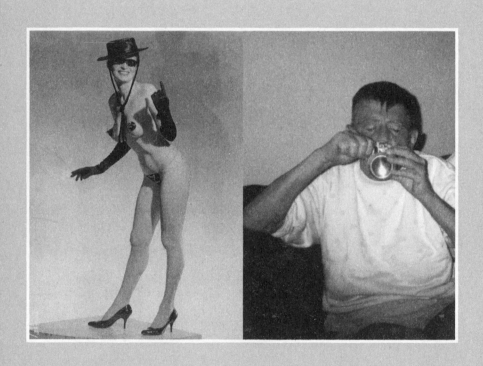

Every Friday night of my life I drink. An alcoholic one night of the week, a workaholic the other six. My shrink had even agreed that seemed like a good plan for me. Only I'm better these days. Now I don't work *either* day of the weekend unless I have a speaking engagement. And I still only drink too much on Fridays. "Was it fun making your movies?" people always ask. "No!" I respond. " 'Fun' is being home in Baltimore and going out to scary bars." So here goes: My Night of a Thousand Drinks.

Bars have always been a big part of living in Baltimore, and the good ones have no irony about them. They're not "faux" anything. They're real and alarming. True, Baltimore is changing, but what I make movies about is still there, lurking on the backstreets, the unheralded neighborhoods, off the beaten track. When I was a teenager, before I could legally get into bars, I hung around *outside* of bars. My mom used to drive me downtown from our safe, then almost countrylike neighborhood to Martick's, a bar known (at the time) for its bohemian customers. "Well," she'd sigh as she dropped me off outside, knowing I couldn't get in because the owner was aware I wasn't twenty-one, "at least here you might meet some people you could get along with." I sure wasn't having much luck elsewhere. I didn't realize this at the time, but what a brave wonderful chance my mother took by doing that! Even though she was horrified by what I was hoping to become, she encouraged my chances. And she knew that Maelcum Soul was the barmaid there and that my best friend Pat Moran (we met because we had the same boyfriend) sometimes joined her behind the counter selling drinks. I hung out in the alley, or as we started calling it, the "alley-a-go-go." Pretty soon other lunatic bar customers would come outside to talk to this skinny underage longhaired kid who wanted to make movies. I was in seventh heaven.

My mom didn't know it, but I *had* already gotten into a Baltimore bar with fake ID. Pepper Hill was a semi-legal gay club located right next door to the main downtown police station. Who wouldn't wonder about payoffs? There I saw "Pencil," my first other-side-of-the-tracks drag freak. He was Baltimore's male Tralala, and I used to see him in the daytime, too, when I'd hook school and eat at that awful, aptly named Little Restaurant on Howard Street. Pencil was tall and weighed about one hundred pounds, and wore skintight, black girl's jeans, an angel blouse, and his own bleached hair in some kind of makeshift beehive. He would screech and sashay up and down the street having nell-fits and mincing to horrified truck drivers who would shout insults back. I was shocked. I had already met David Lochary when I was in high school. He was the first person to use the word "gay" to me as we watched Rock Hudson in *Pillow Talk* at the Hillendale movie theater. "He's gay," David sniffed, pointing to the screen before turning to me, "and so are you." I mean, I had seen "Peaches," the amazing black drag queen who performed at local frat dances with the very white and hetero-sexual rock-and-roll band the Upsetters (not to be confused with Carolyn Wasilewski, also aka "Peaches," the white fourteen-year-old girl delinquent who inspired my movie *Cry-Baby* by being murdered in 1954 with the name "Paul" written in Mercuro-chrome on her right thigh). I remember thinking it was strange that all the straight guys in the audience would cheer gay Peaches onstage with the Upsetters, but then beat him up after the show. Already I was learning how confusing show business could be.

I had never known Pencil, but I wanted to know *about* him. I had heard that he lived with his parents in East Baltimore, way out near the barn where the streetcars turned around and came back toward the city. Rumor had it that *this* was where Pencil "got lucky" late at night. I also used to see Pencil with his best friend, "Cleopatra," who, at 6'6", hardly "passed." Together they would cause quite a ruckus when they showed up at the Municipal Band concert in Mount Vernon Park, which was mostly attended by little old blue-haired ladies. For some reason Pencil always made an appearance just to horrify the crowd. I watched his every move.

Later in life Pencil seemed to vanish from the streets. Once, Pat Moran and I were in my car and we saw him and I told Pat to yell, "Hey, Pencil!" and she did, but he just gave us a dirty look. We had heard that he had hissed to others that he "wasn't Pencil anymore, but Miss Streisand." Could have fooled us. I tried to locate Pencil for this book but at first had little luck. "I know someone who saw him on the bus once" was about as close as I could get until I found Doris, the beloved and retired long-time barmaid from Leon's—Baltimore's oldest gay bar. She filled me in. Pencil had graduated to "serious drag," become a hairdresser, and gained weight. He drank too much but had good friends right up to when "he had stomach problems," moved with his mother and sister to Startex, South Carolina, and died in the late 1990s. Pencil was erased for good. But not from *my* memory. I never once in my life had so much as a conversation with Pencil but he was a great influence on me—defiantly courageous in the face of hatred, rabidly enticing despite his repellent packaging, and soooo happy to be living a life totally against the laws of the time.

Of course, before Pencil there was "Zorro"—"Lady Zorro." I wrote about her briefly in *Crackpot*: the lesbian stripper from Baltimore's notorious red-light district The Block, whom Divine and I used to go see at the very end of her burlesque career in the sixties. Zorro was so butch, so scary, so Johnny Cash. No actual stripping for her at that point; she just came out nude and snarled at her fans, "What the fuck are you looking at?" To this day Zorro is my inspiration. She gives me courage to go onstage with no props for my spoken-word act. Brave. Without makeup. Like Tilda Swinton at the Oscars.

Imagine my sadness when I saw in *The Baltimore Sun* the 2001 obituary for Sheila Alberta Bowater, sixty-three years of age. Since part of the headline read "dancer on The Block," I scanned down and there it was—"Appearing as Lady Zorro . . . she danced at The Oasis and The Two O'Clock Club . . ." I couldn't believe it! Lady Zorro was dead! But then I kept reading and the real shock came. The obituary mentioned her daughter, who lived in Tigard, Oregon. Zorro had a daughter?! I immediately wrote Eileen Murche to express my sympathies and she wrote back: "Dear John, How bizarre that you should contact me regarding my mother Zorro . . . My mother spoke of you many times. She loved how outrageous you are."

I was speechless. Zorro knew who I was?! She actually had followed my career later in her life? Eileen confided to me that she had gone to Catholic school as a child and enclosed great "glamour" photos of her late mom.

"How could Zorro's daughter possibly be like other little Catholic girls?" Eileen wondered in her letter, adding, "My childhood memories are of strippers, drag queens, drugs, the race track, The Block, and the many faces that passed through the doorway of [her family's downtown rowhouse] 301 E. 28th Street." In other words, the exact opposite of how I grew up in an upper-middle-class family at 313 Morris Avenue. What could it possibly be like to have Zorro, the lesbian stripper, as your mom?

I hopped on a plane to find out. Eileen lives in a lovely suburban home outside Portland. She was going through a trial separation from her husband of eleven years (whom I met). Her two small children were in school the day I visited. Eileen was down-to-earth, pretty, and full of gallows humor and amazingly graphic memories. We sat in the club room and she got out her box of Zorro memories. Eileen had quite a story.

Lady Zorro was born out of wedlock on May 23, 1936, in New York City to a mother who wanted to avoid the disgrace of being pregnant in her hometown of Providence, Rhode Island.

The child was raised in three different foster home/orphanage environments that were later described as "hellish." The grandparents somehow found out about the baby, took her home, and legally adopted little Sheila when she was nine years old. She was a hellion from the beginning, butch once she got to high school, with the added problem of having very large breasts. Later, Sheila briefly tried to be a stewardess, but as Eileen remembers hearing from her mom, "a passenger grabbed her ass, and she threw a drink in his face and told him to 'fuck himself.' " So much for the friendly skies. Sheila somehow ended up in Baltimore working as a stripper with the name of Lady Zorro. The new moniker, her daughter explained, "was because she needed a costume" with a mask "because her face wasn't that attractive. She had a crooked nose and they wanted to cover it up." Sheila also got her first girlfriend, fellow stripper Rachel, better known as "Ray." Lady Zorro and Ray. Ray designed Lady Zorro's costume and suddenly a star . . . of sorts . . . was born. "Z" (as she was known right up to the end by people in the life) had a real rage she brought to the stage, which added a demented hostile sex appeal. An angry stripper with a history of physical and sexual abuse with a great body and the face of a man. Now, *there's* a lethal combination. One thing I knew from the moment I laid eyes on her: Lady Zorro, this alternative Blaze Starr, was my kind of burlesque queen.

Z hung with a tough crowd on The Block. The Oasis Nightclub owner, Julius Salsbury, and his stripper girlfriend, Pam Gail, both legendary Baltimore gangster icons, were her close friends. When Julius's mob connections got him in trouble in 1970, he fled the country and a fifteen-year sentence, never to be heard from again despite decades of publicity since wondering about his whereabouts. "My mother told me the story," Eileen remembers, "how she drove him dressed in drag because she wore size eleven shoes [which he could get into] and dropped him off at Friendship Airport [now BWI] outside of Baltimore, for a flight to Miami."

Z may have been a tough cookie in the workplace, but she was a pothead at home once the sixties began. The height of Lady Zorro's career was between 1956 and 1962, and by the end she gave up even pretending to be a sexpot. And then Zorro surprised everybody by doing something *way* ahead of her time. This lesbian stripper got pregnant and wanted to have the child. In 1966, when Lady Z was twenty-nine years old, she had a baby girl, Eileen, named after Z's new girlfriend, who, despite being straight, stayed with Zorro for eighteen years before breaking her heart by running off with a male bookie who "sometimes used their phone." "And your dad?" I pry. "His name was JC and he wanted to marry Mom even though she was a lesbian. At one point, my mother met his mother with her family in Delaware and the future mother-in-law was just horrified. I only saw my father eight times, but at Christmas and on my birthday he would show up with a gift. But then he went to Florida and I never saw him again."

Eileen's first memories? "The racket of drunk people coming in downstairs after [Mom's] work, the loudness of their voices, the smell of marijuana, the smell of alcohol." "But when did you begin to realize this wasn't normal?" I wondered, remembering sitting at the top of the stairs in our family home, feeling safe, listening to my parents and their friends singing show tunes around our piano or playing charades. "When I went to Catholic school and some of the other kids invited me over to their house and their moms stayed home and picked them up from school. I had two mommies, Eileen and Zorro." But these "mommies" weren't anything like the gayly correct ones that Heather had in that classic book for children of gay parents. Of course there were benefits of having these two mommies that the other kids didn't have, such as "making a thousand dollars a night when I was eight years old." "They had poker parties and would take bennies and stay up for days playing cards." Eileen recalls the job title I have heard many times in Baltimore: the "hey girl," who waits on illegal gamblers at a clandestine den. As in "Hey, girl, bring me a beer!" "I served drinks and they would throw quarters in a big box, then dollars, then later in the night it was tens and twenties." "But how did you get up to go to school?" I worried, like a good dad. "I didn't," she said, shrugging.

Yet little Eileen was a straight-A student in Catholic school. Zorro may have been drunk and stoned on weed at home, but she had her daughter "baptized, went through her first communion" with her, and "wanted to give me everything she never had." "You're nothing without a college education," Z would rant as she taught her daughter to sift marijuana seeds. "I smoked pot and drank at eleven," Eileen says, chuckling. "Rather than play with Barbie dolls I had a little joint-rolling machine. I rolled a mean joint. My mother's friends thought it was funny. I started to drive then, too." "What? You drove at eleven years old?" Yep, Zorro "had a Lincoln Continental then and I used to pick her up at the bar because I was worried about her drinking and driving.

She was an obnoxious mean-spirited drunk; she would pick fights with anyone. Men, women—she'd kick their ass!"

But Zorro tried in her own misguided way. Eileen remembers being included on Sundays, which all the strippers had off, when they would come over and talk about "what sick fucks men were." Eileen may have been a child, but the girls were "always nice to me and gave me money." Instead of bedtime stories Eileen heard about "a guy who would pay a hundred bucks" to a girl "to walk around the dirty floor of the bar and then lick her toes," or a guy from Hampden "who used to have sex with his mother." "Motherfucker," they'd curse at him, but as the strippers explained to the child, "he liked that." "I'd walk by people having sex in the house," Eileen remembers with little trace of anger, almost amused at the inappropriate memories that seemed so normal to her at the time. She was even abused by a prominent businessman in Baltimore who, even though he died last year, should still feel guilty in his casket. Starting to feel bad myself for holding Zorro in such high esteem for years, I realize in her defense that I guess lesbian mothers have the same right to be bad parents as straight ones do.

Then it got worse. Eileen's other mother left and Zorro "had a nervous breakdown and things went downhill after that." "Z never had sex again," her daughter remembers. "She never recovered." Little Eileen would call big Eileen and beg, "Please take me with you," but her "other mother" was ill-equipped to deal with the situation. "I can't," she sadly responded; "you're not my daughter." Big Eileen would call sometimes, Zorro's daughter remembers, trying to give her the benefit of the doubt. "Mostly when she was drunk. I only saw her once or twice after that."

Zorro went on welfare and was in and out of mental institutions. When she was released, "they had her on chloral hydrate and Elavil and she just lay on the couch for years." Zorro would try to commit suicide and little Eileen would pull the gun from her hand. Eileen even got raped when Zorro's wallet was stolen by some psycho at a bar who looked at the address on the ID, went to the house, and attacked the youngster. Zorro's reaction? "Why didn't you fight back?"

Yet Eileen continued to excel in school. "My friends thought [my mom] was cool because they could come over and smoke pot at my house and drink. I didn't care what she was; I just didn't want her to be fucked-up all the time." When Zorro was committed for long periods, Eileen remembers trying to keep it a secret and "taking care of myself." She walked to school every day and the nuns never suspected that their little honor student was living completely unsupervised by herself in the ghetto. "I felt like I was stepping out of one world and then into another. I kept those worlds very separate."

But then Eileen got caught. The electricity at home was cut off for nonpayment of bills and she "overslept and was late for school," so she forged her mother's signature on a note. But the nuns spotted the fake and told Eileen that her mother "needed to call." "She's gone," Eileen blurted out. "But when will she be back?" the nuns asked, startled. "I started crying and told them what happened," Eileen remembers matter-of-factly, "and they called Child Protective Services and the people across the street lied and said I could stay with them. I did stay with them sometimes but I wanted to be by myself." "You never said, 'Help me'?" I wondered. "Never," Eileen answers proudly. Why should she? She was president of her class!

Eileen never seemed judgmental about her unconventional mom and tried to remember Zorro's good points for me. Lady Z "read the newspapers every day," "liked classical music," and, much to my thrill, "loved Johnny Mathis." She may have been nuts, but Z was always incredibly proud of her daughter's academic success. "The roof caved in on our house," Eileen recollects with a grin, "so the nuns called the St. Vincent de Paul Society to come fix it. We didn't have heat for a couple years in the house, so my mom wanted the nuns to come. Sister Mary Francis, principal of my school, showed up," and Zorro "only had a small buzz. She knew how important this was for me." Zorro, the good mom, "went to turn on the oven to put food in [to cook] and a thousand cockroaches started walking up all over the wall." And people wonder where I get my movie ideas? Could there be a better scene than this?!

"One of the founding things that saved my life is the Catholic Church," Eileen admits, and for once I don't make a religious wisecrack. Here is what the Catholic Church should be doing instead of condemning movies and denying science. "There were two old ladies who lived next door, and one was a seamstress who used to make me dresses and wanted to save my soul." Later a priest offered, " 'Hello, Eileen, we need help at the rectory, can you come after school?' All the people at the church helped me." "Are you a Catholic today?" I ask. "I am," she answers evenly.

Eileen continued on to the College of Notre Dame, moved

out of her mother's house into the dorms, and finally got a boyfriend who "was always there for me—until he slept with my
best friend and that was that." When Eileen graduated from college, Zorro "came and brought a cooler full of beer. Some of her
friends from the bar came. She did get drunk." By then, Zorro
had had all her teeth pulled out, so there went the possibility
that anyone could imagine she had at one time been a stripper.
"Amazingly," Eileen remembers with a laugh, "even though my
mother got welfare, she was a Republican."

Zorro started hanging out at the Porthole, a local gay men's
neighborhood bar. Suddenly Z was a fag hag! "She could draw a
crowd," Eileen remembers with a shudder, "her voice was so
loud!" Then, like the old days, everybody from the bar would
come back to the house to smoke pot. "She was so down and out,
I moved back in for a year," her daughter says, sighing. "Bums
would hang out, mentally ill people, people with AIDS. She'd
give her shirt off her back. I once stepped over this black woman,
six-foot-four, and thought, 'That's the ugliest chick I've ever
seen!' Then I saw the dick." After Eileen moved out again, she
would "show up every other weekend" and say, "Please don't be
fucked-up," but Z would announce, "I'm a fuckup! After you are
six years old you are a child of the world." "So I'd drive her to
the Rite Aid for cigarettes [Z smoked four packs of Benson &
Hedges a day] and buy her a couple of beers." An enabler? "I
never bought her hard alcohol," Eileen argues with a shrug.
"Did you ever try to get your mom to AA?" I ask. "Always tried!"
Eileen laughs. "She had a couple DWI [convictions] and she was
supposed to go but she traded pot with someone who would sign
in for her at meetings."

Finally Eileen had had enough. She moved to the West Coast. The only thing she really wanted was to be normal. But Eileen still tried to keep an eye on her mom. "I flew her to Florida when I was on a business trip, fresh out of college, making $30,000. It was a big conference and I told her, 'Just stay in the hotel room. I have a function I have to go to. Here's a six-pack of beer, don't drink anything out of the mini bar, it's too expensive. I'll be back.' Later, I walked into the hotel lobby and I could hear her voice and I looked up to this elevated bar where she was with *my* name tag on! She had crashed a competitor's party and was just ranting."

"So did that do it?" I say with hope. "Had you finally reached rock bottom?" "No, I kept coming back for more," Eileen sighs. "I flew her out to my wedding here." Eileen had warned her future in-laws and they had politely said, "All families have issues." "You have no fucking idea," Eileen remembers thinking. "But she [Zorro] would ask people, 'You got any good shit to smoke?' and I'm like, 'Mom, these people do *not* smoke pot. Stop asking every person that walks through the receiving line!'"

"Then I went on my honeymoon," Eileen says with a forbidding pause, and her mom said to the new mother-in-law, "I'd like to have you and your husband over and your next-door neighbors who were so nice in helping my daughter plan the wedding." So they came and the hostess-with-the-leastest tried to do her best, but as Eileen later heard the story, Z "had this big jug of red wine she told them she needed for the spaghetti sauce, but she drank the entire gallon and took a Xanax and forgot and took two more and smoked pot so by the time people showed up she was completely fucked-up, dishing all the relatives, the hus-

band—'He's adopted! You don't know if his mother had AIDS.' "
The guests just ran. "Did Zorro ever apologize?" I wonder.
"Never," Eileen answers. "I didn't talk to her for six months af-
ter that."

But then Z (or Sheila, as she was back to being known by her
non-showbiz neighbors) "fell, broke her hip, got a staph infec-
tion and pneumonia." Eileen went back to Baltimore to old home-
sweet-home and "broke in the door," and her mother was almost
dead. "Had she called you?" I quizzed. And then Eileen responded
with the only answer from our interview about her mom that
ever shocked me: "She never wanted to be a burden to me."

So, out of "guilt," Eileen moved Sheila/Zorro, who by now
looked like an old haggard man from Baltimore, into her house
in Oregon. "People had died of AIDS in there [in her mother's
old place]; everything was ruined. I sold the house, to the crack-
dealing lady neighbor who liked Mom, for $11,000 given to me
in cash in a paper bag." When Zorro moved in with her daughter on the West Coast, it was "just hell. I told my husband, 'I
know it's going to be hard. She doesn't like you. You don't like
her.'" Eileen tried to make reasonable "house rules"—Zorro
was allowed two cases of beer a week, an ounce of pot a month,
and whatever pills the doctor would give her. But "she would go
crazy and the neighbors across the street told me that while I
was at work, my mother would knock on people's doors and say
she 'had DDTs,' meaning DTs." "Once I was on vacation in
Mexico and the neighbors were watching Z, and one day there
was no answer at the door, so they went in and my mother was
sitting out back, naked, listening to the radio. She had a joint in
one hand and a cigarette in the other."

Eileen can admit that her mother's death from cancer "was a relief." "I had to sleep with her at night because she had a morphine pump she kept pulling out." Eileen even tried to find her father to tell him, "Mom's dying." "I found his brother and called but he told me JC 'never had kids.'" "'Yes, he did, I'll send the birth certificate,'" she argued, and "I finally got my father's address and I was going to call him, and the day before, the phone rang and he said, 'Eileen, this is your father.' He explained he left because he had been involved in a scandal with some hookers in Baltimore and it was in the newspapers and he 'didn't want to embarrass me.' He said he didn't have anything to offer me and I told him I wanted to see him but he said he wasn't up to it. He had cancer, he explained, and 'I'm dying.'" "'Well, you have my number,'" Eileen told him hopefully, "and then I started to get angry and I didn't call him again and then he died." No happy endings here.

"Did Zorro ever get mellow as her last days approached?" I wondered, hoping for a little good news somehow in this story. When "the doctors told her she had twelve weeks to live," Eileen recalls (she lasted thirteen), her mother wasn't fazed. "When it's your time to go, it's your time to go" was Z's immediate response. "I was crying," Eileen remembers, dry-eyed, "and she looked at me and sang 'Don't Cry for Me, Argentina.'" Was Zorro ever nice to you?" I ask tactfully. Eileen pauses and answers without rancor, "No; she made me dinner. She showed me her love by feeding me."

Remembering the life of one of my longtime idols, Eileen is quite levelheaded. "Could you ever see the comedy in your situation when Zorro was alive?" I ask. "NOT AT ALL!" she answers emphatically. Zorro "tormented me, she abused me, and it wasn't until after she died that I started to appreciate her. I got that phone call from you . . ." But Zorro obviously did *something* right, I argue. "She raised a daughter who is reasonably happy and well-adjusted, and isn't that the best you can say about any mother?" "I always hoped I could have a relationship with her," Eileen says quietly. "But you did," I plead. "You were the bright spot in her life always." Can living in a real John Waters movie ever bring any kind of joy? "I spoke at my mom's memorial service and said, 'I spent my whole life trying to not be like her, only to find out at the age of thirty-five, I *am* like her. I can walk into a room and within ten minutes everybody in the room is standing around me. I'm not in show business, but I *am* in marketing. I learned how to talk to people . . ." "To hustle, just like your mom did?" I ask. "Absolutely!" Eileen admits with a twinkle in her eye.

A sad story? Maybe not. Months later Eileen wrote, asking, "Would you please save that tape we did together for me? It would be a great way for my children to learn about their grandmother after they are twenty-one. They ask me about her all the time, and what was she like? I always smile and tell them she was a piece of work."

Boy, I need a drink after the Zorro saga! But where to go? All my really favorite Baltimore monster bars are gone. Like Hard Times, the aptly named blue-collar or no-collar bar once located at the corner of 28th Street and Huntingdon Avenue in the Remington neighborhood, which got closed down in 2001 as neighbors "breathed a sigh of relief" according to the press reports. City environmental and sanitation inspectors had found there was no running water on the premises while it was still open to the public. So what? I mean, I guess you had to piss in the alley out back, but at least there were cute Baltimoreans inside. Dirty drinking glasses? What's the big deal? Just rinse them out when it rains.

I wish Morgan's was still there. I had a real soft spot for this obviously illegal after-hours club in Hampden, which somehow stayed open for years. I think cops went there themselves when they were off duty. This is the only bar in my life that refused me admittance. And for a long time, too. "But he made a lot of movies," I even heard a friendly mutant stick up for me to the mean, but handicapped, doorman. "Never heard of them," he sniffed. "Besides, he don't live in the neighborhood." Hampden had yet to be discovered by homesteaders, yuppies, and starter families, so my celebrity was meaningless here. I could waltz into Studio 54, the Mudd Club, or any New York "in" restaurant, but not Morgan's. Finally, after months of my showing up and pleading, the owner, who looked like a weirdly handsome Robert Mitchum on a bummer, came down and we met. I guess by now a couple of locals had vouched I wasn't undercover. "Go ahead up," he snarled with a subtle hint of pride in his establishment. Once I climbed those long steps up to the fully operating bar (with booths, for chrissakes!), I wasn't one bit disappointed. Once again, the local dealers, alcoholics, and hillbilly chicks were partying big-time, and some of them looked great! Here, I realized, was the "upper lower class," a segment of society that I had never heard described properly in any sociological studies. Not only were they high on drugs, the bar was open and ready to serve beer, and at rock-bottom prices! Believe me, not one hipster would dare go in this joint. Even I, a veteran extreme-bar cultist, was frightened here. I avoided eye contact and tried to watch people in the mirrors on the walls so they didn't notice me. I started to take friends from New York there and they *really* seemed to like it. Especially some of the stylish women I know who mostly had only gay male friends at home. Here, they got cruised by real heterosexual men who definitely weren't closet queens. These guys had never even heard the term "fag hag." I still laugh with one of my women friends who went home with a really cute guy she met at Morgan's when she was visiting me. When she complimented him on his accidentally cool wildly patterned thrift store shirt, he answered sexily, "It's made of rayon. AND I'M A RAYON FOOL!"

"Isn't going to these places dangerous?" many of my friends ask me, and they have a point. My notoriety usually protects me in the beginning, but if no one is friendly, especially the bartenders or barmaids, I leave immediately. It's a slow process getting accepted in the bars, and pretty often my judgment has been solid. Maybe it came from teaching filmmaking to convicts. I mean, what is prison, really, except a good bar without the liquor?

For many years I went to the now-defunct Atlantis, a male strip club located next to the Maryland Penitentiary. I called it "the Fudge Palace" in my movie *Pecker*. I always took out-of-town guests there, everybody from Gus Van Sant to many of the New York art dealers (both gay and straight) who were participating in the Print Fair at the Baltimore Museum of Art. Even my friend Judge Elsbeth Bothe went with me one night after a long day on the bench. When I told her that "sometimes you get teabagged by the naked dancers if you sit too close," she didn't chicken out; she just wore a hat for protection. God, how I miss that place.

But I like girl strip bars, too. As long as they're bad ones. No thanks to the high-end "gentlemen's clubs," with Playboy Bunny types who want to give you a lap dance while reminding you there is an ATM right inside the lobby. Boots was a favorite go-go-girl place. Located on Eastern Avenue, between Fells Point and Highlandtown, this may have been the lowliest strip club ever. So naturally, for about a year, I hung out there every weekend in the early 1990s. The "talent" was definitely unnerving. One we called "the Moose." She was a big ox who was a lazy stripper. One night, when it was her turn to dance, she was still in the bathroom located next to the stage, so when she heard her musical cue, she just kicked the bathroom door open as she still sat on the toilet and shook her tits for the audience. Boots was very David Lynch. One regular, a woman customer with a greasy ponytail, jitterbugged with the valve of the radiator every night for hours and nobody questioned it. The barmaid had a hair-trigger temper but I liked to get her talking. She used to tell me "bring Johnny Depp in" as she thrust topless photos of her legal-age go-go daughters into my hands for me to give him. I stupidly invited her to my Christmas party one year and she brought her boyfriend, who entered with a bad attitude and would stop in front of any male guest, glare scarily, and snarl, "Are you a faggot?" Many weren't but didn't quite know how to respond, and everybody complained to the bouncer, who had to throw the barmaid and her boyfriend out. I never went back to Boots until many years later, but the same bartender was working there. She was "sober now," she announced, giving me a *very* unfriendly look, and I left quickly. Boots closed not too long after, and when the gay Atlantis sadly shut its doors (the location became yet another swanky men's club), the gay strip club reopened in the old Boots space under the name of Spectrum, which immediately became known as "the Rectum," and due to the really hideously nelly go-go boys with awful Baltimore accents that some obviously unseasoned manager had hired, it closed down quickly.

I guess I could go to the Bloody Bucket; it's still open. That's not the bar's real name, but locals call it that. It's located at 1619 Union Avenue, across from the Pepsi plant in the area of Hampden commonly referred to as "the Bottom." I wish I owned this place. It's totally untouched. I'd rename it the Pelt Room but otherwise I wouldn't change a thing. The crowd that hangs there is unpredictable but definitely not one you'd bring home to Mom (unless she's Zorro). I love Blanche, the bartender, a woman of a certain age who is an R. Crumb comic come to life. A big, big girl with giant thighs who looks so sexy and powerful in her micro cutoff denim skirt. Cellulite is, in this case, a true beauty mark. Having her serve you a drink while you listen to the customers' amazing stories is such a great way to start off the weekend. "I was in this terrible car accident," a drinking buddy there once told me, "some Chinaman [what all blue-collar guys in Baltimore call any type of Asian] ran through a red light and smashed into the car I was riding in. My head went partially through the windshield, there was glass everywhere. My friend who was driving was pinned behind the steering wheel. I was so pissed off that I wanted to beat up the Chinaman, so I got out of our car, went over to him to punch him out, but when I opened his car door I saw his head was part cut off and he was dead. So I stole his wallet." "How much did you get?" I asked, excitedly picturing the movie scene. "Twenty bucks," he said, sighing gloomily.

The only guzzling events I've never had the nerve to attend in Baltimore are "blow-roasts." Blow-roasts are even more excessive than the scariest straight bars, but they are a local one-night tradition and sometimes even the cops organize them. Tickets are secretly and selectively sold weeks in advance to working-class men at their local neighborhood bars, usually in the county, and the location (union hall or biker clubhouse) is revealed right before the big night. A blow-roast is just like a bull roast; oyster shuckers, pit beef sandwiches, gambling, kegs of beer, and medleys of mayonnaise-based dishes. But at a blow-roast there are also blow *jobs*. A "two-tier level of hookers works these events," explains a friend who has attended several times. "The good-looking ones are the strippers and they specialize in acts such as 'dildo shows,' where they penetrate each other for your enjoyment while you eat. One of the girls' specialties was she could shoot a banana from her vagina." Before I can stop him from telling me more details, he adds, "I saw one guy pick it up off the dirty floor and eat it." But the real horror are the "b.j. girls," the "rank ones," who give blow jobs to men who win them in a raffle. "Biker types escort them around table to table," my friend continues to explain, "and sell the raffle tickets, and when they sell one hundred dollars' worth, they draw a number and the winner goes into this dirty little side room where they've set up partitions with blankets or sheets and you get blown." "But what kinds of girls work blow-roasts?" I ask, thinking that this job is surely the lowest one in show business. "Pretty ugly ones," he remembers when he is forced to picture their faces. Imagine, just imagine, waking up and knowing your job for the day is working a blow-roast! "Suppose a blow-roast girl runs into her father's friends" I wail, "or even her father?!" "I don't know," my friend begs off, "I only went a couple times." "You went *back*?!" I marvel, trying to imagine the horror of these events. "Did *you* get blown?" I finally demand. "Nooooooo!" he shrieks, wishing he had never told me about blow-roasts in the first place. I wish he hadn't, too. And I'm sorry I had to tell you! But I don't have a choice—I've been drinking.

There's only one place left to go and that's the Club Charles, the hipster hangout I have been frequenting for the last thirty years. It may be an "old reliable" but it's located right across the street from the Charles, the best movie theater in town, and it's still, weirdly, the coolest bar. But it used to be even better. In the 1970s it was still called the Wigwam and it was known in the press as the scariest bar in Baltimore. You couldn't even get buzzed in at the front door unless you were a bum. A real one.

The owner was a Native American woman named Esther Martin, and I lived in awe of her. Born in Oklahoma in 1923, she ran away as a teenager to New York and got a job as a hat-check girl at the Stork Club. Moving to Baltimore in hopes of studying to be a nurse at Johns Hopkins Hospital, she ended up instead working in the nightclubs here until 1951, when she bought a bar and got married to Kent Martin. The Wigwam was the politically incorrect name of their new nightspot, and the teepee-shaped sign advertising "Grub and Firewater" immediately attracted a good clientele. By the time I met Esther in 1980, the neighborhood had changed drastically, and she was a hardworking divorced mother of four. She ran the joint like an iron-fisted Elaine's, only her clients weren't celebrities, they were alcoholics, mental patients, and vets. If you received any kind of government check, you were eligible to drink in the Wigwam. If not, get out! Esther would cash the checks, keep all the money, and dole it out to her collection of lunatics because, as one of her daughters remembered her mom explaining, "If they had all their money, they'd just drink it up." She kept "tickets," or IOUs, on scraps of paper only Esther knew how to decipher. For some reason, Esther let me and Pat Moran (who was managing the Charles Theater at the time) inside her secret society. It was like being cast in the banquet scene in Buñuel's *Viridiana*, where the bums take over the mansion and wreck it, except nobody froze in a tableau of *The Last Supper* the way they did in the film. No, Esther was watching. And you were *allowed* to go wild. I saw one homeless guy bite off the nose of another and spit it out on the bar. If you left a cash tip, withered hands would appear from all sides and try to grab it away, but Esther didn't care. She wasn't interested in chump change. She wanted your very soul.

Through the years, Esther and I became friends. In 1980, when the Wigwam became the Club Charles, Esther was okay about artsy hillbillies, gay outcasts, and cool gearheads taking over from the bums. She still owned the joint but the neighbors and police were giving her such a hard time over her clientele that she was afraid they'd take away her liquor license. It was time to retire from behind the bar and go down to her little cubbyhole office in the basement, count the money, and watch over her kingdom. I used to plug the Club Charles on talk shows, and Esther and I both hooted when we talked *Lifestyles of the Rich and Famous* into using the bar as one of the locations when they did an episode on me. Long before Esther died from diabetes in 2003, she instructed her staff and future staff never to charge me for a drink. And you know what? Somehow, to this day, even new kids who just recently started working behind the bar honor her request.

But the real reason I loved Esther right from the beginning was her mouth. No one in the world cussed more! She gave the phrase "cursing a blue streak" a refinement that seemed almost noble. "That motherfucking cocksucking son of a bitch" was used as a prefix to almost every name she uttered. When Esther died, I went to the funeral home to pay my respects. I had heard that Esther's last words were "Move your coat, asshole," but even though I had gotten to know her four children, Kim, Joy, Dick, and Battle, I felt this wasn't the time or place to set the record straight. So years later, even though it was hard to *ever* imagine what kind of peace Esther was resting in, I invited her family to come over to my house to talk. They knew I had a great respect for their mom. And like all children of insane mothers, they had learned to view their upbringing with a certain bemused detachment.

"Don't put your fucking on the fucking table, asshole!" was her actual last message to her kids, written on a Post-it note, her favorite method of communication. Not one of the kids is exactly sure what the missing word was, but they agree it could have been "coat." "Cocksucker!" they immediately shout in unison when I ask what their mother's favorite cuss word was. Sometimes, Kim remembers, Esther would leave notes that read "Fuck you! Shit! Shit! Shit!" "Mom's father paid her to cuss as a kid," explains Dick before Kim adds, "He was a mean asshole. He beat her [remembering her mom's words] till she pissed herself." Just a mention of Esther's foul language makes each sibling go into hilarious imitations of their mother's tirades. "As my dear sainted mother would say"—Dick laughs and then mimics Esther's voice—" 'You're as worthless as a cunt full of cold piss.' " "Shit and fall back in it!" Battle hollers out in loving imitation. Kim remembers fondly her mother telling her and her sister, "A cunt hair will pull a twenty-mule team!" "FUCK! SHIT! PISS! MOTHERFUCKER!" they all start barking joyously, laughing and missing their mother's almost anti-Tourette's-syndrome, all-voluntary form of cussing.

All Esther's children worked at the bar at one time or another, and they get misty-eyed remembering the bum clientele, or "smoke hounds" as their mother used to call her customers, her army who "took care of stuff" for her. Farmer, Country, Russian George, Hillbilly, Jim Dandy, Indian Willy, Frenchie—and Fay Girl. "She was the hottie," Joy explains, "long in the tooth, but all the bums loved Fay Girl," the queen of the grizzled set. "Esther felt love for these people," Dick remembers. "She'd visit them in the hospital," Kim adds before Dick continues, "She'd go to Social Security, the VA hospital. She'd look for their veteran's papers." "When they died," Battle remembers proudly, "she'd bury them." Esther took photographs of them, too. "All around the house," Kim remembers. " 'Oh, there's Mary in her coffin.' Mom always thought she would get a big payoff," she adds, "and as kids we'd see the suitcases . . ."

Ah yes. The mythical suitcases of the dead bums whose souls Esther owned. Up in the attic, still there in the family house where Joy continues to live. A kind of bum burial ground for Esther's subjects. A carnival of lost souls that shines in the dark of a forgotten harsh kindness. As Esther's children got older, they had to help their mother go through what was left of the bums' stuff. " 'You got to help us clean the Captain's apartment,' " Kim remembers her mother saying. "He had a massive artery blow, and his bed was soaked in blood and Mom had me go down there and dig through all his shit!" "Did he have a diamond in his pocket?" Esther always wondered. "Well, did you ever get left anything of value?" I ask, knowing Esther had somehow amassed a home for her family and five other properties she rented out. Joy remembers, "Earl, a customer, not a real bum, annoying, but he loved Mom, and he told her, 'I'm leaving you everything.' He lived a month. And then Mayflower [moving] trucks pull up—not one, not two, there's a whole block taken up. And they started unloading the most unbelievable antiques. His entire estate was left to Mom."

You certainly didn't want to be on Esther's bad side. Her clientele was "all alcoholics or mentally ill and Mom was keeper of the asylum," Battle remembers correctly. Sometimes they needed a stern mother and sometimes they got one. "She would punch somebody full in the face with her fist," Kim remembers with awe. "There was a rage with Mom," Battle sighs; "demons." When one of her bum ladies got hassled by another bar patron, Esther was there to protect her, Dick recalls. "She cold-cocked that son of a bitch." Battle laughs. Dick continues, "And when the fool reached out and kicked at Esther, she went off. She was kicking his guts and saying, 'This is Esther. You don't fuck with Esther!' She worked on the element of surprise," he marvels, remembering his mom's fighting methods. "She'd pull out a 'slapper' she carried, a rubber hose with lead in it and taped up. I saw her use it on some guy in Rite Aid once. He wouldn't get out of the way. She walked up and said, 'Excuse me,' but he just looked back." "God, she had that look!" Battle blurts out with fear and admiration. "She just . . . Boof! Boof!" Dick explains, whacking an imaginary slapper in the air. "She just beat this guy. He just went down on the ground cowering."

I try to picture my own very proper mom beating the shit out of somebody as we shopped for back-to-school clothes, but I just come up blank. It's hard to imagine a slapper done in tweed. But would I have been excited if my mom had punched out my junior high math teacher who signed my yearbook "To someone who can, but doesn't"? You bet! Maybe Esther was a real inspiration for *Serial Mom*. I mean, as one of the ad lines I suggested for that film read: "She *meant* well."

Esther "worked every single day." Kim remembers, "She loved being behind that bar." Esther didn't drink except maybe "a beer" or "crème de menthe." She was "old school," her kids tactfully try to explain. "She loved Nixon" and "hated John Kennedy," they remember, acknowledging the irony. She "had a gun" but for good reason. "She had to pay off the cops," Joy recalls sadly. "They'd be in there every day playing pinball. She'd get them beer. 'So-and-so needs a case for a bull roast.' Then they'd come in with a list—'This is for the Sergeant.' Old Crow liquor, four, five hundred bottles, and then she said, 'Fuck the Sergeant!' and stopped." "I'd rather have a daughter in a whorehouse than a son in the police force," Esther used to rage to anyone who would listen.

But Esther, in her own way, believed in law and order. "She got robbed every week in the bar," Joy remembers. "She had a gun to her head many times. I remember being taken shopping with my mother in Hutzler's [the nicest Baltimore department store] downtown," Joy continues, when "on the escalator to the mezzanine Esther sees the store detective chasing this black guy. 'CATCH THAT MOTHERFUCKER!' Mom yells as the other women looked at my mother with that look I always got [from other mothers] from the time I was a child—the look of horror." Esther was touchy, too. When she heard two customers complaining about Judy Garland's live performance in Baltimore, the notorious one where Judy was drunk and staggered around the stage, Esther threw the couple out of the bar. "Here goes Mom," Joy remembers the tirade, " 'You're fucking barred! Get out of my fucking bar! If she [Judy] didn't do another motherfucking thing but *The Wizard of Oz*, you cocksuckers!' "

But it wasn't all fun and games. After Esther and her husband divorced in 1962, "they never spoke but had affection for each other," Kim recalls. Neither "ever dated anyone else again," Dick remembers, as Kim adds incredulously, "She did go to the funeral and was that grieving widow." When the children became teenagers, it got intolerable at home and they ran off to Arkansas and lived with their dad, who got full custody, but the family dynamics were still confusing. "They took us into deposition and asked, 'Did she [Esther] abuse you?' and I said, 'No. I mean, she beat us,'" Dick remembers innocently. Kim and Joy lasted two years and then came home and moved back in with their mother, who acted like nothing had happened. Dick was more bitter and didn't see Esther for five years. Battle "got Dad the divorce lawyer."

Yet all Esther's children have a great affection for her. "My mom was a beautiful woman," Battle says proudly. "She made us very independent," Kim says, laughing good-naturedly. "She loved to take us shopping," Kim continues. "All her tips were in her bra and she'd pull down her girdle and all this money would fall out." "She was very pro-education," Joy remembers, and like Eileen, Zorro's daughter, all Esther's kids "loved school." "It was away from the madness," as Joy puts it without a hint of sadness. None of them seem overly angry about their alternative upbringing. "It was so much better than childhoods I hear from my girlfriends that were so boring. There never was a dull moment," says Joy, the one whom all the siblings agree is the most like Esther and who still runs the Club Charles from the same downstairs cubbyhole office as her mother did. Maybe that's why I interviewed Joy alone, away from the other family members. She married a cop ("He's an honest one") and has left all of Esther's belongings as they were in the house. "Her nightgown is still hanging in the bathroom," Joy admits.

"You could have asked Esther the day before she died what we did for a living," Kim remembers with a shrug, "and she wouldn't know." "Because you were no longer working in the bar, it wasn't real?" I wonder. "Right!" Kim, Battle, and Dick agree instantly. "She would say she was so proud of us to other people,

but never to us," Kim remembers with resignation before adding, "She also never wanted to get involved in our personal lives.
'Don't bring that shit in here!' she'd yell if you were ever moan-
ing about a boyfriend." Before Dick got married, he said, "we
went out with Esther and she started to tell my future wife stories. We were driving cross-country and an in-law in the car was
sick as could be. Mom turned to my fiancée and said, 'Honey, her
breath smells like your asshole.' I only knew Robin a couple of
weeks then . . . ," he trails off good-naturedly. "Nobody lived a
life like we had," Battle says proudly with a warm grin.

But can I go too far in being inspired by someone else's good
"bad mother"? Can other moms' militant lunacy ever be funny,
even if their ideals are based in raw naked pathology? It's a
question I wrestle with daily. The mother of a friend of mine is
a case in point. Jake used to be my FedEx man. Even though he
was straight, he had a great sense of humor and sometimes left
me Polaroid shots of his penis. I didn't mind. Just another reason to love FedEx. I originally met Jake at a hetero bar and he
drove a souped-up, repainted, secondhand police car. Once we
went on a "date." He strapped a video camera to the hood of his
car and we drove around while he filmed us smashing through
piles of old dead Christmas trees that residents had left in the
alleys and he would set on fire. I could never get Jake to "put
out," but it still was a really romantic night for me, so I stayed in
touch. He hinted that his mother was quite a bizarre character
and asked me if I'd like to go have dinner at her house. Always
up for meeting people with their parents, I eagerly accepted.

She lived in a normal suburban garden apartment by herself and looked like anybody's mother. I did wonder why there was no visible food being prepared as we joined her at the kitchen table. Suddenly she announced, "I decided not to make dinner because I didn't feel like it." Oh. Well, okay, I thought as my stomach growled with hunger. Suddenly, with a look of insane glee, she said to her son, "Go on, Jake, tell John what we used to do as a family every Easter." Jake suddenly paled and tried to change the subject, but she was unstoppable. "We'd ride around in our convertible," she blurted out, "and laugh at niggers!" Stunned, I sat in my chair, trying to believe my ears. Jake laughed nervously but didn't deny it. I tried to picture this awful script in my head, wondering, If I turned the races around, could it be a funny scene in a movie? A black family riding around in a convertible laughing at white people? Maybe. If handled properly, with the joke *really* well set up, and directed by a young, cutting-edge black auteur. But my insane hostess wasn't finished yet. "I hate women, too!" she cried out for no apparent reason with a bone-chilling happiness. "Go on, Jake," she continued, much like the insane female storytellers in *Salò*, "tell John about the time we left a note for our landlord that said"—and here she sang out the words—"WE SAW YOUR PENIS!" By now I was mumbling excuses, gathering my things, and making a run for the car with Jake right behind me, but she wasn't fazed. "Here!" she yelled to both of us as she chased us to the car, thrusting out two cans of cold beer. "Take a drink for the drive," she hollered as we leaped inside, me in shock, Jake giggling like a good son, I guess used to his mom's outlook on the world.

I'm not sorry I met this woman. Racists are the dumbest

people alive, but Baltimore is filled with nutcases who think they are totally levelheaded and their antics have to be repeated to be believed. Like the story this late friend of mine, Gary, loved to tell in horrified remembrance. Gary got in the elevator in his building to go down to the lobby to exit. Already on board was a neighbor lady he barely knew. The elevator stopped again on a lower floor and another female resident silently boarded and then got off one floor below. "You know," the neighbor lady still in the elevator commented to Gary as they resumed their descent, "she blows niggers." Gary gasped in horror and ran out as soon as the elevator doors opened but claimed he always re-gretted not answering truthfully, "I do, too." Which brings us to the question: If someone is a racist and really cute, could you still have sex with him? I had to admit the answer is yes. I have. You just change the subject or shout, "La la la la la la la," cover-ing your ears when he speaks his nonsense. If all else fails, stick something in his mouth to shut him up.

I'd buy you another drink, but didn't somebody just yell "Last call!"?

BOOKWORM

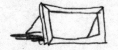

I've jitterbugged with Richard Serra, eaten Thanksgiving dinner with Lana Turner, had tea with Princess Yasmin Aga Khan, gone out drinking with Clint Eastwood, and spent several New Year's Eve parties in Valentino's chalet in Gstaad, but what I like best is staying home and reading. Being rich is not about how much money you have or how many homes you own; it's the freedom to buy any book you want without looking at the price and wondering if you can afford it. Of course, you have to read the books, too. Nothing is more impotent than an unread library.

I have, as of the day of this writing, 8,425 books, all cataloged but no longer in complete order on my shelves. Each week I read *Publishers Weekly* not so much for the business news but to see what books are coming out and when I can buy them. Like all avid readers, I sob about the death of my favorite bookshops in each city I visit, but I'm secretly thrilled at how easy and cheap it is to order from Amazon.com. But couldn't they at least reward us with frequent reading points like the airlines? I'm always amazed at friends who say they try to read at night

in bed but always end up falling asleep. I have the opposite problem. If a book is good I *can't* go to sleep, and stay up way past my
bedtime, hooked on the writing. Is anything better than waking
up after a late-night read and diving right back into the plot
before you even get out of bed to brush your teeth?

You should never just read for "enjoyment." Read to make
yourself smarter! Less judgmental. More apt to understand your
friends' insane behavior, or better yet, your own. Pick "hard
books." Ones you have to concentrate on while reading. And for
God's sake, don't let me ever hear you say, "I can't read fiction. I
only have time for the truth." Fiction is the truth, fool! Ever
hear of "literature"? That means fiction, too, stupid.

Okay, everybody likes to hear about a good book. Oprah has
made book lists a middle-class phenomenon. So what about the
rest of us? The outcasts who have no desire to assimilate and
love to read about the "little horror stories in other people's lives,"
as Mary Vivian Pearce said in *Female Trouble*. What should we
read? Not to escape but to dwell on all the delicious insanity we
are still learning to embrace? Well, I've got a list for you, and
believe me, it was hard to narrow down. From thousands and
thousands and thousands of twisted volumes, here goes—John
Waters's Five Books You Should Read to Live a Happy Life If
Something Is Basically the Matter with You.

And yes, it's all fiction. Maybe there is no better novel in the
world than Denton Welch's *In Youth Is Pleasure*. Just holding it
in my hands, so precious, so beyond gay, so deliciously subversive, is enough to make illiteracy a worse social crime than hunger. Published in the U.K. in 1945, ten years after the terrible
accident in which the author, riding his bicycle, was hit by a car

and permanently injured, this amazing (and thinly disguised) autobiographical novel is the graceful and astonishingly erotic tale of Orville Pym, a creative child who has lost his mother to some mysterious disease and "has not yet learned to bear the strain of feeling unsafe with another person." Hating "other people" who imagined "that they understood his mind because he was a boy," our elegant but damaged little hero, "longing for escape, freedom, loneliness and adventure," wanders around the grounds of a hotel where he has been taken by his father to vacation with his older brothers.

Have the secret yearnings of childhood sexuality and the wild excitement of the first stirrings of perversity ever been so eloquently described as in this novel? When Orville discovers an old book on physical culture and begins frantically working out to improve his body, he worries that he isn't sweating enough. Determined, he locks himself in the small bottom drawer of a dressing chest and, immediately "overcome with the horror of being a prisoner," innocently fantasizes that he is in a dungeon he remembers from one of his aunt's mid-Victorian novels. Orville instinctively welcomes the guilt of these thrilling, vaguely sexual yearnings, but he is just a child—how can he yet understand the friendly feel of future fetishes? He knows he is not like other boys, but the wonders of deviancy far outweigh any desire to fit in with his peers.

Orville yearns to be butch. Endlessly experimenting with fashion and different looks, he finally paints the toes and heels of his white gym shoes black, hoping to appear "daring and vulgar." While he leaves his hair "rough" and appears in his new, supposedly masculine outfit, his brother humors him by saying,

"My God you look tough." But little Orville can't help his feminine side. He has always been obsessed with broken bits of china he collects at thrift shops ("No one ever wrote more beautifully about chipped tea services," a writer for *The New York Times* would comment decades after the novel was written). When Orville felt these girly items "pressing gently against his side" as he carried them in his pocket, "it gave him a sudden and peculiar pleasure, a feeling of protection in an enemy world."

It isn't easy being a creative child. As happy as Orville is when he's alone, he still feels the urge to create his own drama. When he sneaks into an abandoned ballroom at the hotel and finds himself onstage (my parents actually built me my own little stage at the top of the stairs in our first house, where I performed endless indulgent "shows" for my very tolerant Aunt Rachel whenever she visited), our little master of masochism uncovers a musical instrument enclosed in a case with a broken strap. Suddenly inspired, Orville runs to the musician's cloakroom and locks himself in, strips off his clothes, and starts whipping himself with the strap. In his furtive imagination, he was "Henry II, doing penance, at Beckett's tomb . . . a convict tied to a tree in Tasmania. A galley slave, a Christian martyr, a noble hermit alive in the desert." This kid knew how to play. God, I wished he had lived in my neighborhood. We could have *really* put on a show on my little stage!

Orville knew that after his fantasy was over, "his behavior, if discovered, would be thought rather peculiar," but he marched on bravely, looking for further stimuli. Stumbling upon a large chain in the meadow outside, he realized one end was "embedded so that it wouldn't come way. Almost automatically, Orville knotted the extremely dirty and heavy chain around his waist and then swayed from side to side, quite carried away by some new reverie." His little scenario continued. "Now he was chained up forever" in his mind and he "would have to drag it [the chain] backwards and forwards on the grass for the rest of his life," "chanting a new dirge-like song." But then reality hits. His brother catches him in full fantasy. " 'Christ! What are you doing?' he howls in utter amazement." " 'You'd be locked up if anyone else found you doing this sort of thing.' "

But nothing can stop Orville's inner drama. When he invades an empty church for more elaborate fantasies, I really identified with this child! First, Orville makes out with a brass statue of a woman on a tomb, reasoning that she "hasn't been kissed for five hundred years." He then climbs under the altar cloths, glad to be "in complete darkness and enclosed on all sides." "A thrill of pleasure" sweeps over our little lunatic, but that isn't enough. "What would happen," he wondered, if during Mass "at the vital moment, I should leap from my hiding place with an unearthly scream? The congregation would rise in panic thinking the devil had come down to earth. For a few moments I would be left to dance about madly . . ." Oh God, Denton Welch, you sure understand childhood rage. I still feel like doing the exact things you imagined for Orville every time I step into a church . . . even today!

Little Orville was a watch-queen, too. He loved to spy on the gruff and rugged schoolmaster and his two "deprived" older boy students, who were camping in the nearby woods on a much more physical vacation. When Orville sneaks back in a rainstorm and finds the schoolmaster alone, he gets caught peeping but is invited inside the hut for tea. Orville is ordered to take off his wet clothes and change into a dressing gown. The erotic tension between Orville and the schoolteacher is so thick you could cut it with a knife, but it might only be real in the child's mind. You're never sure. When Orville admits he has been watching the deprived boys, the schoolmaster asks nonchalantly, "Why don't you come down and help me with them sometimes?" Orville sputters, "They'd think it was queer," but the older man shrugs and answers, "They'd think all those things if you put them into their heads. Otherwise they'd think you were a perfectly ordinary person."

But Orville doesn't want to be a perfectly ordinary person. He wants to be this man's slave, and after washing up the dishes for the schoolmaster, he offers, "Will you be wanting anything else, sir?" The older man, maybe quite innocently, encourages Orville's fantasy by replying, "You can polish my brown shoes if you like." Little does the master realize Orville's lust as he begins the task. "In a dazed way, Orville fetched the shoes and started to polish them. As he thrust his hand into one of them, he thought, 'It's always mysterious inside shoes; like a dark cave' . . . He placed his fingers in the little hollows—like a string of graded pearls—made by the toes. Pressing his knuckles up, he touched the over-arching leather which seemed cracked yet humid. He thought that there was a whole atmosphere and little world inside the shoe."

But that's just the foreplay. The schoolmaster offers to "show him some knots" and then ties Orville's hands and hoists him up. "Let me down," Orville cried, "you'll wrench my arms out of their sockets." But the schoolmaster just "poked him sharply in the ribs and slapped his behind resoundingly" before offering to trade positions. "Now it's your turn . . . you can tie me up exactly as you like." Orville eagerly accepts the challenge and when the man complains, "The cords are cutting into me," Orville feels "great pleasure" before coming to his senses and politely announcing, "I think I ought to go now . . . thank you so much for a very delightful afternoon. I hope we'll meet again." Somehow Denton Welch has captured the undiscovered innocence of the Marquis de Sade and the ingrained perversity that only children can fathom.

"I don't understand how to live, what to do," Orville despairs; and who does when you're this age? Parents should understand that their young kids are *not* like them and need to have the privacy to fantasize both their good and bad desires. What you may find shocking about the perverse behavior of your child may not even be remembered by your offspring later in life. But what you may pooh-pooh as their silly young fears can be more debilitating to your children than you will ever imagine. When Orville later becomes scared by an older boy, roughhousing with him on a train ride, threatening to "trim his eyelashes" (how's that for a new kind of elegant torture?), Orville suddenly begins to scream. "The sound is piercing, like steam escaping. The people in the carriage looked at him with blank faces. And as Orville screamed he knew that he could not stop, that he had been working up to this scream all his life. Through his madness spoke these very clear thoughts, 'Now they'll never touch you again. You can be mad for the rest of your life, and they'll leave you alone.'" Amen, Denton Welch, amen.

Okay, I admit Denton Welch isn't for everybody. But Lionel

Shriver's scary psychological novel *We Need to Talk About Kevin* (2003) certainly is. Here's a page-turner from the Devil's Reading List about a child all parents pray they never have. Fifteen-year-old Kevin, three days before the legal age of accountability, has murdered seven of his high school classmates, a cafeteria worker, and a teacher, but is furious if anyone compares his crime to Columbine. "I just wanna go on the record that those two weenies were not pros. Their bombs were duds and they just shot plain old anybody. My crowd was hand-picked." The story is told in letters between Kevin's parents, who are no longer together. The mother, Eva, "exhausted with shame," desperately tries to understand not only her son's violent behavior but her own vague dislike of him. She hadn't really wanted to get pregnant, but gave in to her husband's demands so he could be a father. She hated giving birth and found breast-feeding unfulfilling. But did she deserve this?!

After his conviction, Eva visits Kevin in the juvenile correctional facility, but her son tells her, "Keep it up if you want a gold star. But don't be dragging your ass back here on my account. Because I hate you." After a moment's hesitation, Eva replies, "I often hate you, too, Kevin," and finally they have somewhere to start in rebuilding their relationship. Now Eva can ask questions about the victims. "Why those particular kids?" "Uh, duh," he answers, "I didn't like them." When she wonders in anguish, "Do you blame me?" he snaps back, "Why should you get all the credit?" Slowly she begins to see his twisted thinking. " 'Now he doesn't have to worry which he is— a freak or a geek, a grid or a jock or a nerd,' she explains, 'he's a murderer.' " In a final attempt to understand her homicidal son, she asks why he didn't murder her. Kevin replies with bone-chilling reasoning, "When you're putting on a show, you don't shoot the audience."

Who's to blame when your kid goes nuts? Is it a blessing to *not* have children? *We Need to Talk About Kevin* became a hit cult book for women without offspring who were finally able to admit they didn't want to give birth. They felt complete, thank you very much, and lived in silent resentment for years at other womens' pious, unwanted sympathy toward them for not having babies. With even gay couples having children these days, aren't happy heterosexual women who don't want to have kids the most ostracized of all? To me they are beautiful feminists. If you're not sure you could love your children, please don't have them, because they might grow up and kill us.

We Need to Talk About Kevin could bring any parent sobbing to his (or her) knees, yet somehow this book is easy to like. The plot twists keep coming and we never anticipate the new shocks until we're gasping out loud. And what a great ending this thrilling yet oddly commercial novel has! The sudden psychological awareness between Eva and Kevin takes the private pain of family torture and reinvents their sadness into a secret partnership. Kevin and his mom now deserve each other. It's a new kind of love story for the criminally insane, so no wonder somebody's going to make a movie version. It better be good, too!

Sick of reading about weird children? Let's turn to the rage in adults. I love to read about anger. A "feel bad" book always makes me feel good. And no other novel in the history of literature is more depressing than Christina Stead's *The Man Who Loved Children*. This devastating portrait of one of the most hateful, spiteful, unhappy marriages ever imagined was originally published in 1940 with little fanfare and some backhanded good reviews ("Eventually, Christina Stead will impose herself upon the literature of English-speaking countries," Clifton Fadiman wrote in *The New Yorker*. "I say 'impose herself' because her qualities are not apt to win her an immediate, warm acceptance"). Her fellow novelist Mary McCarthy was not kind, calling the book "an hysterical tirade" filled with "fearful, discorded vindictiveness." It's hardly surprising that *The Man Who Loved Children* quickly disappeared. But when it was rereleased in 1965, the book finally found the praise it deserved: "a long neglected masterpiece" and a "big black diamond of a book." I became a rabid fan.

Henny Pollit, our furious heroine, is trapped in a marriage to a sanctimonious bore who keeps her pregnant. Worse, he constantly lectures her on "love and goodness." When he begins one of his pompous sermons and sees Henny is frantically scribbling something down on paper as she listens, he thinks his wife is so inspired she's taking notes, but when he looks over her shoulder he reads, "Shut up. Shut up. Shut up. Shut up. Shut up." Henny hates her husband with such venom that the reader feels like visiting the emergency room of a hospital after hearing her tirades of vitriol.

"How dare you say that! How dare you——" her husband sputters, but when Henny starts, nobody can control her bitter attacks. "You took me and you maltreated me," she rages, "and starved me half to death because you couldn't make a living and sponged off of my father and used his affluence, hoisting yourself up on all my aches and miseries . . . boasting and blowing

about your own success when all the time it was me, my poor
body that was what you took your success out of. You were breaking my bones and spirit and forcing your beastly love on me . . .
slobbering around me and calling it love and filling me with
children month after month and year after year while I hated
you and detested you and screamed in your ears to get away
from me."

Let's form a "Hate Book Club" and read the dialogue from
this amazing novel out loud. Come on, you play Henny and I'll
play the husband and we'll shout out the malignant taunts and
experience together the group horror of a failed marriage. Go
on, give Henny's furor a voice! Rant aloud what she's had to put
up with: "Your everlasting talk, talk, talk, talk, talk . . . boring
me, filling me, filling my ears with talk, jaw, jaw, till I thought
the only way was to kill myself to escape you . . . I'm through;
you can pack your bags and get out." Okay, build now! Start
bitching about his family, "your loudmouth, dung-haired sister,"
shout out, "Take your whore sister with you!" like Henny did.
Now I'll play the husband and smack you. And then just like in
the book, you attack me with a knife. Maybe the neighbors
downstairs will hear all the commotion coming from inside our
Hate Book Club and will rush up in concern to investigate. Once
we get them inside, we can force them to read *The Man Who
Loved Children*, too, and then they can imagine the terrible
calm at the end of this scene, when Henny lies defeated on the
floor and I, playing the husband, whisper the most maddeningly
abusive dialogue of all: "The worst part of it is, Pet, that you
love me still in a way; everything you do—even this!—shows
me that. I know it!"

Okay, you want something happier to read? Even absurd? The author was an alcoholic and spent a lot of time in mental hospitals, but Jane Bowles's *Two Serious Ladies*, Tennessee Williams's "favorite book," might just perk up your mood. I remember when Elloyd Hanson, the late, great co-owner of the Provincetown Bookshop, recommended this novel to me when it was rereleased in 1966. Once I read it, I felt insanely grateful to have gone beyond the door of literate lunacy into a world of complete obliviousness to emotional reality. I've never come back. *Two Serious Ladies* made a real reader out of me, and if you give it a chance, it will do the same for you.

Originally published in 1943 to confusion ("To attempt to unravel the plot . . . would be to risk, I feel sure, one's own sanity," the *New York Times* reviewer sputtered) and then trapped in out-of-print limbo for years, this peculiar piece of fiction's street cred never quite faded. "Few literary reputations are as glamorous as the underground one she [Bowles] has enjoyed since her novel . . . was published," remembered another *New York Times* critic on the book's revival. "The extreme rarity of the book once it went out of print," he continued, "has augmented its legend. When a London publisher wanted to reprint it . . . even Mrs. Bowles was unable to supply him with a copy." For years and years I wanted to own the first edition of this hardback and I finally got it. Sometimes when I want to feel smarter, I sneak up on this volume on my bookshelf and kiss it.

Two Serious Ladies is the parallel tale of a pair of ferociously eccentric women who search for crackpot adventures and some sort of cockeyed inner peace. Their unfathomable sexual attractions are completely wrongheaded. Mrs. Copperfield goes on a dreaded vacation with her husband and wanders away and falls in love for no apparent reason with a female hooker named Pacifica, who certainly does not return the feelings but half-heartedly plays along for the money. "You can't imagine how I dread leaving you," Mrs. Copperfield tells her startled new friend just after meeting her. "I honestly don't know how I'll be able to stand it . . . I'm so terrified you might simply vanish." "She wants to stop thinking," says Pacifica, the whore, as she struggles to explain Mrs. Copperfield to a male customer. When Mrs. Copperfield suddenly throws back her head and starts to bellow a song, the john asks politely, "Did you ever sing in a club?" She answers happily, "Actually I didn't. But when I was in the mood, I used to sing very loudly in a restaurant and attract a good bit of attention."

When the Copperfields' friend the wealthy widow Mrs. Goering gives up her family estate to move into a run-down house in the country, with a bunch of hangers-on in order to find her "little idea of salvation," she realizes even this impulsive action is not enough. So she decides to go on a little adventure to explore the seamy nightlife of towns both near and far. But Mrs. Goering seems to bring out unexpected hostility in other people. When she tries to make small talk to a woman on a train, this stranger reacts with unexpected anger. "I won't stand for this another moment," she yells. "I have enough real grief in my life without having to encounter lunatics." Even the conductor joins in the furious scolding of Mrs. Goering. "You can't talk to anyone on this train, unless you know them," he lectures. "The next time you're on the train stay in your seat . . . and tell this to your relatives and your friends." Unaffected, Mrs. Goering gets off the train and fearlessly enters a crummy bar, where she meets Andy, a motley bum, and immediately falls in love and moves in with him the next night. "You're some lunatic," Andy marvels, and he's right! After living with Andy for just eight days, Mrs. Goering dumps him to run off with a fat businessman named Ben who drives a hearselike car and mistakenly thinks that she is working as a prostitute. Andy moans, "You, as a decent human being, cannot do this to me." "Well, I'm afraid I can, Andy," Mrs. Goering replies. "I have my own star to follow, you know."

When Mrs. Goering and Mrs. Copperfield reunite at the end of the book in a hotel bar, accompanied by their inappropriate love interests, these serious ladies' blurting out of rude truths reaches a crescendo of loony reasoning. "I am completely satisfied and contented," the deluded and cluelessly loyal Mrs. Copperfield announces even as her supposed girlfriend Pacifica runs off to meet a boyfriend she has announced she plans to marry. When the fat businessman Ben totally ignores the smitten Mrs. Goering and leaves her stranded at the hotel, he barely notices her distress. "Hey, you," he calls out to her as he gets in his car to leave, "I forgot about you. I've got to go big distances on some important business. I don't know when I'll be back. Good-bye." Both women respond with astonishing rationales. "True enough, I *have* gone to pieces," Mrs. Copperfield explains, "which is the thing I've wanted to do for years." "Certainly I am nearer to being a saint," Mrs. Goering reflects, and I for one believe her.

Want to go further in your advanced search for snobbish, elitist, literary wit? Of course you do, but I should warn you,

you'll have to work for it. Try reading any novel by Ivy Compton-Burnett. She was English, looked exactly like the illustration on the Old Maid card, never had sex even once, and wrote twenty dark, hilarious, evil little novels between the years 1911 and 1969. Pick any one of them. They're all pretty much the same. Little actual action, almost no description, and endless pages of hermetically sealed, stylized, sharp, cruel, venomous Edwardian dialogue. "Once you pick up a Compton-Burnett," Ivy commented about her own books, "it's hard *not* to put them down again."

Since *Darkness and Day* has been called "one of her strangest novels," I guess I'll recommend you start with this one. She wrote it in 1951, when she was sixty-seven years old. It is her insanely inventive revision of *Oedipus Rex*. A family returns from exile to reveal the deep secrets of their accidental incestuous marriage only to learn that their innocent truths cause even more complicated shame. Ivy Compton-Burnett was obsessed with the *exact* meaning of language, and she hated describing anything that wasn't included in what her characters actually said. She would paint a verbal picture of the people in her books but once and *only* once (usually when they are first introduced) and you'd better remember it, because often there are thirty pages of dialogue before someone else is identified again. When readers finally reach these tiny islands of rest between speeches, they steady their eyes, take a deep breath, and plunge back into Ivy's turbulent whirlpool of language. No wonder a critic called Miss Compton-Burnett "a writer's writer." Her dialogue constantly deconstructs what her characters actually mean to say.

Once you get the rhythm, the sparkle, the subtle nuances of family dominance in her character's words, you will feel superior to other people and how they struggle to speak in real life.

Sure, you'll get lost reading *Darkness and Day*, maybe hypnotized, probably even bored. But as soon as you realize you aren't concentrating, not paying enough attention, BANG! A great line will hit you right between the eyes and give you the intellectual shivers. You certainly can't *skim* this book. One editor complained after reading long passages of dialogue, and having to turn back page after page to figure out who was saying what to whom, that the author had forgotten to write that one of the characters was speaking on the telephone. Ivy grumpily admitted he was correct and added two words to the text to explain: "He said."

The monstrously intelligent and all-knowing children in *Darkness and Day* speak like no other children in the history of youth. "Do you remember your Uncle?" a relative asks his nieces Rose and Viola. "You used to be younger," Rose says with steely reasoning. "That is true," the uncle answers, "and I feel as young as I did." "People do feel younger than they are," she quickly responds. "They don't get used to a new age, before they get to the next one. I feel I am nine, and I have been ten for a week. I am in my eleventh year." "I don't often think as much as that," her sister Viola comments. "I always think," answers Rose with a vengeance.

Simple truths are told in the book in bafflingly elegant ways. "You can't help what happens in your mind," one character comments. When the family worries about a scandal, a member logically surmises, "People don't forget things, unless they do."

After the housekeeper catches little Rose reading in bed past her bedtime, she scolds, "Dear, dear! I did *not* see you hide that book." "Well if you had, it wouldn't have been hidden," Rose answers without flinching. Even something as simple as saying good morning can be tortuously debated. When the children don't answer, the teacher makes another attempt. "Well, I will try to do better. Good morning to you both again." "We don't say things like 'good morning,'" Rose answers, "we don't see what use it is." "Well, perhaps you are not old enough to realize that," the teacher tries to argue. "We don't want to be old," Rose answers back, "people don't really know much more. They only learn to seem to." When the children have so tortured their teacher that she quits after only two days' work, she tries to put her frustration into words. "The use of patience is not to encourage people without proper feeling to be intolerable," she says, but the children are unmoved. As their governess discovers a mean prank the children have pulled involving the teacher's chair, she tries to discipline them. "The thing that occurs to me, is too bad to be true." "Then it can't be true," Rose answers, ever the debater. "I don't dare ask about it," the governess proclaims. "Then there is the end of the matter," the children declare with intellectual victory.

And on death, Ms. Compton-Burnett's writing can be just plain brutal. After the children in *Darkness and Day* are told of a passing in the family, they are asked to "run upstairs and forget what is sad. Just remember the happy part of it." "What is the happy part?" wonders Viola. "There is none," answers Rose. "Why do people talk as if they are glad when someone is dead? I think it must mean there is a little gladness somewhere."

Right up to the end of her life, Ivy Compton-Burnett's irritable, nitpicking, obsessive love of words never ceased. According to the great biography *Ivy*, by Hilary Spurling, an old friend came to visit Ivy and she woke up from a catnap and snapped, "I'm not tired, I'm sleepy. They are different things. And I'm surprised that you should say tired when you mean sleepy." That Ivy! She was a real laff-riot. Her last spoken words before death? "Leave me alone." I have to. I have all twenty of her novels and I've read nineteen. If I read the one that is left there will be no more Ivy Compton-Burnett for me and I will probably have to die myself.

LITTLE RICHARD,
HAPPY AT LAST

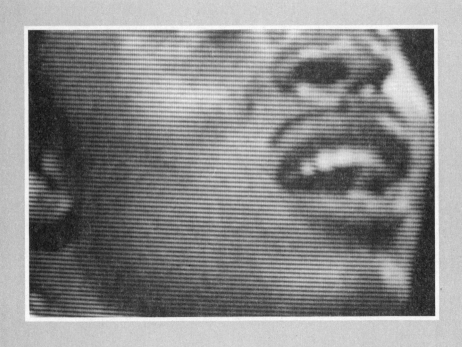

L ittle Richard scared my grandmother in 1957. I was eleven years old, on the way to her house for dinner with my parents, and had just shoplifted a record in the five-and-dime. Mom and Dad hadn't even noticed. Easy pickings—the 45 rpm of "Lucille" on the Specialty label. My favorite tune. I felt happily defiant in the backseat of the car with the sharp edge of the single jabbing my stomach beneath the sweater. Once inside Mama's (as we called Stella Whitaker, my mother's mother), I made a beeline to her out-of-date hi-fi and let it roll. "Lu-CILLE! You won't do your sister's will!" came blaring through the house like a pack of rabid dogs. It was as if a Martian had landed. My grandmother stopped in her tracks, face ashen, beyond comprehension. The antiques rattled. My parents looked stunned. In one magical moment, every fear of my white family had been laid bare: an uninvited, screaming, flamboyant black man was in the living room. Even Dr. Spock hadn't warned them about this.

Ever since, I have always wished I could somehow climb into Little Richard's body, hook up his heart and vocal cords to my own, and switch identities with him. Admiring his processed pompadour on my own head in the mirror, feeling his blood pulsating in my veins as I looked down at the twitching pencil-thin moustache over his lip, I'd stomp through the world screaming, "A-wop-bop-a-loo-mop-a-wop-bam-boom!" and finally feel happy! Strangers would jump back and shriek, "Good Lord, it's the Bronze Liberace—Show Business Personified!" while others genuflected to the inventor of rock and roll, and for once, just once, there'd be a real reason to live.

But are there some role models you should never meet? When *Playboy* magazine sent me to interview the then fifty-four-year-old Richard Penniman in 1987, it turned into kind of a disaster. At first all went fine. When I called him to try to set up our meeting, Little Richard was receptive but would have none of the gushed compliments. "No, no, no, John," he cried in mock indignation over my flattery, still sounding as hysterical as his early recordings. "That will get you nowhere!" I knew that His Highness was foaming at the mouth over the recent *Jet* magazine cover story on him headlined LITTLE RICHARD TELLS WHY HE QUIT BEING A MINISTER. Yes, he'd recently made another Hollywood comeback in the hit film *Down and Out in Beverly Hills*; had recorded his first all-new-material album in eight years, *Lifetime Friend*, with a video to match; had made guest appearances on Johnny Carson and *Hollywood Squares*; had been honored by the Rock and Roll Hall of Fame; and was planning yet another world tour, but he had definitely *not* left God! "Why would *Jet* magazine do this?" he wondered, genuinely upset. "Little Richard has never quit the ministry! I believe in God! My music itself *is* the ministry." As he complained about telephone calls from his concerned religious constituency all over the country, I tried to calm him down with the information that writers usually don't do their own headlines and it was possibly an innocent mistake. "Okay, baby," he purred wearily, agreeing to the time of our interview, "my bodyguards will get you. God bless you."

Little Richard, at the time, was living in a surprisingly ordinary hotel room in Los Angeles, while recovering from a 1985 Santa Monica Boulevard car accident that almost killed him. He was a king without a castle. The first home he bought at the height of his fame, next door to Joe Louis in West Los Angeles, was long gone. His household possessions from his last estate in Riverside were in storage or had been given to relatives. His dog, Fluffy, was staying with his sister. The piano his grandfather gave him was at his brother's. God, fame, family, and a small staff, including a physical therapist named Madison, were enough right now. Little Richard was thankful to be among the living.

Mark, who looks like a younger version of his boss, comes down to the hotel lobby to escort me up to the room. He had met Richard in his studio while they recorded "Great Gosh A'Mighty" and has been working for him, both privately and in his backup band, the CIA, for about a year. We wait outside while Richard finishes a phone conversation with one of his sisters. Hotel guests pass in the hall, unaware that a legend lurks on their floor.

Finally, the door opens and I feel as if the Supreme One of Color has appeared before me. Looking trim and healthy (he has recently taken up bodybuilding) and, as always, a little frantic, he ushers us in, dressed in a red open shirt, pleated brocade trousers, and red ankle boots. He doesn't look his age ("Lord, when the time comes, I'm gonna have a face-lift, jaw lift, eye lift; everything that is falling will be lifted and the things that can't be lifted will be moved!"). His hair, once raised to new heights by "Willie Brown in Atlanta, Georgia—my beautician at the time" is more conservative now, and he does it himself. The pencil-thin moustache has mysteriously widened with the years.

One wishes that Little Richard were still crowned and be-jeweled as sweating flunkies carried him about on an ornate throne; but unfortunately, there is only a couch to sit on in this very generic modern hotel room. File cabinets are in one corner and the family snapshots have been tucked into the frames of the "art" on the walls, but otherwise, there are few personal touches. I take my rightful place on the floor at his feet and turn on the tape recorder, resisting the urge to kiss his boots, as fans once did in Germany. Mark sits in front of the TV, watching with the volume turned off for the rest of the evening.

I tell Richard of the pilgrimage I had made that evening to the house he had bought for his mother. A very nice Christian lady named Mrs. Wilson now lives there, and she invited me in and told me that fans still come around at all hours searching for their idol. "She's probably getting my checks," Richard roars, then laughs so hard one can notice his perspiration rising. "I wondered where they was going. I'm goin' by there and get them. Sister Wilson, where did my check go?"

Little Richard remembers his palace fondly. "I had velvet and silk in the living room, green and gold—I had all this gold hanging down. In the bedroom, I had blue silk coming out of the wall with my bed in the middle. I had dreamed of that as a little boy—it was my design for my mother." He plans on getting another house soon but feels "better here now in the hotel, around people. Mark is one of my main people. I need two more. My niece is my secretary, I have two bodyguards I travel with, and a twenty-four-hour limo. I need to get over my mother's death. I don't want to be by myself in no house. Everybody is gone at night; that's lonely. You need responsibility, someone to take care of. My mother died and I couldn't stand to look at her bedroom anymore. I'd get sick. I've always been a momma's boy. My father was a bootlegger; he sold stump whiskey in Macon, Georgia. He hid it under the peppers and corn and the collard greens. There was a black lady who used to watch me named Ma Sweetie, she would let him know when the police were coming—he would leap the fence in a single bound."

As Richard was beginning his career, his father was murdered. "I was appearing at the VFW club and I came home . . . It was pouring down rain, and those houses with the tin tops and you could hear the rain. This guy had killed my daddy and I saw his coat lying on the porch. A raincoat with all this blood on it. It was just . . . something. I walked in the door, seein' my mother. I looked at this beautiful woman and she said, 'Bru?' My mother called me Bru and I called her Mu. She said, 'Bru?' and I said, 'What is it, Mu?' She said, 'You don't have no more dad,' and I just cried. 'Oh, no! Lord!' Everything inside me just broke. 'Cause my mother, that's my heart. When my mother cried, boy, that shakes my mind! I can do some drastic things behind Mu! I ain't scared of lions, tigers, snakes, puppy-dog tail, or *chickens*! It [segregation] was so hard then. But you still had a peace, a serenity: that joy, that hope, that determination, that perseverance that someday, somehow, I *will* make it!"

Resisting the urge to leap up and scream a honky hallelujah, I just sit there listening, a one-man congregation in the Church of Little Richard. I half expect Mark to pass a collection plate, but he's still glued to the TV; maybe he's heard it all before. On the other hand, when Richard's on a roll, he's not easily interrupted. "I look back on my life, comin' out of Macon, Georgia, I never thought I'd be a superstar, a living legend. I never heard of no rock and roll in my life. Black people lived right by the railroad tracks and the train would shake their houses at night. I would hear it as a boy and I thought, I'm gonna make a song that sounds like that. In the studio, we got low-down and they said, 'We ain't never heard anything like this.' I would sing and scream and make those high notes and low notes. Oh, I was a wild child! I sent a tape to Specialty Records and they didn't get back in touch with me. I was in this hotel and I had a Chrysler my mother had mortgaged her home to get me. I went into the studio anyway, and they had me singing like Ray Charles, B. B. King. They wanted me to sing the blues and that was not me. I got on the piano and started singing, 'Woooooo!' They said, 'Oh, boy, where did you get that voice?' 'A-wop-bop-a-loo-mop-a-wop-bam-boom!' and they said, 'That's a hit,' and the rest is history."

The fame came, all right, like burning lava, and today, Little Richard seems a happy prisoner of it, resting on his laurels, fretting and planning, unable to go out—even for a walk. "I'm afraid to. I might meet somebody who will try to take me away. My chauffeur picks me up in the limo and we pass the girls and they start screaming. I'm talkin' fourteen or fifteen years old. They scream, 'Aaaaaghh! Aaaaaghh!' and I say, 'Oh, thank you,

Lord.' It's such a good feelin'. It's a blessing sometimes and a lesson. It makes you feel good you're a living legend and not a dead one. People expect so much from you, you got to live so much down. The burden of all this falls on you. It's hard to have a friend when your name's a household word."

He's quite well aware of his place in history, thank you. When I quizzed him on the best reviews he ever received, his voice shot up like a tape recorder on fast forward. " 'There's only one originator, there's only one architect, Little Richard'— I love that. I saw that in so many write-ups. And when the people say my music inspired them—the Beatles, when James Brown was my vocalist, when Jimi Hendrix was my guitarist, when Joe Tex was singing with me, Otis Redding, when Billy Preston was my organist at thirteen—it makes me feel good!"

Little Richard will admit to being hurt by bad press, especially by a caricature that once offended his vanity. "They called me big-headed with a little body. I didn't like that. In New York, they had this great big *heeeeeaaad* in the paper and a little bitty piano and a little body like Humpty Dumpty on a wall." But he's not complaining. "I believe a star is living a lie if he doesn't want his picture taken. Be a dishwasher. Take my old job at the bus station! It's a joy when people holler. Mark will tell you, I go down to the slums. I go to poor people's houses; they don't even know I'm coming. I buy food and go around and hug them. I get out of the car and hug the winos. This is a joy to me, because I came from the slums; you can't forget!"

As I ponder the mental picture of a welfare family of six eating their last food-stamp dinner as a hyper Little Richard followed by squealing fans bursts through the door, uninvited,

thrusting bags of groceries at the hungry, I bring up the book—
The Life and Times of Little Richard, perhaps the best and most
shocking celebrity tell-all book ever written. Penned by Charles
White with Little Richard's full cooperation and published in
1984, it is copyrighted in the names of the author, the star, and
his longtime, now-deceased manager, Robert "Bumps" Black-
well. It's a real lulu. Detailing his early life, in which he traveled
with a minstrel show, sold snake oil in Doctor Hudson's Medicine Show, and performed in drag as Princess Lavonne, it touch-
ingly included early childhood anecdotes, such as the time
Richard gave an old lady neighbor a bowel movement in a box
for her birthday. (What a coincidence! Divine was on the receiving end of this exact same gift in *Pink Flamingos*.) Halfway
through the book, you realize that you are in a stratosphere of lunacy. The bizarre lifestyle you'd fantasized for Little Richard is
small potatoes compared with the truth. His onetime drug addic-
tions and alcoholism, his hilarious threesome with Buddy Holly
and his longtime stripper friend Lee Angel (with a "fifty-inch
bust"), his obsessions with voyeurism ("Richard the Watcher")
and masturbation ("six or seven times a day"), are all topped off
with truly staggering photographs of his many fashion state-
ments. Just when you start thinking Nobel Prize, you get to the
final chapter, a compilation of Richard's religious testimony
that seems to sour the entire volume and turn off the very audience for whom the book was written. He seems to want it both
ways.

"Some things that is said in the book are not really accurate
in certain ways." He falters when I bring up some of his quotes
about religion, rock and roll, the Devil, homosexuality, and his

then-current view on sex in general. Does he regret telling all? "No, I think it's time for people to be truthful. I got so much publicity, the book is bigger overseas than here. It's a great book, the best I've ever written; it's the truth about my life and thinking. I don't know how you put this, 'cause I don't want to hurt Dr. Rock [Charles White]. Some of the things accredited to me, I didn't say. I never fought it. I appreciate it . . . This man left his business [to do the book]; he's a foot doctor. Traveled all over the world."

Richard tries to set the record straight. "I love gay people. I believe I was the founder of gay. I'm the one who started to be so bold tellin' the world! You got to remember my dad put me out of the house because of that. I used to take my mother's curtains and put them on my shoulders. And I used to call myself at the time the Magnificent One. I was wearing makeup and eyelashes when no men were wearing that. I was very beautiful; I had hair hanging everywhere. If you let anybody know you was gay, you was in trouble; so when I came out I didn't care what nobody thought. A lot of people were scared to be with me."

Politically relieved, I wonder aloud, "Is the 'good' Little Richard battling it out spiritually with the 'bad' Little Richard? Has he turned umpteen times from rock and roll to God only to be lured back by Devil fame and worship?" "No, I don't think that way," he states emphatically, admitting that he's "amazed most people don't believe me. My God, I haven't grouped in so long. It's been almost twenty years since I've been out to have a good time. Life has changed for me now, I'm older, that's not my interest anymore; but at the time, it was. I was young, never had enough of nothing. When I was first started in the business, I used to look for that in every city so we could have a ball, do it all, in the hall, even on the wall! When I was in Baltimore [at the Royal Theater] the girls would take off their—people didn't call them panties then, they called them drawers—and throw them on the stage. It was terrible, but at the time, we didn't know better. All the girls would want to come in the room and you'd let them in and they'd never leave! I was shocked! Girl groupies, boy groupies, dog groupies, cat groupies! She would say, 'Give me a pillow,' and I'd say 'My God, ain't she going home?' And they'd stay for a week!"

Maybe I'll stay, too. As much as I believe that Richard's wild days are over, I can't help thinking that his onetime lunatic libido can't lie low forever. "Is sex out completely?" I finally ask point-blank. "Well . . . uh . . . uh . . . ," he stammers, "at this age, you don't have a lot of choice. I'll say this much. We still see a lot of cake in the showcase, but we closed the bakery." Sex? Drugs? Rock and roll? He's not buying any of it. "I'm not into drugs at all. God is the only cure for crack; He is the only one can bring you back. You can get over 'herrone.' Once somebody slipped LSD in my food. My chauffeur and bodyguard kept me. I cried. I was afraid, like a little boy. I didn't take speed. I was going *too* fast. I needed to take some breaks and I did. God gave me a break. Do you know what I enjoy now? Tellin' people the right way to go, the pitfalls, how to love people."

And I believe him. But deep down, selfishly, I wish *somebody* could tempt him to fall from grace just one more time. Imagine that demon style rearing its ugly head in maturity! I still want him rippin' it up, screeching, scaring all the white folks. Getting a hold of myself, I resist the urge to whisper conspiratorially,

"Come on, Richard, let's put on some false eyelashes, take some pep pills, and call Lee Angel, your onetime sex magnet, and see what's cookin'!"

Richard looks distractedly at the silent late-eighties news show on TV. "Excuse me; didn't the Ayatollah get killed today?" "He did?" I ask, alarmed (he didn't). "Didn't Iraq bomb his home?" he asks, before blithely getting back to our conversation. The thought enters my mind that maybe World War III has broken out and I don't even know it. I'll spend the end of the world with Little Richard in a hotel room. Religion might come in handy, after all. Preach to me, Richard! The best of Reverend Ike and Marjoe rolled into one.

"I only came out of show business one time," he states, unaware of my inner turmoil. "I was in Australia and I saw Sputnik and I got afraid. When I was quitting, I was admitting I was scared of Sputnik. You know I came from the country; I'm not from the city, what a pity. I was scared to death to get back on the plane to come home. I was scared Sputnik would run into our plane, Russia done set this thing up. I had read about the Tower of Babel; you have to remember my people are Seventh-day Adventists, my people go to church on Saturdays . . ." "Are you Jewish now?" I inquire, repeating published reports that Richard had followed in the footsteps of Sammy Davis, Jr. "There's something I prefer not saying," he teases mysteriously. "I will say this. I'm a believer in the God of Abraham, Isaac, and Jacob. I believe the seventh-day Sabbath is God's way. I believe we should eat kosher. I was invited to a party night before last. Rod Stewart's. I didn't go, because I open the Sabbath on Friday."

"How about the rumor that it was Bob Dylan who converted

you to Judaism on your deathbed following your accident?"
"Bob Dylan is my brother. I love him same as Bobby Darin [deceased] is my baby. I feel Bob Dylan is my blood brother. I believe if I didn't have a place to stay, Bob Dylan would buy me a house. He sat by my bed; he didn't move for hours. I was in pain that medicine couldn't stop. My tongue was cut out, leg all tore up, bladder punctured. I was supposed to be dead. Six feet under. God resurrected me; that's the reason I have to tell the world about it."

"I wish you had been Pope," I blurt out, all whipped up in a religious frenzy, throwing caution to the wind. Richard doesn't miss a beat, and I wonder if he has already considered the possibility. "I idolized the Pope when I was a little boy," he says reverently. "I liked the pumps he wore. I think the Pope really dresses!" But there were other, more low-down ecclesiastical fashion casualties who seemed a bigger influence. "There was Prophet Jones of Detroit—he used to walk on this carpet. They would spread this carpet out of the limo and he would walk on it. When I got famous, I had the guys just spreading carpet for me to walk on, and they would kiss my hand . . . and I used to like to live like that." How about one of my personal favorites, Father Divine, the black messiah who ruled his fanatic flock of millions with an iron fist and blatantly proclaimed, "I am God"? "I [tried] to have dinner in one of his kingdoms in Philadelphia, but the lady put me out . . . I just had on one of my typical outfits, my hair hanging down, and she said, 'The Father don't allow nothing like that in here.' I felt bad, 'cause I went there to eat, they had a good dinner, you could eat all you wanted for a dollar. I'll never forget it."

It's time to go. The phone is ringing. The Grand Ole Opry. The Joan Rivers show. Richard is getting a headache. "What about the future?" I lamely ask, hoping for a few more minutes. "I was just offered a role with Gary Coleman. They wanted me to be his father. And they wanted me to weigh three hundred pounds. He was to be a bad little boy, like a demon. My management people thought it was not a good idea, 'cause there wasn't no other name people in the cast. I'd like to play a detective. I can see myself playing something really rugged—macho!" Little Richard starts growling, and this tears Mark away from his silent TV program. He laughs out loud. "Mark, that ain't funny! He always laughs when I say 'macho.' I can't be macho? Shoot, I'll be macho if I want." Vainly trying to picture him calmed down, alone, reflecting, or, God forbid, falling asleep, I ask, "What kind of music do *you* listen to?" "I like classical music," he answers bashfully, "something quiet. Strings. It just makes me think, relaxes me. I've been doing that for years, but I was afraid to tell anyone. They might not like my music anymore."

Suddenly all business, Richard rises and hands me a typed release. "This is something we give everybody. I'd appreciate it if you'd sign this here." Good Lord, what is this? I wonder, reading, "We agree that you [Little Richard] shall have approval of the content of any article written hereunder predicated in whole or in part upon the interview." "But, Richard," I sputter, mentally cursing *Jet* for causing his press paranoia. "I can't sign this; all freedom of the press is gone. If you had shown me this first, *Playboy* would never have sent me." "Why not?" he asks. "I don't want people to hate me. I saw Elizabeth Taylor do this. I've seen Michael [Jackson] do this." I call information and get my editor's home phone number in Chicago and wake him up. I explain. Richard is adamant. "Can't you just leave?" my editor quizzes. "Is somebody going to pull a gun?" "Who knows?" I say, eyeing Mark, who has politely backed up his boss, and wondering if maybe even *I* could beat him up. "I'd rather you not publish it at all. Just leave the tapes; I'll pay you," announces Richard. Church is definitely out. I feel as if I've been excommunicated. Oh, great, I think, I'm going to be in the first fistfight of my life with my favorite role model over some goddamn tapes! Richard then debates my baffled editor. "John asked me about my peeping! I'm so old I can't even see through the hole!" Suddenly I'm afraid I'll start laughing hysterically. Why is Little Richard so worried? All his fans love him for his outrageousness. The book had just been published in the United States; of course reporters will ask about the content. As for his religious followers, what are they doing reading *Playboy* anyway?

By now, an hour or so had passed. Are all celebrity interviews this hellish? Would Barbara Walters bolt? I then argue with Little Richard's lawyer on the phone. Talk about putting a damper on things! Being over budget and behind schedule on a film shoot would be a picnic compared with this. Finally, under extreme duress, we make up. Richard explains his worries. I explain my job. We hug. He signs his book to me, "God Always Cares, Little Richard." I think about how I used to sign mine "See You In Hell, John Waters" and realize the miles we're apart.

I rush out of the room and realize my own world did end today in its own peculiar way. Maybe I don't want to switch identities after all. A few days later, a press representative calls me at home, announcing that Little Richard is threatening to call the NAACP. Later, I hear he's calmed down. He is still the undisputed king in my book. The man can't help it. But I learned one thing that day. Not all role models turn out the way you want. Pssssst, Richard? More than twenty years have passed— wanna come over to *my* house this time and try again?

OUTSIDER PORN

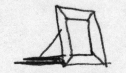

Marines like three things," confides outsider pornographer Bobby Garcia, "beer, porn, and blow jobs." He should know. Bobby is obsessed by male Marines and has been chasing, filming, and having sex with them for the last thirty years. "Never tell a Marine you are gay," Bobby advises anyone who shares his taste in presumably heterosexual men; "tell them you are a cocksucker." From the look of Bobby's amateur porn tapes, his advice seems to have worked.

Bobby Garcia is a great artist but doesn't know it. His filthy little "screen tests" are all shot in his apartment, usually in the bedroom, filmed just like Andy Warhol's *Blow Job* but with the camera zoomed back a little further to reveal all. A lone Marine begins by taking off his clothes, folding them military style, and lying down on either Bobby's bed or couch. Watching hetero offscreen fuck movies, they know they are supposed to jerk off on film, some going along with Bobby's cockamamie story of this being an "audition for a straight porno shoot." Bobby can tell how far they might go. "I look them in the eye . . . and then to the crouch" (as he pronounces "crotch"—just the way Edith Massey did!). His movies all have the same story arc—sometimes the Marine just jerks off; sometimes he looks embarrassed, sometimes not. Sometimes the good ones feel exhibitionism throbbing in their veins and Bobby's antenna goes up. You see Bobby's hand creep in from the side of the frame to "pose" their Hollywood loaf (semi-hard) dick. If the Marines don't object, he blows them. If he sees they are touching their asshole in any way, he rims them. Bobby wears breakaway exercise pants for easy access to his hole. He's a director, so he knows time is money, and this way he can save screen time—he's fuckable with his pants still on! "Marines don't want to see a dick," he has said; "they want to see your mouth and your ass." Once in a great while, the Marine will reach over and touch Bobby's dick and you can see his disappointment at the hint of the soldier's being gay. Bobby likes dominant abuse. "Call me names," you can hear him order on camera, but these reluctant studs usually are pretty lame in the ad-lib department and Bobby has to cue them the phony taunts he wants to hear, like "Bitch!" or "Cocksucker!" The worst for Bobby is when they want to blow *him*. This seldom happens but he goes along with it because he doesn't want to waste valuable videotape by starting over and knows that his appreciative audience will be just as shocked as he is that every once in a while he discovers a real gay live wire. And woe to the unlucky Marines who reveal (usually after doing the poppers Bobby always has on hand) that they want Bobby to fuck *them*. "Disqualified!" you can imagine Bobby yelling in his mind in desperation and sexual letdown. Bobby is a bottom, but he's a "bossy bottom" if there ever was one. Bobby is not only the best porno director there is; he also knows how to "top from the bottom" with style, wit, and a raw sexuality that speaks to the voyeurs who lust after hetero-flexible men everywhere.

It isn't easy to find Bobby today. Sure, you can buy his videos from Frat House Boys through the mail or go to "AWOL Marines" online and see his later work with daily updates, but Bobby long ago sold the rights to his tapes, and he's not even aware of their distribution. How could he be? He doesn't even have a computer. He barely has a house. After years of searching, finally I got a lead to Bobby's phone number from a Bobby benefactor. I call him and he agrees to let me come to meet him in Twentynine Palms, California, where he lives. I have no idea of what to expect. I have seen so many of his tapes that I know the couches in his apartments and the sound of the train coming by that you hear in the background of all that whacking and slathering of baby oil. (Bobby loves baby oil. In one eye-popping tape, Bobby takes a big drink of baby oil straight from the bottle before he goes down on a startled Marine.) But all those apartments are gone. Long gone. Today Bobby is renting or maybe squatting in a run-down home surrounded by jail-strength industrial chain-link fencing. As I pull up in a ridiculous Mercedes-Benz that I didn't order but was upgraded to by the car rental place, I feel a sickening sense of entitlement. I hate fancy cars. In real life I drive a plain Buick that looks like a narcotics-agent car or the vehicle of the local monsignor. Who wants to be noticed in his car? Suppose I still might want to commit a crime? Who would ever want a car a witness could describe? Anyway, here I am at the home of the most notorious underground Marine pornographer in the world, the one who caused the big scandal at Camp Pendleton, for chrissakes, and I'm in some fancy Hollywood-executive-type vehicle.

As I step out of the car, a pack of snarling dogs runs from the front door and leaps up on the fence, barking and baring their teeth. Bobby follows, yelling at them to calm down and welcoming me. He looks much thinner than he did on the tapes. But, oh God, it's him all right—Bobby Garcia, the in-his-forties Mexican American man who has blown hundreds and hundreds of really cute Marines and lived to tell about it. The Almodóvar of Anuses, the Buñuel of Blow Jobs, the Jodorowsky of Jerking Off. Here is an auteur who devoted his life for you to be able to enjoy Marine porn, a man whose work makes me so happy, so jealous of his dirty dedication, that I am, quite simply, thunderstruck.

Bobby calls the dogs off, breaking up the ones who have paired off to fight wildly among themselves, and unlocks the padlock of the gate. I drive onto his property and the dogs jump up on the car, barking in the hastily rolled up windows on both sides as Bobby screams commands for them to stop. The dogs sort of listen and calm down. I get out of the car and shake hands with Mr. Garcia, and he invites me into his humble abode.

I am stupefied to see the interior. Well, I use the word "interior" freely—his home is part outdoors, too. Times are tough for Bobby these days. As we search for a comfortable place to sit, I notice a trough with two real pigs waddling around, weighing in at a total of 750 pounds. *Inside* his house. Bobby actually lives in a pigpen! As we sit down and I get out my tape recorder, I look up in alarm at a giant rooster (one of two) who is also one of Bobby's roommates. I soon realize this is not Bobby's house—it's his Noah's ark! "I live with eleven dogs, two pigs, two roosters, and more than five hundred rats—one thousand, or two thousand—who cares?" he announces happily. I suddenly actually feel some sort of critters moving under the newspaper covering the kitchen floor. Good God. "Do the other animals like the rats?" I ask in shock. "They could care less," he laughs. "The rats don't bother you. You give them scratch [chicken feed] from Wal-Mart." He tells me he feels them crawling over him when he's sleeping, and I momentarily consider making a break and running to the safety of the rental car, but something about his sweetness and hospitality makes me stay. The rats "no bother me," Bobby says with a shrug. "They don't make no mess. They eat at such and such time." He even has *names* for the rats! "When you live in the house you get to know the mama and the papa. And the mama gonna have ten, twenty little rats so you know the mama's name. I have a special whistle for mealtime. I invite them in . . . I don't want to kill them." He's no Willard, though. "I wish they were gone, absolutely," he admits, but then suddenly is inspired by my horror. "I video if you want," he offers. "I'll film the rats next week." "No, that's okay," I sputter, wondering if we should team up and make a John Waters–Bobby Garcia coproduction: he is servicing the cutest Marine of all time and a rat jumps out when I blow Bobby's whistle and bites the Marine right on his ass.

Jesus, I'm embedded with Bobby and the sun is going down and I'm suddenly not even sure Bobby has electricity. The more the pig grunts and the rooster eyes me with pent-up rage, the more antsy I get. Bobby takes me into the bedroom where his tapes are kept, but there's no light and I keep hearing scampering noises of God knows what, so I suggest, "for sound purposes on the tape recorder," we sit in the car to continue the interview. Bobby's fine with that, so we go out front with the dogs fighting in the dirt and get in my rented Mercedes. Bad idea. The dogs jump up again on both sides of the car and I can hear their claws scratching the doors and I pale, imagining the damages I'll have to pay the car rental company. "Put down the windows," Bobby advises, seeing my alarm, and he's right; the dogs back off. We continue talking about a career that deserves some kind of grant. If only there were a MacArthur award for porn, Bobby Garcia would be the ideal recipient.

Marine lust this strong must have started somewhere, and Bobby quickly agrees. "I grew up in Acapulco. That's where I became a queer," he explains. He then moved with his family near Fort Hood, Texas, next to an army base. "My father was killed when I was six years old." His civilian mom "used to run a business; she used to take care of a motel where all the boys from the army lived, so my job was to wake them up to go back to work." Whatever happened during those "wake-up" calls seems to have lit the fuse of a lifetime explosion of sexual mono-mania.

Before VCRs, before camcorders, in " 'seventy-five or 'seventy-six," Bobby moved to L.A. and started shooting 8 mm loops, peep-show stuff of "always" straight men, but burned the film in what one would imagine was artistic frustration. It wasn't until Bobby (working under another name) was hired as house-hold help by a "showbiz lady," who he quickly claims was Raquel Welch (!), that his calling in life revealed itself. "I drove to San Diego for Raquel and ran out of gas in her Jaguar, pulled off in

Oceanside, saw the beautiful boys [the Marines at Camp Pendleton] on Friday night. I went back to Beverly Hills but that was in my mind. Then I went back [to Oceanside] and stayed for good."

"I filmed where I lived," Bobby states emphatically, like some confident location manager on an independent film. He bought a VHS camera "for hobby, not to make money." "When I moved to Oceanside I was in my small little studio paying $150 a month. I was one block from the main street. I only have to walk a half a block to get a Marine. I say, 'Hi, do you want a beer?'" "I'm not twenty-one," they would answer, but Bobby knew eighteen years of age was legal for what he had in mind. "I live nearby, I have some beer at home," Bobby would coyly offer. "Fuck, yeah!" was a response he told me was typical.

Bobby's apartments, his soundstages, were what Cinccittà was for Fellini. Here is where he would always shoot his Marine masterpieces. Many of his fans can still identify the bedrooms of the three different places in Oceanside; the next one in Camp Lejeune in Jacksonville, North Carolina, where he relocated for about a year and "did some of [his] best work"; and the other one near the Marine Corps Air Ground Combat Center in Twentynine Palms that he has long since vacated. Bobby got laid more than anyone I ever knew, if you called what Bobby liked "getting laid." "I make them feel good" is his only comment on why he is so successful in luring straight Marines to whip it out. "How can a guy like me who can barely speak English get this beauty?" He laughs as he looks through his "talent" scrapbooks, which rate his corps of military stars in sexual power. "Everything I did was to make them comfortable," Bobby remembers as he gazes lovingly at the long-gone heterosexuals who at the beginning of his career were more handsome than any professional porno stars working today. And at first Bobby didn't even pay them! "The main thing you tell them is [you will] keep your mouth shut with other Marines. If I see you in the street, I keep going, I never see you again. If you want a good blow job or some man-pussy you know where I live."

"But aren't the Marines nervous about what other Marines are going to think?" I ask, bewildered. "In some of the tapes," I remind Bobby, "you can hear other Marines laughing and waiting off-screen in another room in your apartment for their turn to jerk off for the camera or to be blown by you." "Absolutely," Bobby confirms. "I just put a sheet over the door [to where he was shooting]. They know what is going on because they are going to do the same fucking thing." Just as in the lives of many gay men, I notice the attractiveness of his Marines diminish slightly as Bobby gets older. "Is there such a thing as an ugly Marine?" I ask, wondering just how stringent his casting process was. "Yes," Bobby reluctantly admits but you can tell what really tests his patience is not how cute or not the Marines are; it's when they have trouble reaching a climax on videotape. In one hilarious vignette Bobby looks right at the viewer through the camera lens and rolls his eyes in frustration as he jerks off a nervous and panicked Marine who can't come no matter how much baby oil Bobby applies to his "blue balls." There's never been a Bobby blooper reel, but I can have a dream, can't I?

In the early eighties, "somebody from Long Beach" came around, saw the tapes, and recommended "someone who could help [Bobby] get money" for his movies and get them distributed on VHS in video shops' porn sections all over America. Bobby was thankful. "I started paying the boys," he remembers, "a good-looking boy for a good blow job got twenty dollars." The new cash "helped with beer money for the guys." Bobby's tapes were released by an L.A. company and were an instant sensation: some of the first "amateur porn tapes" to offer supposedly "all straight guys," a genre Bobby helped start that is widely copied today. Bobby Garcia was suddenly a brand name. "Right next door to Camp Pendleton in the small town of Oceanside," the promotional material screamed, "Bobby lives smack in the middle of 44 thousand Marines." Porn enthusiasts were amazed at the raw sexuality of his stars. *Shoot to Kill*, *Bomb Squad*, and *Basic Training* were just a few of the hilarious titles, but their taglines were even better: "*Discharge* means only one thing to Bobby—get off or get out!" Each Marine was given a lurid screen-test profile: "Johnny a big beefy hairy-chested Nebraska farm boy. He worships his cock with one hand while fingering his asshole with the other." Or "Tom—this is a cocky little son of a bitch. He has a mean streak when it comes to sex . . . He also demonstrates how male he is by humping a pillow. This tape is an ass-lover's dream." Stars were being born; lots of them.

And then, in 1993, the scandal happened. Bobby remembers, "A Marine came over with some girl's income tax check. I endorsed it and cashed it for him, and the girl claimed she never got the $600. I got arrested for receiving stolen property, or whatever . . . They came looking for me and found some tapes. When I was in the federal holding tank, two guys from D.C.— one guy showed me the tape. The next person, a military person . . . offered to me—no more jail time [if he'd talk]. But I walk away. I keep my mouth shut." According to the *Los Angeles Times*, "Pornographic pictures accompanied by notes, asserting that Marines at the Twentynine Palms base were being recruited by other Marines and offered money to pose naked, were sent anonymously to Commandant Gen. James Jones who commented that participating in pornographic activity is 'incompatible with the ideals upheld by the United States Marine Corps.'" Somebody snitched. And according to the other published reports, "two Marines were ultimately discharged [!]" But nothing happened to Bobby. What he was doing wasn't exactly illegal. The men were of age and nobody could possibly imagine them being bullied into doing anything they didn't want to do. Compared to most porn, the tapes were fairly tame. Bobby went to jail, not for his smut, but on the stolen property charge. "Seven months in jail," Bobby dreamily recalls as his eyes roll back in joyous ecstasy at the memory. "The most *wonderful* time," he sighs; "ahh . . . federal jail!" Snapping back to reality, he laughs, "I got out and went back to Oceanside."

Back to work. Buy the beer. Order the poppers. Stock up on baby oil. True, there were some rules he must have learned from his new distributors. No more swallowing. Even though he "never feared AIDS," mistakenly believing that all straight men are safe, he reluctantly made the Marines wear rubbers when they fucked him. Such was the price of success. "Every day I had six to ten guys," Bobby recalls proudly. At times, other pornographers would show up outside Bobby's apartment to try to lure away Marines who were lining up to get inside. Imagine! A traffic jam of horny Marines! Next came the copycat Marine porn, but as Bobby says of his "so-called competition" at the time, "anybody can get a five-to-ten-dollar military haircut!" He could spot the fake Marines in a minute and knows that if you ever see Marine porn where the men are dressed in uniform, the tape is bullshit. "A Marine will *never* wear the uniform in the scene. No money in the world for them to do that!" In other words, Bobby's boys may have been amateurs in the porn world but were hard-core pros in the military life. "What percentage of the Marines you ask to be in your films turn you down?" I wonder. "Mmmm . . . ten percent," he estimates, before adding that some of the ones "who won't let me do anything [except watch them jerk off]" eventually "come back" for more.

Bobby works alone. He is his only crew. Because Bobby encourages his talent to shoot their loads anywhere—on him, on the bedding, on the furniture, even on the rug—one imagines cleaning and laundering are his biggest budgeted items. Wherever semen lands, Bobby then zooms in with the camera with an almost religious, mystical respect for the Marine load and then lingers, sometimes endlessly, before panning up to the embarrassed shooter cleaning himself up.

But what about individual stars? Like Troy, Bobby's onetime costar, whom he picked up in a mall in Oceanside, one of the few "names" who reappeared and had sex in Bobby's place with a lot of the Marines? Was he a surrogate? A son figure for Bobby? An heir apparent to Bobby's world of "trade"? "No, he just did it because I paid him," Bobby remembers unemotionally. "He was straight; he had girlfriends." "Were you ever attracted to a gay man?" I ask. "No," Bobby says without a moment's hesitation. "But did you ever fall in love with any of them?" I probe. "I only fell in love with one," Bobby admits sadly, "Chris. A long time ago. He was from Michigan and he fucked me. I was just watching his tape last night." Relieved to hear that Bobby *did* have electricity *somewhere* in his house, I listened as Bobby explained. "I sucked his cock. Yes . . . I used to call him one, two, three o'clock in the morning and his wife would answer the phone. Ten minutes later he'd be here."

"Do you know where any of your Marines are today?" I quiz Bobby hopefully. "Very few," he admits. "Did any of them turn into friends forever?" I ask. "No," he states matter-of-factly. But Bobby has the tapes of them; that is all that counts. Unlike most directors Bobby continues to watch his own work over and over. The only pornography that can turn Bobby on is his own.

"Did any of the guys regret what they did for you? Did they ever freak out when they heard their tapes were for sale or easy to see online?" "I never hear from no one, not even once. Straight guys never watch gay movies. Marines are the toughest; the killers, they never talk." "Did they ever beat you up?" I ask, fearing the worst—"the gay knocks," as old Baltimore queens used to call getting roughed up by straight hustlers. "No, no one beat me up. Did you ever notice in some of my films the Marines have their hands behind their necks?" Sure, I'd noticed, always assuming this was a "no reciprocation, full service" pose, one Bobby asked them to assume so they would not feel the obligation to touch him back. But no, I am wrong. It was just Bobby being practical. "It's because I wanted to see where their hands *were*!" "You mean, to hit you?" I asked, amazed at the sober reasoning of a man who admitted he had been an alcoholic when he made a lot of his movies. "Yes." Bobby smiled. "Or strangle me. You can see me in the films move their clothes away [after they took them off]. I don't want a knife or something hiding there."

How about the scariest Marine Bobby ever filmed? Keith, the psycho drunk who locks the front door of the bedroom in the middle of his scene so Bobby can't get out and growls, "I'm gonna make you suck my cock." True, this isn't much of a threat as far as Bobby is concerned, but when Keith starts his violent, homophobic, sexist tirade while he jerks off and Bobby then blows him and eats his ass, you begin to fear for the director. "I may be from the backwaters of Tennessee," Keith snarls, remembering "a fifty-three-year-old woman who loved my twenty-one-year-old dick." By the time he's boasting, "I like to beat the shit out of faggots," you really feel guilty. But for what? Being turned on by a once-removed danger? "I set the whole thing up," Bobby reveals with a Hitchcockian twinkle in his eyes. "I told him what to say." For the first time, I think Bobby may be lying.

I bring up my personal favorite of his stars, the Johnny Knoxville look-alike with the huge dick and the sunglasses, the cutest porn star in the world. Or the Quaaluded-out "Baby Face Marine" who obsessively shows off his ass while mumbling, "Bitch, fucking cunt, whore." To whom, Bobby himself? "Call me names," Bobby says again and again, never changing his lines except to order the talent to "make noises." How about the lughead with the broken leg in a cast who did a solo? "Just once," Bobby remembers wistfully about his appearance, knowing exactly whom I mean instantly. Bobby knows them all! "Joe," from the *Kink* series, with the big thighs who shot the biggest load ever seen in porn. "Ah yes," he sighs; "he wouldn't let me do anything." In his amazingly tender tape *A Message from Bobby*, he leafs through his scrapbook tallying his conquests and shyly boasting, "Thirty-eight boys in one month!" He locates Polaroids of my favorite stars in his stable and gives them to me. Beautiful, sexy, naked shots that everybody in the world could see were art. These incredible photographs should be in a museum and could be if Bobby would just leave the porn world behind and upgrade his beat to contemporary galleries.

But no, Bobby has little talent for money or business. "What I do, I do for love." Bobby shrugs. He claims to be unaware of the many videos and DVDs released of his past work, and is totally surprised to hear of the great "AWOL Marine" website that is a film festival tribute to his work. Bobby admits to running his "little classified" in *The Advocate* in the past to "make money to pay my rent and buy beer." But I wonder how he could possibly fill any orders from the place he was now living. He "never returns calls." In other words, he is the Gloria Swanson of the Marine-porn world: a recluse who never quite realized the power he has over the sexual fantasies of his loyal customers. "I never knew people liked the tapes. You see where I'm living. I don't own nothing. I live with my animals. I want to help animal shelters."

Bobby may have a one-track mind but he puts the "gentle" in gentleman. He remembers not only big dicks but kindnesses, too. Like the time he "was out of my luck, only had a few bucks— in Los Angeles." Lauren Hutton was in a show called *Extremities* (1983). "I wanted to see it so bad, but I had no money. Sitting on the curb . . ." Suddenly Bobby starts crying as he continues his tale and I realize the goodness in people can give Bobby an emotional hard-on. "She [came out and] said to me, 'You go in the back. Give him food,' she told the ushers. 'Let him in.'"

Bobby is against the Iraq war, too, and before you cynically surmise it's because there are no Marines left in the United States who can perform for Bobby, he'll set you straight. "My heart goes out to the families over there and the families over here. It's bad, hopefully we get out soon," he says sadly. When I tell Bobby how guilty I felt when I caught myself scanning the photographs *The New York Times* published in 2008 of the "most recent 1000 service members in Iraq to die," to see if I had ever been turned on by any of them in Bobby's films, he doesn't hear. "I don't like nobody to get hurt," he mumbles, "not even a butterfly."

But Bobby can still shock me. He tells me his favorite movie is *The Hours*, based on my friend Michael Cunningham's novel. "I saw it at least twenty, twenty-five times," Bobby remembers with great respect. Just as I imagine the thrill of telling Michael about his newest fan, Bobby brings out from a special hiding place a treasure box filled with letters from English, Spanish, and Greek royalty. Real queens, not gay ones. Bobby's hobby is writing to anyone who wears a crown. And they write back! He even shows me a polite response from Princess Di to Bobby's fan mail! "But how do you know which ones will respond?" I ask in dumbfounded amazement. "I subscribe to *Majesty* and *Royalty* magazines," and he starts by writing to "ladies in waiting" in each country and "they usually write back," and then he works his way up to the top.

Bobby is royalty, too, but I have trouble making him believe in himself. I offer to take him out to dinner and he's willing, but he picks a nearby fast-food restaurant no matter how much I stress we can go somewhere nicer. "Aren't you proud of your great work?" I ask. "No, I no proud," he says without ever touching a single morsel of the food we order. "I no proud. I no ashamed. I just think that was part of my life." "Are you in touch with any of your family today?" I wonder. "No. Barely," he says with little obvious sadness. "Is your mother still alive?" "Yes," he admits. "Does she know about your films?" I pry. "I don't think so. Maybe. You never know," he reasons with a slight hint of concern. "But you don't work anymore—why?" I plead, pretending I don't realize he is so poor that he has no equipment left, no editing facilities. "I adore my dogs, more than movies." "But you've stopped having Marine sex?" I blurt out in concern. Have no fear: Bobby still scores, just not on videotape. "Maybe in my pick-up truck or a hotel," Bobby laughs. "Then nobody's knocking down the door." I don't mention there is no door to knock down where Bobby lives now, much less the fact that even the horniest Marine might have erection issues with the pigs and rats in Bobby's squat. Eyes lighting up, Bobby offers me a walk on the wild side. "My friend, we can go to a Marine bar three blocks away and get a guy." Although going cruising with Bobby has a certain appeal, I cling to my journalistic standards and beg off, at least for this visit. I take Bobby back to his . . . ranch . . . hideout . . . whatever it is. I feel sad for Bobby and encourage him to make some more deals, get an advance from a new porn distributor, and start making movies again. He tells me he wants to go back to Oceanside and work again. All he

needs is money for some cheap video equipment and he feels he
could be back in business. Back on his knees. Back in the baby
oil saddle. Poppers ready. Porn loaded.

Bobby gets out of my car and once again the dogs come
charging out from his house, hurling themselves against the
chain-link fence. He leans his head back in through the passenger window to say goodbye and wishes me well writing about
him. "Be kind," he whispers in a suddenly serious voice that
doesn't reveal if he is quoting the famous Deborah Kerr line
from *Tea and Sympathy* or not. I will be kind, Bobby. And every
time I rewatch one of your tapes and hear you say, "Call me
names," I will. You're a genius, Bobby. A goddamn genius.

Then there is David Hurles. Maybe he is even more fanatical
than Bobby in his sexual tastes for the outer limits of straight
men. Danger is the turn-on for Mr. Hurles. Marines aren't butch
enough or scary enough. No, David likes psychos. Nude ones.
Money-hungry drug addicts with big dicks. Rage-filled robbers
without rubbers. And of course, convicts—his ultimate Prince
Charmings. In the last three decades David Hurles has picked
up rough trade off the streets of California, out in front of the
Doggie Diner and Flagg Brothers shoes in San Francisco, and
the Oki-Dog in Hollywood. Bars like the Old Crow and the Spot-
light were his own personal Schwab's Pharmacy. Only David
wasn't looking for an unknown Lana Turner in a tight sweater to
turn into a star; he was looking for handsome criminals. These
mostly long-forgotten locations in hustler history have become
almost like stations of the cross in the mythical ritualization

217

scenarios of old-fashioned "cruising." Hurles took these outlaw studs, who may never have even realized they could be sexy, to his home like a fool-saint, paid them money, and photographed them for your sick, self-loathing enjoyment. *Old Reliable* models snarled at the camera nude. They gave you the finger, bent over with their asshole showing, looking through their legs. And in what became Mr. Hurles's signature photo pose, they smoked a big steaming cigar, nude, with an angry leer. These danger-to-any-community Romeos burned their way into the consciousness of my generation of gay men. In the same way Douglas Sirk's romantic films could make some straight people feel real-life love was disappointing compared to the melodramatic cinematic kind, David Hurles's photographs forever scarred some gay men's ability to be attracted to another average gay man. Without these pioneering *Old Reliable* photographs, homoeroticism in the art world couldn't have existed. Robert Mapplethorpe was a pussy. Mr. Hurles is the real thing.

Like Bobby Garcia, David Hurles is not easy to locate. These outsider pornographers are mavericks, but few understand—especially not their neighbors. They move a lot. I manage to get Mr. Hurles's phone number but am warned by a fellow *Old Reliable* fan that "David will never pick up, he is a total recluse." But when I begin leaving my message on his answering machine, David *does* pick up. He sounds kind and gentle. He's a fan of my work, too! What a thrill. We are a deviant mutual admiration society. He invites me to come see him on my annual upcoming trip for Oscar weekend in L.A. I wish I could bring him *and* his boys to the *Vanity Fair* party—just think of the purses they could steal.

Today, David Hurles lives in a large studio apartment in old Hollywood—not the gentrified part. As I walk up the stairs to the third floor, I realize how lucky I am to be in a profession that enables me to be this nosy. David greets me warmly and we embrace. He is a great man to me, one I have always revered. Nice-looking, too, about my age, and he doesn't look like the stereotypical pervert like I do. He has almost no possessions but a computer, his bed on the floor, and boxes and boxes of his product—*Old Reliable* VHS tapes (a few transferred to DVD), audio cassettes, stills, and catalogs.

"So you still *are* in business," I marvel, thrilled that my favorite studio since Warhol's is still going. "What's left of it." He sighs. "I used to be successful . . . I made a half million dollars one year and paid the tax." "But you still are successful artistically," I gush. "You risked your safety for your customers." "If you ask me cold I'd say I've had very little trouble. But if you sit down and think about it I've been robbed a lot . . . it was expensive." When I bring up the "arousal of fear" his work celebrates, he fondly remembers a critic who claimed "that danger is my only hard-on." "That's one of the joys of psychopathic [men]," he explains, trying to convey his models' mind-set. "It's a control thing—'Look how much I turn you on.' " Few besides David Hurles have made such a stunning, if quasi-legal, career out of their neuroses. I'm so happy he's happy he's fucked-up.

It all started when Hurles ran a classified sex ad in *The Berkeley Barb* in the seventies, when he was living in San Francisco. "What did it say?" I wondered. "Oh, straight guys, you know, blow jobs," he vaguely recalls. But then, from what most people would call trouble, came the inspiration for a great career in filth. "A nineteen-year-old straight guy, straight out of San Quentin" answered the ad, David explains, "beautiful, big dick, great sex. When we were finally done, of course, [he] pulled a gun, wanted to rob me. 'Please don't tie me up,' I asked him, 'bondage is not my thing.' 'Okay,' the criminal trick said, 'but I'll come back and kill you if you call the police.' Of course I had no intention of doing that," David admits. "As soon as he was gone I realized I was turned on, you see. I had to jerk off." Oh.

So David started taking naked pictures of guys who scared him. Truck drivers. Vagrants. Speed freaks. Halfway house hunks. Tattooed mutants. With hard-ons. Wrestling (a Hurles favorite), boxing, shooting up in their dicks. All glaring into the camera looking like they wanted to rough you up. At first "lowly mafia" bought the stills from David to sell in porn shops, but then when he was peddling his smut photos himself in Washington, D.C., Mr. Hurles "met the most important man in my life," the "three-hundred-pound albino from Mississippi," Dr. Herman Lynn Womack, who owned and ran Guild Press, one of the first distributors of nude gay magazines. I remember seeing these forbidden magazines in Baltimore when I was underage and overaroused at Sherman's Newsstand downtown. I was way too uptight to buy these titles, so I shoplifted them. When I tell David this he admits gleefully that he did, too! To get Womack to distribute his photos David "had to trick with him." It was worth it. Hurles started getting paid a hundred dollars for each still shoot after "paying the models fifteen dollars." "Did you have sex with the 'talent'?" I ask. "Usually afterwards," he fondly remembers. "I usually gave them fifteen to twenty dollars extra. The cuter ones got more."

David had been a "model" himself. "One of the books Guild published," David explains, "was *Auto-Fellatio and Masturbation* and I was in it." It sold for a "$7.50 cover price—a *lot* then." He remembers bragging, "I'm so talented I can not only suck my own dick, but I can take pictures of it at the same time." But there was always trouble. "Dr. Womack went to prison," David sighs. "I visited him. I was subpoenaed by the grand jury four times—that's a hassle," but he was never ashamed of his arrests. "No, I was rather proud," he admits.

Suddenly David was on his own and "it was time to get creative. I had the idea for audio self-help tapes. I had a roommate who was a bartender and he used to bring home someone to fist fuck him every night and it was a turn-on to listen. I had taken this course on hypnosis once . . . so I put the two together . . . and made this tape, *Painless Anal Intercourse*, and it did surprisingly well."

David Hurles agrees with me when I say, "You invented verbal-abuse porn." One hopes *The New York Times* remembers the accomplishment when it is time to write his obituary. David would lock his boys in a room in his home and tell them to talk dirty into a microphone and then leave them alone to vent their sexual pathologies. Like Andy Warhol with a hard-on, David gave them little direction except "Talk about yourself." "Did you tell them to be mean?" I quizzed. "I never directed. They felt they had my permission. I encouraged. I suggested. They pretty soon figured out where to go. When they were done, they'd give me the tape and I'd give them the money." *Old Reliable* distributed "over four hundred" verbal-abuse audio tapes. "I was afraid to release some of them," he admits. "They were so raw."

One of the tapes is titled *Ty Meltdown*, and the unedited sexual ad-libbing of this psycho performer will raise the hair on even the biggest masochist's neck. "Good voice," David notes in his own handwriting on the label of the tape. "Criminal. Scary, and taking advantage of guys. Box their tonsils with his dick." Ty's calm, masculine-voiced monologue about fucking and brutalizing young punks in jail is audio sadism well beyond the comfort zone of all sexual role-playing. But not David's. He still listens to the tape and it still turns him on. As with Bobby, the only erotica that works is his own.

Old Reliable struck a nerve in the guilt centers of radical gay porn. "Every man has a hustler in there somewhere" is how David explains his recruiting technique. Of course, he had help. Bob Mizer, the Walt Disney of beefcake, had his own big studio of musclemen, and he traded stars with David over the years. "Bob was very generous to me. I met him in 1970 and he was my closest friend for twenty years, right up to when he died." They both worked the trenches of the hetero-hunk gutter circuit, fought the police, went to jail, and unrepentantly started right back up again. Boyd McDonald, the better-than-Maxwell-Perkins editor of *Straight to Hell* magazine, aka *The Manhattan Review of Unnatural Acts*, was later a big supporter, too. And no wonder! With titles such as *Homosexuals Are the Only True Radicals*, *Ten Surfers Pissed on Me*, and *Closet Queen Cop Gets His*, this all-true, reader-written journal about having sex with strangers must have been the Holy Grail to David Hurles. "Boyd was the kindest person," David remembers, "gave me such encouragement." He continues, "I made a lot of money," moved from San Francisco to L.A., and became known as "the Prince of Hollywood." He bought a "very nice condo" and later a house "near the reservoir, near Madonna's." He was known for his sartorial splendor—"wearing pastels"—and at the height of his career in the late eighties he "was doing two shoots a day."

But David's "stars" were beyond difficult. "I have always tried to be judgment free," he confides, leafing through one of his catalogs of past product, reminiscing about each of his psycho escorts the same way Vincente Minnelli might recall the singers and dancers he had once directed. "I made a lot of money on Mike." David beams, showing me a photo of a hillbilly trucker with a giant dick. "From New Orleans," David remembers, "last time I heard he was in Las Vegas. Don't believe he *ever* had to buy a beer [for himself] since those pictures came out." But most of David's memories are not so joyous. He stops and points to a specific model, one, like all of David's boys, who looks like a homicidal maniac. "I kept track of the money I spent on this one—after a quarter of a million I stopped. You gotta understand—I got a letter from this sugar daddy back in New Jersey. He had a picture of this awful messed-up ex-model of mine and he said, 'This is what cost my friend his home in Paris and $100,000.' I don't doubt it. It happened to me." David begins turning the pages again, looking for a special one. "I had a boyfriend named Andy who's in here somewhere . . ." He shows me the photo and continues, "Andy had to suddenly go home for his father's funeral and his mother said [to me], '*Please* don't let him come.' But he did, so it was a cold and rainy night and I had a chance to go out and pick up somebody [else]. Danny looked awfully cute in his tight pants. Then the next twenty to thirty years whenever he had a problem he came to me. And believe me his problems added up! Each one cost money. Heroin, speed . . . I can go through my catalogs and point out the junkies. I couldn't stop them from doing it. They didn't come to my house to take orders from somebody . . . This one here said he'd be dead by age twenty-five and by God, he made it with a month to spare." "Were you a drug addict?" I wonder. "I've done plenty of drugs with tricks," he admits happily. "Speed was my favorite, MDA, and then Quaaludes."

Was David also a gay man who could only be turned on by straight men? "I try to avoid the gay ones," he admits, but he's more of a sexual liberal than Bobby. "Sure, I go to bed with gay people. I like getting fucked and gay people do that quite adequately, too." He continues his capsule biography of sexual attraction as he gazes at the photos of his past leading men. "Stephen got out of prison. I was sick and he nursed me back to health but I didn't realize he was cleaning out the house. Suddenly my linens were gone, clothes closets were empty. I never called the cops, but you couldn't ignore his emergencies. He would climb up on the roof to get attention. He got arrested and did nine and a half years. And guess what? He's out again and he's been calling me!" David looks at the model on the back cover, a horse-ish oaf with a beer-can dick who either looks retarded or sexy depending on your taste. "He's from Long Beach." David sighs. "I remember the day he fell down my steps and broke the neon sign I had on the landing." "But do you know where they are today?" I ask. "I know where a great many of them are," he replies. "Six feet under."

What ruined David's business was not police busts or the revenge of malevolent hustlers. It was a wrestling accident in

1990. "The truth of it is, I got kicked in the eye," David sadly admits. He was "having fun" on videotape, filming himself wrestling with some trick, and the stud turned David around and accidentally poked him. David's vision in one eye began to go, a terrifying thing for a photographer. "That's when I realized I couldn't drive. That's when things began to fall apart. For six months I was a codeine addict." He sold his L.A. house and bought a trailer in Long Beach and continued to video men with no visible means of support. "The boys there stole my equipment so I couldn't shoot. Those people in Long Beach were bad. They found me—the new pigeon in the trailer park. The worst ones were their girlfriends—one tried to stab me one time. Sometimes they'd come for diaper money and I would give it to them."

And then, lo and behold, David Hurles photographed a twenty-three-year-old man named Mike, and despite the fact that Mike is straight, they hooked up and this happy couple has been together for the last twelve years. "He looks like the world's oldest hippie." David smiles, shyly showing me a photo of a very handsome tough guy who so personifies David's type. "Does Mike work?" I hesitatingly ask. "No, he's basically illiterate," David laughs. "Is he a drug addict?" I sheepishly question. "Yes, sure," David instantly admits, amazed I'd even have to ask. "Speed," he explains. But as for all Americans these days, the economy is an issue. "We can't afford for him to be a speed freak," David sighs.

Long Beach didn't exactly embrace the new honeymooners. "Every day we were in more and more danger—home invasions twice with guns. They took everything but my work." In declining health, David moved in with a friend for eighteen months, but his friend didn't like Mike, so Mike was homeless. Finally, "I got this place [in L.A.] for me and Mike," and they moved in. Mike's mattress is on the floor on the other side of the apartment, and he is supposed to show up to take a photograph of David and me, but Mike never appears. "My building manager hates us," David admits, "for no good reason. We've got to move, been here fourteen months now. They don't like the look of the people who come to see me."

But all his work! What will he do with it? Does he have an archive? "I already lost a lot. I have a storage place. In two years the rent has gone from $198 a month to $256. I can't keep paying it. I'm stuck with Social Security. All I have is a still camera; I don't have a Hi8 video." David Hurles has no idea what will happen to his work after he dies. "Do you have a family?" I hesitantly ask. "I loved my mother more than anything," he says bluntly. "She absolutely knew everything I did." He is one of four living siblings, but when his "mother died three years ago none of them bothered to tell me. I didn't ask why they didn't tell me. What do you do?" True, he has had a minor revival lately. In 2005, Green Candy Press put out a beautiful coffee-table book of his photos entitled *Speeding*, and he got an actual cash advance. Some of his work is also featured in Taschen's incredible *The Big Penis Book*, but his artistic estate and critical reputation are very uncertain. "There are still some *Old Reliable* men out there," David says, "fewer and fewer every year. I wish I could shoot them." "Did AIDS ruin rough trade?" I ask sadly. "Yes," he answers glumly, "that and the Internet." I ask David to sign his book to me and he writes, "To John Waters, a co-conspirator and fellow traveler. You led and we followed. My best, David R. Hurles." But David is wrong. Without the pioneering pornographers who changed what we thought was indecent, and on rare occasion, subverted artistic lust, I could never have had the nerve to make my movies. Isn't there some sort of Purple Heart for the auteurs of amateur porn? Can't some hotshot university start a Legion of Honor for David Hurles and buy his collection of smut to preserve it forever? The wonderful, terrible, beautifully scary life of David Hurles has been an inspiration to my inner filth for years and it's high time he got the academic respect he so rightfully deserves.

Am I a pervert for loving the work of Bobby Garcia and David Hurles? Well, yes, I guess. But a healthy one. I made friends with my neuroses through psychiatry. I believe in the talking cure and you should, too. Freud *was* right about a lot of stuff, but these days insurance companies won't even pay for therapy. No, they want you on pills: one visit to be diagnosed for anxiety and a second one to get you zonked. None of this expensive open-ended treatment with no cutoff date. Don't get me wrong: Prozac-type medicine saved the lives of a few of my friends who really *were* manic-depressive. You know the type—staying in bed for days sobbing under the covers and/or beating up their pillows in an endless rage. For these people mood stabilizers are a godsend. I never bring up the sexual side effects—I keep thinking I'd rather be depressed *with* a hard-on than happily blank without one, but, hey, I'm all for choice. But for all the neurotics who may have felt a little blue one day and were unfairly diagnosed and overly medicated before they could even try to talk out their problems, I have some advice. It's appropriate to be depressed sometimes. Who wants to be "even" day after day? If you just killed three people in a DWI accident, you should feel bad. If your whole family molested you in a giant basket on Easter morning, you have the right to be grumpy every once in a while. But feeling down can make you feel up if you're the creative type. The emotional damage may have already been done to you, but stop whining. Use your insanity to get ahead.

"But what about love?" you may ask. That terribly exciting disease that, to me, feels like another full-time job. Isn't love just trying to get back what your parents didn't give you before you were three years old? One thing I learned in therapy is you'll *never* get this back, so move on, for God's sake. Make friends with your neuroses. I know that true love is supposed to be companionship, growing old together, blah blah blah. I thought that was what *friends* were for, not sexual partners! Some of us want hot lunatic porn sex and we want it forever!

Everybody has his or her "love map," as the late, great, sadly discredited Baltimore sexologist Dr. John Money once called our predetermined sexual types. And we can never really change our love maps, but we can learn to see them coming. A healthy neurotic knows his type can and probably will bring emotional trouble combined with a powerful sexual wallop. But we can see, through effective therapy, that we have a choice. Yes, our love maps may be bad for us but WOW! I won't find this kind of sex in a healthy relationship. So is it worth it? If it is, yes, you are fucked-up, but as long as you *choose* it, you are also neurotically happy. When Bobby Garcia and David Hurles build up the self-esteem of their masculinity-troubled stars by lowering their own in the name of sexual excitement, who am I to say these artists would be better off in a mature relationship of self-respect? Maybe being fucked-up is *why* they are so original.

And I know what you are thinking from reading this chapter, but you are wrong. I don't only like straight men. As a young man, I had three gay boyfriends, two beatniks and one hairdresser, and in my adult life three relationships that were important to me: one with a gay man, one with a guy who today identifies as straight, and another who is completely bisexual. I'm friends with them all today, too. And for the record, I may be an alternative Father Flanagan, but I never slept with any prisoner I taught or counseled professionally, even though one of their relatives good-naturedly, and almost approvingly, yelled, "Payback time!" after he was paroled and I went over to pick him up at his family's house for our first night out in the free world. It just wouldn't have seemed right. I am in the "corrections" field and I take my responsibilities seriously. But sure, I can still go for a confused dick. My real type, these days, is a blue-collar closet queen—they're the best. They don't want to go to premieres with you, they don't want to be in your movies, they don't want to meet your famous friends, they don't even want to be seen with you because then people would know. They just want to come over. The perfect boyfriend.

I've never really dated age-appropriately either. I have a sixty-five-year-old friend who shows me photos of similar-aged guys he meets online and he says, "Aren't they cute?" No! I think. They're old men! Even though I know I, too, am an old man. I'm just not as healthy as my friend and I don't really want to be. I guess I'm looking for a sexy gerontophiliac (an ugly word for a lovely thought), even though I know anyone searching for a sexual father figure wants to *punish* his father, not reenact their functional relationship.

What could my personal Internet sex ad read? I've seen my own name mentioned in other people's "dating" profiles—something like, "Come on over and we'll watch a John Waters movie." I wonder how they'd respond if I answered, "I *am* John Waters and I've got *all* his films. I'm on my way!" Should I place a classified in *Boxoffice*, that great trade magazine for middle-American theater owners I've been subscribing to for decades? Maybe buried beneath all the ads for popcorn-machine parts and chewing-gum removal chemicals, my notice could read, "The Sultan of Sleaze seeks lunatic usher with good bod and a crooked smile. Let's rob a multiplex together and hole up at my place afterward. Send photos c/o Atomic Books, 3620 Falls Road, Baltimore, MD 21211." Go ahead, try answering my ad. I'll get your response. For real.

Having a sense of humor about your neurotic love maps can make things a lot easier. At Elton John's fancy L.A. dinner party/ Oscar gala, a fellow neurotic and good friend, for no apparent reason, whispered in my ear, "What's better than rimming?" Surprised at the seemingly inappropriate riddle told in the middle of all this glamour, I answered, "Okay, what?" "Nothing," he said with the self-satisfied grin of a happy pervert. I had another dear white friend in Baltimore whose shrink was so concerned over the patient's sexual compulsion for sleeping with scary heterosexual black men that he prescribed Depo-Provera, the drug authorities force sex offenders to take to erase all sexual desire. But my friend *still* could get a hard-on after he'd taken it! To watch him in action was amazing. He'd bravely approach whatever ghetto gangsta he so lusted after, look him dead in the eyes, and then throw an entire ring of keys at his feet without saying a word. They got the point. And if my friend was lucky, some of them picked up his key ring, went home with him, and looked a gift horse in the mouth.

Of course you can go too far. There are sexual neurotics who lose their sense of irony about their compulsion and let their love maps destroy them. Like poor, poor Uncle Ed, real name Ed Savitz, the most notorious pervert ever to come out of Philadelphia, who for years paid teenage boys cash for their sweaty socks and skid-marked underwear and caught their turds in cellophane and saved them like a butterfly collection. Who would choose to be Uncle Ed? When the police finally moved in and arrested him after he'd spent decades supplying "beer money" to young blue-collar hustlers, who viewed him without guilt as a convenient cash machine ("No big deal," one commented, "he was a nice guy and a faggot"), they found 312 garbage bags filled with soiled socks and underwear. A neighbor in his fancy Rittenhouse Square condo building told the press Uncle Ed "cooperated with the rules of the building," but others weren't so understanding and called the police complaining about "smelling shit."

When the headlines screamed and Uncle Ed was put in prison with a twenty-million-dollar bail, everybody but the delinquent "victims" wrung their hands in dismay. "If you was a boy, you'd understand," one of Uncle Ed's more liberal fecal friends tried to explain to the press. "It was like a natural thing," another said, "you need money, you go up to 'Fast Ed's,' sell him your dirty socks, spit in his mouth, sell him your shit." Another sixteen-year-old, perplexed by the outrage of misunderstanding adults in his Philadelphia community, commented, "If selling socks and underwear were illegal, Woolworth's would be out of business."

Then they found out Uncle Ed had AIDS and the whole world went crazy. Prison officials took away his bad wig and let him get beaten and robbed in jail before his trial began, until he was incoherent. There was never any credible evidence that anyone ever got AIDS from Uncle Ed, but who cared? True, he had given some "bro-jobs" to straight boys, but all doctors agree the main way you can sexually transmit this disease is by being the passive partner in anal intercourse, something these boys never were. And surely turning over your moldy underpants was safe sex! Uncle Ed died in prison, the ultimate Frankenstein's monster of homophobia.

I don't feel sympathy for all outside perverts. Sometimes the worst ones are heterosexual insiders like the Connecticut businessman (I won't bring up his name in case he is in recovery) who became the laughingstock of the country in 1995. Flying business class on United Flight 976 from Buenos Aires to JFK, our passenger was guzzling cocktails in an alarming manner, so the flight attendants cut him off. According to police reports, this frequent flyer rejected "last call" with a ferocious resolve. He shoved his way into the first-class cabin and began serving himself another drink. When the crew tried to stop him, he shoved a flight attendant into a seat, climbed on top of the serving cart, dropped his pants, and took a shit.

Imagine if you were reading your book or watching the movie and you looked up and saw a middle-aged man shitting on the service cart. Arms outstretched for balance as the cart careened up and down the aisle toward you with bowel movements flying. Surfing turd! The president of Portugal and the Argentine foreign minister were on this flight, heading to the United Nations' fiftieth anniversary—just think of their later cocktail chatter! Would they share the details of their sky-high horror on Flight IOU A #2? Would they whisper to international ladies in evening gowns that this air-rager had "used linen napkins as toilet paper, wiping his hands on various counters and service implements" as the *New York Post* reported? Would they confide their relief when the pilot "then canceled further food service"? I guess he did! How many frequent flyer reward points do you get to make up for a turd in your lap between courses?

Think of how this mad shitter must have felt when he began to sober up in his jail cell. Whom did he call? His wife? "How was the flight, honey?" must have been the one question he feared the most. Did he tell her the truth—"I got drunk and shit all over the plane and I'll be on the front cover of all the tabloids tomorrow"—or did he just mumble, "I'll be a little late"? Did he warn his three daughters to "maybe take off from school tomorrow—there may be some cruel jokes about your daddy making the rounds in the cafeteria"? Or was he a serial shitter who was hiding his past turd terrorism? Had he been doing "upper deckers" for years in his community? Was he the one who thought up the revenge tactic of shitting in the top tank of the toilets of your enemies so they can never locate the odor?

Did his turd tirade start a trend? How would he feel years later if he read *The Great Deluge*, by Douglas Brinkley, and learned the details of the looting following Hurricane Katrina in New Orleans? Did he secretly sympathize with the riot community who *somehow* spread the word in the middle of a national disaster, with *no* electric power, *no* radios, and *no* telephones, that it was proper looting etiquette to take a dump in the beds of the homes you'd just ransacked? To leave individual turds wrapped up in the clothes you didn't take from the damaged stores you broke into? How faulty toilet training caused a new minority? A turd community?

I mean, it gets worse. I know your eyes are not garbage cans, but somehow I feel it is my duty to share with you the depths of depravity some of our long-lost brothers have fallen to. Just so you will know there are *good* perverts and *bad* perverts; like snowflakes, no two are the same. And I'm not talking about lightweight neurotics-in-denial like Idaho senator Larry Craig. Any respectable tearoom queen could have told him how to have sex in a public bathroom in an airport without getting caught. All you do is have one man sit on the toilet while the other stands with each leg in an empty shopping bag. If any nosy vice cops are looking under the stall, they'll only see one set of legs and two shopping bags. Duh! Larry, it's fucking easy!

No, I'm talking about real perverts, the ones who make happy neurotics like me look bad to the rest of the world. Like Donald H. Baker, for example. I'm really glad I'm not friends with this man. Not even once did I entertain the idea of finding him to interview for this chapter. But I have to admit, I secretly feel bad for him. Let's call Donald "Shithead." He was discovered by police under a woman's outhouse in a state park in Santa Barbara, directly below the toilet bowl opening. In the pit of shit. He was "covered in human waste," according to the press, "wearing only drawstring briefs and tennis shoes." Mr. Baker was ordered out by the police, told to hose himself down, and then arrested and booked. He later explained to investigators that he "liked the dank and the smell of the outhouse." Picture the policeman's face as he jotted down this comment. Imagine the horror-movie-like scream of the girls who used the restroom and saw him down under. Try not to chuckle when you picture the mother sputtering to reporters that her daughters "are now afraid to use the restrooms" anywhere near the park. Who uses outhouses in public parks? Aren't perverts *always* lurking in bathrooms of public places? One would think an unperverted mom would require her daughters to eliminate *before* leaving the house for a day of public running and jumping. It's just common sense.

I guess I should feel guilty that I caused a sex crime with one of my own films, but I don't. A fan sent me an amusing clipping about a fifteen-year-old New Hampshire boy who had gone public with his complaint about a hazing incident he had been a victim of in football camp. The young lad explained that his fellow teammates had held him down and "teabagged" him. He claimed the upperclassmen got the idea of dragging their testicles over his face "from a scene involving a male stripper in a movie by cult director John Waters." Yes, I guess they did get the idea from *Pecker*, but my teabagging scene was blissful, and not quite so aggressive. Still, I was secretly delighted that my comic sex act had crossed over to real life. I mean, there are so many worse things that could have happened.

Like necrophilia. The only perversion besides scat I haven't tried. You have to save something for the autumn of your years, don't you? A healthy neurotic never says never to a new sexual fantasy. Isn't necrophilia the ultimate fear of performance? Ask Karen M. Greenlee—she ought to know. This twenty-year-old self-described "morgue rat" worked in funeral parlors (where else can you meet a body?) and had sex with a corpse. She got caught by police in the back of a hearse after stealing a body from a Sacramento mortuary. She told police she "intended to stay with her dead lover until the body got so ripe she couldn't stand it."

Which made me wonder—do all celebrities get fucked after they're dead? Should I be so liberal that I accept this fact? When Anna Nicole Smith passed away, didn't word go out on the necro circuit, "Okay, you've got thirty-six hours and the bidding starts at $200,000." Was Elvis blown postmortem? Was Piaf gang-banged?

What dead celebrity would you like to fuck? Come on, it's a question all healthy neurotics may have to ask themselves one day. Most of my friends pick the obvious choices—Marilyn Monroe or James Dean. But not me. I'd go for director Luchino Visconti. In that plush elegant coffin that his onetime boyfriend Helmut Berger must have wanted to throw himself into at the funeral. Or better yet, "Rotten Rita" (real name Kenneth Rapp), the biggest speed dealer to the early gay male stars of Warhol's movies in the Silver Factory period. Maybe Ingrid Superstar (the so-called missing Warhol star who wandered away from her mother's house decades after her stardom diminished, never to be heard from again) could join us for a threesome. And then, if we're lucky, Andy, from beyond the grave, could film us!

ROOMMATES

I live alone but I have a ton of roommates. Luckily, they're not human beings. I couldn't stand the idea of having someone else's belongings around. I don't have the mental space. Worse yet, suppose they suddenly hung on the wall something I didn't like? I can't listen to someone else's music or borrow their books either. No sirree, no real-life people sharing my bathroom or reading my newspapers before me! Instead, I live with artists.

Mike Kelley is one of my roommates. Yes, the man who made pitiful seem sexy by turning grimy thrift store stuffed animals into heartbreaking, jaw-droppingly beautiful sculptures by placing them on stained blankets on the floor or facedown on card tables next to one another like dead Jonestown suicide cultists. Suddenly a museum or an art gallery took on the appearance of a coroner's office displaying corpses of toys after an airplane crashed into Santa's sleigh mid-flight on Christmas Eve. Mike Kelley lives with me everywhere. In my New York apartment on the living room wall hangs his *Dirty Mirror* (1997) with its disgusting leftover cocaine lines painted in acrylic. A bloody hep-C trace can even be noticed as you look at the repulsive stain that totally obscures the mirror's reflection of the viewer, not that you'd want to see your face after a night like this. What a terrible drug-over this artwork suggests: reckless, misleading moments of chemical joy that seem so sour an hour later.

Mike is a really "shitty" roommate, but he knows this is a compliment. His *Wedged Lump* (1991), a large painting on paper that suggests a giant turd surrounded with comic-strip stink marks, hangs in my dining room in Baltimore, where my dinner guests are forced to confront the fate of their meal no matter how gourmet the initial presentation appears. I live with Mike Kelley in my workspace, too. Right above my writing desk in New York is one of his *Garbage Drawings* (1988), isolated refuse from the original *Sad Sack* cartoons that features fumes of filth that I hope will inspire my screenplay or book ideas.

Even my library is defiled by Mike Kelley. Hanging in Baltimore is one of the hilarious 1989 *Reconstructed History* vandalisms—a real page from a history textbook that Mike defiled with glee, the same thing all gifted and pissed-off kids did in high school, hoping to turn their rage into art. "BARF" adds Mike to the historic signing of the Declaration of Independence illustration, and now every Fourth of July I can feel patriotic thanks to Mike Kelley's troublemaking, defiant reinvention of this dull textbook.

My assistants live with Mike Kelley, too. Outside their office is the *Auditions* sign he created for a Los Angeles Museum of Contemporary Art exhibition in 2004. Mocking the hastily drawn cardboard signs casting agents put up in the halls of hotels to lead actors to their correct tryout rooms, my roommate Mike celebrates the sadness of Hollywood, the despair of missed appointments, failed careers, and the ever-present cliché of the casting couch.

Some of my friends make fun of my roommate Mike. "How much was *that?*" a usually liberal-minded friend shrieked when she saw *Child Substitute* (1995), the pitiful collage Mike did that looks like a five-year-old retarded boy began cutting out pictures of animals from Sunday newspaper supplement ads but lost his train of thought and abandoned the project. "It cost enough," I answered vaguely to her snorts of contempt. Every time this friend comes to my New York apartment she notices new details of the crudely cut out and lumpily glued-on photographs of pets, framed in the cheapest way possible by the artist, and shakes her head in bafflement. I *love* how mad Mike's work can make some people. Isn't that the job of contemporary art? To infuriate? The real naysayers who can't see the reverse beauty of Mike's sculptures or paintings *should* be outraged because they secretly know that his art *does* hate them and they deserve it.

Somebody else lives with the one Mike Kelley piece I desperately wanted and missed out on buying. I first saw *Storehouse* (1990) in the traveling "Just Pathetic" show at my late and great dealer Colin de Land's gallery, American Fine Arts in New York. The "sculpture" is nothing but a cardboard shipping box filled with soiled, packed-up cat toys, uneaten pet food, and wormer medication that obviously didn't work. Pushpinned to the wall above are two Hallmark-type greeting cards from a vet expressing sympathy for the "death of your pet." This mundane still life of sadness and private mortification made me remember Mike's quote to the *Los Angeles Times* about another sculpture he had done: "Everything in this piece is a failure." I suddenly felt like selling everything I owned at the time to buy this incredible "failure." So I asked Colin the price. True to his legend, he took months before he got back to me ("Hope the delay did not cause terrible anguish," he wrote) with the answer: $10,000. Stupidly, moronically, I didn't have the art nerve at the time to pounce. I could see this grubby little sculpture of refuse was beyond financial value. Why was I such an art chicken? Now fucking MOCA in Los Angeles owns it and I'm pissed. Every time I look at the slide that Colin sent me, I fantasize about breaking into the museum and stealing *Storehouse*. Guards, trustees—you have been warned. I like that sculpture more than you do!

My roommates need to be illusionists and Mike Kelley certainly is. He's a companion who can make you see something supposedly shameful in a beautiful, hilarious, radical, subversive way. Isn't he really a miracle worker? *Art and Auction* magazine called Mike an "apocalyptical vulgarian" but who cares about a roommate's reviews? I call him a terrorist and a healer and he never has to pay rent in any of my abodes. Matter of fact, I'll pay him!

Cy Twombly isn't thrilled to be my roommate, and who could blame him? He's got better apartments and houses to move into than mine, believe me. Isn't Cy Twombly beyond a doubt *still* the most cutting-edge artist working today, even if he is over eighty years old? According to my close friend the writer and former museum curator Brenda Richardson, he can make even the most seasoned art collectors and accessions committees seethe in skepticism and rage over his work. My walls and floors are not worthy of Cy Twombly's drawings, paintings, or sculpture.

Just look up his *Untitled* (1992) and you'll see what I mean. No, I don't own it. You think I'm made of money? But I can fantasize, can't I? If I ever won the stupid lottery or suddenly made a fortune with *Pink Flamingos* being turned into a video game, Cy's sculpture would be my midlife crisis purchase to impress *myself*. To hell with sports cars (no one over thirty years of age should *ever* be seen in a convertible), yachts, or ridiculous bling. Owning this shockingly ugly and elegant work of art would make me feel young again.

I first saw this *Untitled* (catchy title, eh?) at the opening of the Cy Twombly Gallery at the Menil Collection in Houston. Rich people, art critics, and museum heads never looked more vulnerable as they turned the corner and came face-to-face with the rudely witty, obscenely imperious sculpture. Yeah, yeah, yeah, I know it's supposed to be about "time and meaning," "transformation," and "metamorphosis and myth," but to me it looks like a most confident and graceful depiction of Godzilla's semen discharge. A big load. Steaming. In wood and plaster. Go see it. It's still there.

"Bad handwriting" is what the general art public always squawks about when they think of Twombly's stunningly messy and sometimes sparse paintings and drawings, which to the untrained eye can certainly be mistaken for the penmanship of an "outsider" artist. But on closer inspection, the lucky ones, like us, see the exact opposite—the poetic Palmer Method of a true insider. And we Twombly cultists can get quite obsessed with

trying to focus on each and every one of Cy's mysterious cod-
ings. Take for example *Cy Twombly: Catalogue Raisonné of the
Paintings, Volume 1, 1948–1960*, a book I read every word of like
I was following a mystery novel. Imagine my thrill when I saw
the tiny "note" beneath the provenance, exhibition history, and
references to *Blue Room* (1957), Cy's elegantly painted and pencil-
filled canvas of his signature scratch and scribbles. "The center left part of the painting," this footnote read, "contains one
drawn element, a looping line that is not by the artist." Amazing! But what art vandal would dare add even the tiniest mark-
ing to a Cy Twombly painting? Maybe I *am* for the death penalty
after all. I mean it—in the scheme of things, this is grave! I knew
Blue Room had been on loan to the Baltimore Museum of Art for
a while. Oh my God, had it happened here? "No," I was told by the
curator at the time, "it was exhibited in Baltimore on loan from
Ileanna Sonnabend and the painting was already framed in Plexi-
glas," obviously to prevent repeat offenders. But most important,
who was the insanely observant inspector who *noticed* this one
small squiggle in the millions of others in Cy Twombly's work and
had the courage to first tell Cy and then us? Who else but the art
historian Heiner Bastian, the editor of this scholarly volume,
and to this day, I am in awe of his obsessive eye for detail.

You see, Cy Twombly is, quite simply, better than you and
me and has the right to feel superior to all collectors. He *should*
judge us because he makes perfect mistakes and laughs at the
concerns of the moneyed class, who deserve the problems of
abstraction. For me, his thoroughbred so-called scribbles celebrate an ecstasy that only a dyslexic child prodigy could feel over

his secret code words and alternative alphabets. This exclusive, violent, erotic handwriting that may seem illegible to others *can* be read if you just give it a chance.

Look at Cy's thirty-eight separate drawings entitled *Letters of Resignation*, which he did between 1959 and 1967. Critics have called them "a confession," "a farewell," "a dialogue," but I think none of these descriptions are exactly correct. *Letters of Resignation* is a rant, an agonized response to the lack of power this fictitious author feels. His terrible impatience and obsessive frustration turn the very act of writing and revising into a torturous revenge against authority. Art historians *are* right when they describe these scratched out, erased, painted-over, and rewritten drawings as "violent," "ritualistic, almost fetishistic," but they are wrong when they speculate that Cy Twombly "does not allow the meaning of the markings to extend to the real world." Bullshit. I can read them and so can you if you just give up everything you've been taught in elementary school.

Come on, let's try. Drawing I. You see violent angry pencil scratches and undecipherable words all written together without meaning? Well, be a little looser! Yes, you can see that this handwriting may be illegible to the artistically impaired, but remember, even the most basic psychology textbooks explain that a child's first scribbles make "sense to the ear even though what is written might be meaningless to the eye." Got that? Let's try again. Chicken scratch? Not so fast. Let's translate and pretend we are inventing and deciphering secret dialogue written for an office worker that only Cy Twombly understands. Here goes. Look again at Drawing I. What could he be saying?

ÐRAWING I

"I'm going to try to write this letter and then I'm going to throw it out."

Maybe, you think. Remember, you can't be wrong when you are translating from an abstract language. Go to Drawing II. See the three sections that look like some sort of deranged outline? Notice the indecision of the pencil markings? See how thick the lead is in the middle of the paper? Let's try to "read" it.

ÐRAWING II

"Okay, I've got to get organized, make a list of my gripes, pay back the fuckers who do the things at work that get on my nerves. No, cross that out. Let's start again. I've got to be calm or no one will listen . . ."

See? You can understand Cy Twombly's insanely looping penmanship if you just open up your mind. Jump ahead to Drawing VII. That whirlpool of scrawls, angrily spinning out of control. Go on—you can do it!

DRAWING VII

"So I have to go up, up in the air above your stupid heads, or better, get down! Down under your awareness, floating in the knowledge that even though I am beneath you in salary, I am richer because I can see what you can't."

Now you're getting good at translating what Cy Twombly's character is saying. Experiencing the rage of his powerless letter writing, the blindness of authority figures who would ignore his authentic complaints even if they *could* read what he was writing. Excited? Me too! Experience Drawing XV, my favorite one.

God, looking at it makes me insane! I feel Cy Twombly throbbing in my veins, begging to be heard.

DRAWING XV

"If I took a lie detector test, I could pass it! If they asked me if I liked my job, I'd say yes even though I hate it! I've had to eat humble pie for so long even the cops couldn't tell what was the truth! Do I like my boss? Sure, he's a good man. LIE! I'm a liar but you can't tell. He's a stupid moron but you don't know I'm thinking that, do you? Tell the truth, liar-mouth!"

Jump to the end, Drawing XXXVIII. Doesn't it, at first, look like a paragraph written in real words? Look closer: those are "suggestions" of words; not even one letter is actually in any alphabet. These schizophrenic pencil strokes, consumed by rage and a suicidal decision to throw caution to the wind, free their creator to tell the world what he really thinks.

DRAWING XXXVIII

"I'm okay now, the other side of madness, beneath the valley of ultra-agitation. I finally realize that none of what you now understand matters anyway. I am a person who knows how to write down things. Someone as smart, confident, insane, and in full control of his handwriting as I am always has the last laugh and here it is. I quit. You know my name . . . Ty Rombly."

Cy Twombly has been called a "natural aristocrat" and I have no problem with that. He refuses to speak to me as he hangs on my walls, but that's okay. Silence worked for the amazingly aggressive and powerful female artist Lee Lozano, who in 1971 vowed for "art" never to speak to women again. And she didn't, either! For twenty-eight years she never uttered a word to any member of the female sex. What started out as a statement against the power of men in the art world, entitled *Boycott Women*, got sidetracked into an obsessive lunacy that lasted right up to the day she died. Lee Lozano needed to plan her daily life carefully. "I remember sitting in a restaurant with her once," recalled the artist Sol LeWitt in a published interview, "and a

251

waitress came to the table. Not only would Lee not talk to her, she would hide her eyes. When she came to my studio, if my girlfriend opened the door, Lee would turn on her heels, run down the stairs and be gone." At the end of her life, Lee became ill and had to go live with her parents. But what did she do at the dinner table? Block the view of her mother with her hands and demand, "*Dad*, will you please pass the salt?" This pathological, cockeyed, sexually political plan worked for Lee Lozano's artistic legend, so who can blame Cy for being standoffish?

From what I've heard, Cy doesn't really participate in the mail either. Can you blame him? When your handwriting can be worth a million dollars at auction? I first met Mr. Twombly when we were jurors together at the Locarno Film Festival in Switzerland, and he was a lovely, witty, smart man. On the last day, I got up my nerve and asked him for his address so I could send him the annual Christmas card that I design myself. He very kindly wrote it down on a torn piece of paper in that same handwriting I knew so well from his work. I almost swooned. He even spaced it badly with the letters scrunched at the bottom. What do you do when Cy Twombly writes something down for you? Throw it away after transferring the information to your private address book? Hardly. Frame it? Maybe not. Call the editor of the next volume of Cy's drawings-on-paper catalogue raisonné and ask to have it included? Well, it's tempting.

But I won't, because Cy Twombly doesn't suffer fools. I've always said true success is figuring out your life and career so you never have to be around jerks. Cy has definitely reached that level, but he's not a traditional snob. He's from and still lives part-time in Lexington, Virginia, when he's not at his other homes in Italy, and you can tell he's a Virginia gentleman through and through. He even took arty, hilariously detailed photographs of ugly toys and cheap flower bouquets at the local Wal-Mart and showed them to his publishers. Imagine Cy Twombly in Wal-Mart! Like a space alien. *So* out of place. *So* unrecognized. *So* interested in how earthlings live.

Mr. Twombly doesn't forget the little people. He told *Vanity Fair* in 1994 that he had been raised "by an African American nanny to whom he remains fiercely loyal." He had planned to take her to his big retrospective show at MoMA in New York "though he was afraid she might shock the other guests with her outspokenness." I know what he meant. I had a housekeeper who worked for me for decades whom I truly love, too. Her name is Rosa and she *hates* Cy Twombly's work. Aren't maids the ultimate art critics? When I hung Cy's seven prints entitled *Five Greek Poets and a Philosopher* (1978) in my dining room (can prints ever *really* be thought of as "roommates"?), Rosa moved in close to study them. Seeing only the names of the poets spelled out in Cy's shaky handwriting with no other "art" added, she barked her outraged disapproval. She scowled at the A in Plato that appears to be started over by the artist, certain of the spelling but unsure of the order of the letters. Rosa harrumphed at the R in Homer, so crowded, so sloppy, so excluded like an unwanted child in the alphabet. When I tried to show Rosa this new addition to my collection in the pages of one of the eighty-one books I own on Cy Twombly, the same heavy volume she had been moving and dusting under for years, she let her true feelings be known. "They have the nerve to put this in a *book*?" she howled in disbelief.

Even when Cy is celebrated in a fancy way, there are moments of affluent unease and anarchy. I was lucky enough to be
invited in 1994 to a sit-down dinner to unveil Cy's one new
work—*Untitled Painting* (he loves that U-word!)—at the Larry
Gagosian Gallery when it was still located in SoHo. This was the
only painting in the show and it took up the whole wall. The
guests were seated on both sides of a very long table. Between
courses, the entitled and distressedly dressed-in-elegance crowd
was asked to switch sides of the table so that those who had been
sitting across from them could gaze at the painting as they ate,
too. Was I the only one who noticed the delicious detail that the
waiters neglected to switch the plates, so you were forced to also
contemplate somebody else's leftovers? Did anybody but me put
two and two together that night? The violent burst of Mr.
Twombly's colors compared to the nibbled-on squash that had
once been historically fresh? Or the psychotic markings of the
furious child, which also might be a Roman fishing boat that
caught the very fish whose bones await burial on our overly
privileged dinner plates? Isn't art supposed to transpose even the
most banal detail of our lives? Were poetry, garbage, and genius
ever such a holy mix as they were that rare night in artful Manhattan?

Cy can be scary, too. I remember walking into one of his last
shows in Manhattan at the uptown Gagosian in 2006. There
were nine giant untitled paintings so terrifying and inviting,
repulsive and overwhelming, that you stopped in your tracks.
Here was Cy's massacre of confidence in all its gory detail. This
handwriting exercise of huge, red, dripping, barely clotted loops
of pernicious joy brought to mind crazed celluloid messages like

Stop Me Before I Kill Again, only this time the author was in a trance of twisted magnificence and private memories of classic carnage. This blood was definitely not safe, yet somehow it was beyond disease. Like the *Texas Chainsaw Massacre* of art history madness or the *Saw* of reinvented abstract painting, these works didn't even feel like paintings. They felt like a freeze-frame of the excitement of an idea. Get too close to the detail and you might gag from freedom. Yves Klein may have used the naked bodies of women as paintbrushes, but here Cy appears to have imagined painting with the hacked-off limb of an intruder who interrupted his painting by asking a stupid question about "drips" or how long it actually took to create these works. Like it would matter!

Nobody can overwhelm me like Cy Twombly. He puts me in a rapture of defiance and anger that immediately turns to tranquillity. Even though he lives with me in my Baltimore house only in the form of prints, he once in a while deigns to look at me when I pass his work on my walls, and I'm grateful for the attention. Cy Twombly never disappoints me or makes excuses. He will always be my favorite roommate.

But sometimes you have to lighten up. Fischli/Weiss sneak into my home all the time and make me laugh. They never have the rent, but what do I care? Not only are they the most droll, elegantly witty, and quietly hilarious artists working today, their deadpan, goofily poetic work asks the question, "Can kidding be art?" And, of course, it can. Especially when it is subtle and cool enough not to depend on dreaded cynicism. Unlike so many other contemporary artists trying to move onto anybody's walls, they don't shout for attention at art fairs or translate well to overproduced auction catalogs. This duo of Swiss artists aren't even angry! They're the Dean Martin and Jerry Lewis of the art world and their work has the charm of desperately wiping your nose on a fine Swiss handkerchief while riding the train to Gstaad in a snowstorm for the Christmas holidays.

My love and respect for Peter Fischli and David Weiss began in Zurich in 1990 in Walter Keller's Scalo Bookshop. Browsing through the art books, I came to one entitled *Airports* that had no text but was filled with page after page of Fischli/Weiss's numbingly beautiful but completely unremarkable glossy color photographs of runways, airplanes, luggage carts, control towers, and airline terminals. There was no reason for these photographs to be. Like rejected third choices from some corporate advertising calendar, these nondescript landscapes were so tedious, so overblown, and so dumb that once you finally looked at them with your "art" eyes, you could only feel total exhilaration.

I was too stupid to have heard of Fischli/Weiss at the time, but I bought the book, became obsessed by these photographers, and, in what I now realize was a rather unsophisticated review, praised *Airports* in British *Vogue*. I went on about "purposeful mediocrity" being the only "subtle way to be new" and gushed that I had "glimpsed a fresh kind of 1990s beauty, over and above the banality of pop or the exasperation of minimalism into a shockingly tedious, fair-to-middling, nothing-to-write-home-about kind of masterpiece." My wild enthusiasm for the "second-rate" that Fischli and Weiss so excelled at celebrating peaked at one of the airport pieces I named "FedEx." I described it excitedly: "A parked Federal Express plane sits in an airport with portable debarkation steps at its door. No people. Absolutely nothing is happening. 'Next Day Delivery' never looked so unrushed. A bus used to take passengers to the gate is heavily featured as it drives by, empty except for the unseen driver. We know it can't stop. Packages don't have friends to meet them at customs . . . How much could it cost to purchase this picture? What could it actually be like to have it beautifully framed in your living room?"

Well, I found out. After learning about Fischli/Weiss's past work, the inventively low-grade but expertly produced videos, the tiny, unfired clay narrative sculptures that look like movie scenes exhibited at an amateur craft fair, and their synthetic rubber dog dishes and silverware drawer dividers, I felt more secure. I was lucky enough to purchase their rubber 33⅓ record *Imitation* that my favorite art magazine *Parkett* editioned and offered its readers in 1988. I still chuckle every time I pass it on the pedestal in the front hall of my Baltimore house, where I have been appalled to see guests at my annual Christmas party actually set drinks on it! But I shouldn't worry. You can't really hurt Fischli/Weiss's "record." It's already scratched and scuffed and imperfect. True, it's an album, or rather "an object that can be played" as the artists warn, but only for "those who are not afraid of ruining their record players. If they take the risk, they will not be rewarded. Their record player or rather the needle will hear something like a cross section of average disco music. Average in this case also means decreased quality of sound reproduction—the hi-fi fetish choking on itself."

Graduating to their ridiculously sublime photos of "carpet shops" made out of lunch meats or their "Swiss Alps" imagined as an unmade bed with pillows propped up, I started to feel more sophisticated, more Swiss. And when I finally glimpsed their downscale Gursky-on-Prozac photographs of the almost invisible architecture of European suburban garden apartments, which would make any American yearn to go home, I finally got up the nerve to meet these great artists. My dear friend and art mentor Matthias Brunner (whom my mother *still* wishes I would marry, no matter how many times I tell her we are comrades) knew Peter Fischli and David Weiss. He explained to them my passion for the "FedEx" *Airports* photo, and even though this particular photo from the book had never been editioned or exhibited in any of their art shows, Fischli/Weiss agreed to make me a unique print. I never wrote a check with such unabashed zeal.

Airport—Federal Express (1999), the giant photograph that has no right to be this large, hogs one whole wall in my New York apartment and makes me feel so satisfied. This majestically ordinary panorama greets me proudly every time I come home from some airport—*never* air-raged to have been delayed, *never* frustrated by onboard mechanical problems, *never* crabby because of canceled flights. How could I be unhappy with air travel when every time I look out the window of an airplane, no matter where I am in the world, I think of Fischli/Weiss's glorious views? The ritual, the control, the freedom, and the agony of the airport now give me back the complete joy of being an art collector.

Then there's the rubble. The one piece of sculpture in my New York apartment the maid has never seen. Every time I arrive or depart from home, I go into my bedroom closet, get out my little white art-handler gloves, put them on, and take out the amazing gift I received from Matthias Brunner and Fischli/Weiss for my fiftieth birthday in 1996. Every second I'm in Manhattan, I fear someone who isn't obsessed over art will throw out Fischli/Weiss's tiny piles of painted, hand-carved polyurethane trompe l'oeil scraps of wood that I place lovingly on the floor right outside my kitchen door.

And who could blame them? I remember entering Sonnabend Gallery in 1994, seeing that the new Fischli/Weiss show was still being installed, and, like many other gallery-goers, almost leaving. But suddenly I realized the lumber on the floor, the paint cans, the cleaning supplies, the hammers and other tools, were all Fischli/Weiss sculpture. The leftover nails still hanging on the walls from the last show and the vaguely unfresh paint on the gallery walls were all part of the installation. The fast-food trash on the floor, seemingly left by the installers, was also actually hand-carved by these great tricksters. It was only when you tried to focus on the lettering of any of the commercial products scattered around that you realized they were quickly done, not focused. Being "not ready" for your show, the ultimate nightmare of both gallery owner and artist, was suddenly art.

I love art on the floor. Dennis Dermody hates it, though, and always bitches when he comes in my front door in New York and trips over the thirteen aluminum Carl Andre tiles. "Watch it, ox," I yell, but I'm not mad because you can't really hurt a Carl Andre sculpture. But look out for my Fischli/Weiss! Those eight little pieces of faux scrap wood are so delicate, so quiet, that just looking at them could break your heart *and* theirs if you're not careful.

"You have the worst lighting for your art," a collector grumbled when I was giving a tour of my Baltimore house, but that's the way I like it. "Your art should just be in your house the way everything else is," Brenda Richardson once told me, and I agree. I love going to Brice and Helen Marden's New York townhouse, where you see pictures, drawings, or rare photographs casually leaning on top of one another on the floor, right out in the daylight. Now, *that* is elegance.

And besides, some artists don't *want* you to really see their work. Fischli/Weiss's *Fotografías* (2004/05) are a perfect example. One hundred and eight black-and-white photographs snapped on slide film, "underexposed by 2 or 3 aperture points," and printed on color paper defy you to actually look at them. Only available in a series of six photographs (and you don't get to pick which six, only which series), the four-by-six snapshots of paintings on the front slats of Swiss fairgrounds, carnival rides, children's theme parks, and other locations of promised happy genre "fun" that are always a letdown are the artworks I look at the most every day in my Baltimore living room. But I've noticed that guests who are at all interested in my collection comment on these darkly printed photos of witches, dragons, and spiders the least. You can't really see the photographs from a distance. And if you move in to inspect, you are almost always disappointed. You can see the reflection of their flashbulb. You don't get it and you don't care. You move on quickly, never asking a question about the work or the artists. Fischli/Weiss's *Fotografías* seem to speak to no one. Perfect.

"Originally," these photographs were "just scraping the bottom of the barrel of our archive," the artists explain. "Pictures that hadn't been previously used." Now there is a weak artist's "statement" if I ever heard one! Are these pictures the worst of Fischli/Weiss? I've always thought there will eventually be a show entitled "The Worst of Warhol," but I'm not sure it would work with Fischli/Weiss. Can there really be a "worse" if there isn't a "better"?

I am so happy to be the only Baltimore friend of Fischli/Weiss's *Fotografias*. Are they homesick for Switzerland, the only country where the rich know how to act? The land I love that makes me feel so inferior for not having been born there. These pictures are better than any amusement park ride. They're an expensive cheap thrill that mocks photography as fine art at every level but at the same time winks at me to let me know I'm in on the art. Sometimes right before I fall asleep in my second-floor bedroom overhead, I think I hear them downstairs on the wall giggling together. And then I sleep very, very peacefully.

But I'm attracted to serious roommates, too. Ones that are so smart I usually have no idea what they are talking about when they first move into my house. I don't want someone living with me whose work I can understand. I want an artist who can make me see something amazing from almost nothing—the exact opposite of moviemaking. Richard Tuttle is the perfect choice.

I knew about Richard Tuttle's minimalist troublemaking and respected his early hostile establishment reviews, such as "Less has never been less than this." His bare plywood slat pieces nailed flat to the wall with just one thin side of the depth of the wood painted white were so beautiful, so simple, so plain, that I felt exhausted just imagining how complete the artist must have felt when he decided the work was finished. I had been incredibly moved and shocked at Mary Boone's 1992 show of Tuttle's tiny collages/paintings/sculptures hung at floor level with a single barely visible pencil line drawn down to each from the ceiling. These *Fiction Fish I* artworks are almost invisible when you walk in the gallery. Is this a show for the mice? I excitedly wondered, realizing, yes, to us these assemblages are minute, but to an ant they'd be as colossal as a Richard Serra sculpture is to us. Was Tuttle Tinker Bell's brother? Here, at last, was art made by someone obviously outside the human condition. As Richard Serra once said to me about Donald Judd's pieces, "It was never a question of liking his work," it was "that you could never get over it!" I know what Serra meant. I *still* have not gotten over this Richard Tuttle show.

I decided to get up my nerve and ask Tuttle to move in with me, not that you'd really know if he was there or not. I hung in my New York apartment his amazing nothing-to-it black crayon drawing *Summer 1973* (the same year *Pink Flamingos* really came out), which must have enraged viewers at the time in its very lack of craft, heft, or humor. I look at this hastily drawn "loop" mark with a lot of plain white paper space around it, which must have taken a second to draw, and remember how angry and insane I must have been in 1973, and realize from Richard's example you don't need to get *that* worked up to cause a stink.

I go back to Baltimore, where I always return for inspiration, and stroll by my other Richard Tuttle crayon drawing, *Center Point* (1973). I guess this is maximalist for Richard Tuttle because there are four lines and two colors: the exact rectangle of a 35 mm 1:85 ratio movie screen. Did Richard know he was

bringing in a calming effect to counterattack the anxiety of the
movie business inside my house? Could any job really be as simple, effortless, uncrowded with equipment, and perfect as this
drawing?

By now, Richard knows how much I worship *Peace and Time*
(1993), his unevenly hacksawed wood sculpture I bought from
Mary Boone. The clumsy but strong piece hangs passively in my
Baltimore house, looking like the *That Girl* logo or a failed
woodwork project left unclaimed from summer camp. This work
has enraged people in my home for years, but it makes me feel
better about my life because it certainly doesn't *ask* to be explained. I know Richard has talked about "a threshold beyond
which a self-respecting viewer won't look," but I'm way too self-
ish to offer up this quote to someone who is too cowardly to see
the perfect awkwardness right before their eyes.

Richard hears things from his work and I try to listen, too. I
remember going to see him give a little artist's "talk" for collectors at the inaugural opening of Dwight Hackett Projects in
Santa Fe. The whole event was like a transplanted *New Yorker*
cartoon. The gallery space was almost completely empty except
for a few six-inch bronzed black teepees done by the artist and
placed around the perimeter of the large room. "He is working with the horizon line," the gallery owner explained as the
fashionably-dressed-in-black art mob glanced around nervously,
relieved to see *something* at least but queasy from the heat and
Richard's reputation for being long-winded and impenetrable.
By then, I knew Richard a little, so I went up to him and shook
his hand right before he went on and whispered, "Make it long!"
He smiled, took center stage, and immediately announced with

a straight face, "John Waters told me to make my remarks long." The crowd tittered nervously, gave me dagger looks, and resigned itself to art talk from another reality. "See that piece over there? It *knows* about its shadow! It knows about its space," he enthused to the art mavens who strained to see what he did. "Tell me!" he demanded of his work with complete seriousness. "TELL ME WHAT YOU KNOW!" I was in heaven. Richard Tuttle is *never* funny to me. He's the only artist I respect who's moved way beyond humor. When asked by the curator Marcia Tucker why he made his works, Richard answered with obvious clarity, "So I won't have to do them again."

Everybody knows you need young blood in your house. The way to build a great collection is not to have a lot of money and buy established artists; it's to go to all the galleries once a month and find a brand-new artist you like in a gallery whose stable seems to be up your alley. Go back to the artist's second show and buy something for around $5,000. It *really* means a lot to the artist at this stage of the game, and even though you should never buy art just so you can later sell it for a profit, it *does* perk up looking through the auction results when you see your gamble go sky-high once in a while.

I loved it when Richard Baker came over to stay with me because he seems to have a schizophrenic career. He's been exhibiting surreal, beautifully painted still lifes for years in an uptown New York gallery, but what I go for is his other stuff—the handcrafted deadpan little sculptures of household objects that he only seems to show at the Albert Merola Gallery in Provincetown. I own a faux "pencil," a wooden "kitchen knife," three assorted clay "donuts" (the cheapest-looking kind, which come already stale in a box), a whole collection of fake pills—"downers" such as Oxycontin, Percocet, and Xanax—all displayed on a small mirror (I have to put them away if any ex-junkies are visiting), and a made-to-order large box of Jujyfruits with each hand-made candy spilled out on the table where it sits. I wish he'd just remake every single thing I already live with, even the furniture; then I'd just walk around and gaze at my imitation of life.

Richard Baker's office-related drawings make me crazy, too. Going to these shows is like the very best visit to Staples. He has meticulously drawn on paper a three-by-five-inch file card, the same kind I use daily to list my chores. Every day when I'm working in Baltimore I look up at the small piece of legal paper he also drew and then back down at the exact same style of paper I'm writing this book on. But my favorite of all is the completely realistic drawing of a badly photocopied piece of 8½ × 11 notebook paper. Now, if Richard Baker could just draw the words I have to write before I actually do it—wouldn't that be the ultimate piece of artwork to hang over your desk?

Sometimes I don't mind if my roommates are messy. An artist who doesn't clean up behind herself can be welcome if she does sloppiness with charm, and that would be roommate Moyra Davey. Her work lives with me everywhere, but she keeps a very low profile. She's meek, too, and never shouts out for attention. Once she's inside her own apartment, she never seems to go out. She just snoops around with her camera and photographs formal, lovely still lifes of neglect that demand respect for her low-tech intelligence. And if you look around your own living space, you will realize that everybody has a Moyra Davey still life somewhere in their home; it's just that you don't even notice it yourself. *Greatest Hits* (1999), her photo of out-of-date, probably scratched old record albums in their jackets, wouldn't be worth much to a vinyl collector, but every time I look at this artwork on my wall in San Francisco, I feel so encouraged to realize that nothing ever can be truly "used up." In Baltimore hangs Moyra's close-up of books (1999) stacked on a shelf the wrong way, with the spines turned toward the back of the bookcase. This is a nightmare photograph for me because I need *order* in my own library and Moyra doesn't even notice that she has none! It doesn't matter to her that she'll never be able to find a certain volume because, as she explains in her amazingly obsessive essay, *The Problem of Reading* (2003), there are just so many books to choose from that she's afraid she'll pick the wrong one. I feel less compulsive, freer in spirit, when I stare into the unlit space of unfilled shelving in Moyra's photographs, because she forces me to accept that I have to leave some things to chance, even though I know they will probably not succeed.

Even in my New York apartment, Moyra's smudged elegance can be felt. When you leave my place (nobody would notice on entering), look at the Davey photos (*Untitled, Bottles 5*) hanging right beside the front door and you'll never feel embarrassed for having ordinary moments in your life again. Here are nine empty liquor bottles that Moyra photographed between the years 1996 and 2000 after consuming the contents in a normal unalcoholic way. These are captured so plainly and with such a purposeful lack of force that you are not even sure if she felt like taking the picture in the first place.

Look at some of her other work and you will feel more and

more special to see the off-kilter sensibilities of this artist with a gaze that gives the inferiority complex of forgotten household items the stature of architecture. Can a dirty refrigerator want to have its picture taken (even if it's yours)? Will out-of-date turntables and shelves full of old stereo equipment *ever* be important enough for anyone but Moyra to celebrate? Just the thought of a Moyra Davey photograph makes me want to buy another one, but I'm afraid of one thing. The money she gets for her work might tempt Moyra to hire a part-time cleaning person for her apartment, which would be an art world catastrophe of the highest order.

Cleaning up can be pretty great, too. The artist/painter/ sculptor/photographer Paul Lee has always been helpful around the house, and I've been collecting him from the beginning, right after I saw his work hung in his makeshift summer studio in the artist Jack Pierson's house. Immediately I was taken with his two butch little-boy drawings of the blue-collar workplace. *Stealing Colors* (1999) is a shaky, primitive, part collage, part pencil sketch of a truck filled with meticulously but awkwardly cut out FedEx logos, and you get the feeling the artist was in some kind of enviable trance when he created this work. Same with *Building Colors*, its companion piece, which depicts a cement mixer dumping squares from the old FedEx logo he painted yellow. *Stealing* and *Building* never looked so happy together, almost sexual. If two artworks wanted to sneak off my walls when I'm out of town and have illicit sex, these would be the two I'd suspect.

Later, I let *Before My Eyes* (2000), Paul Lee's Agnes-Martin-meets-Tom-Friedman-on-saltpeter grid of cutout Kodak box exteriors, move in, too, and then all his work started asking me for a place to live. It got to be like a commune. *Anvil* (2002) and *Blacksmith* (2002) came next. Paul's two op-art black-and-white collages hang over my bed in New York to remind me of my own confusion and mixed self-esteem as a youth. I want everyone to feel dizzy in a peculiarly nostalgic way when they look over my bed and imagine what goes on here. Pretty soon his clay-mounted sculpture of a melted "Real Thing" Coke instant camera (2005) was nagging for a place to hang its head, so I put it on the wall outside my Baltimore office and marveled at its Pompeii-like damage. So "swag-bag" rejected, so distressed, so melted down that you were initially depressed over the obviously ruined film inside, but then were quickly put in a sparkling mood, realizing it had been replaced by some new kind of art.

Since I already had Paul Lee's drawings and sculptures, is it a surprise that his *Untitled 4* (2006) of a wispy young boy with a blue square painted over his face jumped right up on the wall next to my Baltimore bed? I hope nobody thinks this sad young man who may have had all his emotions blocked due to some kind of abuse has anything to do with my childhood, because it doesn't. Maybe this vaguely troubled little painting is there just to make me realize that I don't have any excuse to be fucked-up—nobody painted a block over my aspirations and I hope they didn't to Paul Lee's either.

I love it when he recycles. Paul took two photographs of lost boys off the Internet, glued them to foamboard, and bent them— instant sculpture! This creased, damaged little 2004 artwork, so afraid of the entire process of printing and mounting photographs, proves that you can't really fail in the art world unless you try to do it to get rich. His untitled white pop-top of a can mounted on black paper with the reverse framed right next to it (2006) adds a formal touch to throwing you off. The question is, however, throwing you off what?

But Paul's best work, by far, is his soiled washcloth sculptures (2006). These underwhelming cum-rag-dirty, once-smelly linen rejects from the bottom of a hamper exemplify the expression "exposing your dirty laundry." The washrag that has been ripped and sewn together with another washrag, each in a different shade of puke green, adds a touch of bold nerve to the wall right above my desk in New York. Not framed, but pinned to the wall, mated by an insane tailor for sexual reasons clear only to him, this meager rag of shabby craftsmanship and graveyard for bodily fluids never washed *anybody* clean. Here is a cloth that can only wipe away goodness, a rag for all the bile and filth of a sexy night just secretly remembered and celebrated in private.

Paul Lee's crowning achievement so far is *Untitled (Cemented Towel)* (2008), a pitiful forty-three-inch-high Leaning Tower of Pisa from Resurrection City that mocks the pedestal itself, the happiness of clean laundry, and the macho of cement mixing. This seemingly poorly planned, fragile yet heavy-in-weight sculpture comes in two pieces that don't fit together correctly. They lean pathetically like one of the World Trade Center buildings imagining what it had in store for itself before 9/11. The entire sculpture could topple over easily and shatter if a guest in your home accidentally brushed up against it. And to add even

269

more architectural sadness, I have it in San Francisco, where earthquakes lurk. Having it secured to the floor with earthquake-proofing wax made the whole experience of collecting Paul Lee all the more baffling. This incredibly successful artwork is purposely homely, haughtily failed, and passively confrontational. Just like all my roommates—ready to fight.

CULT LEADER

Cult Leader

I'm so tired of writing "Cult Filmmaker" on my income tax forms. If only I could write "Cult Leader," I'd finally be happy. Would you come on a spiritual pilgrimage with me? To Baltimore, naturally. Where I'd deracinate you from your family (after you've stolen all their rare art books and turned them over to our communal library) and together we'd concentrate on what really matters in life—our infallibility. Pope Benedict XVI may have denounced "filth," but we know better. Filth is just the beginning battle in the war on taste. The certain megalomania we all share will strengthen our delusions of grandeur and make it possible for us to go that extra step into what I will call "radical holiness." Fellow faith followers, isolated we are just ex-Catholics or slacker Jews fighting over the limits of shame or guilt. Or worse yet, Protestants turned alcoholic atheists or pussy agnostics who chicken out on the big questions daily. Together we can become saints of sordidness, "the damned, the disinherited, the disrespected and the despised," as Jesse Jackson once so beautifully called his followers. Perverts who are fanatical in their devotion to a new dogma of dirt. Yes, a filth movement for the next century, which will claw its way down the ladder of respectability to the final Armageddon of the elimination of the tyranny of good taste. A rapture of rottenness that will flower like a poisonous mold to cover the prison of acceptance. Yes, we are ready to take over the world.

We'd first discuss Christian doctrine. I may not be what you'd call devout, but I do believe in the basic goodness of people. This is about as spiritual as I get. Brainwashed by angry Sunday school nuns who were furious that a child might think on his own, and later in high school by second-rate Christian Brothers who were impotent when it came to performing the sacraments, I had little use for the dogma that was drilled into my young mind. I mean, "original sin"? The idea that newborn babies come into the world already soiled before they can let out their first cry? Not only hogwash, but especially mean-spirited hogwash. And the Virgin Birth? The supposed miracle of Mary getting pregnant without even the pleasure of the sex act? Now there's a real feminist concept for you! Jesus! Are Catholics all nuts? Now the Resurrection I can maybe understand. Every person who died will get to come back one day and walk the earth. Hi, David Lochary! Hi, Divine! Hi, Edith! It will be so great for everybody to be reunited in eternity. But talk about a housing shortage. What will a two-bedroom condo in Manhattan cost *then*?! And will we be nude? And if not, what will we wear *after* the coffin? The outfit we don for eternity would certainly be important, so I need to have someone begin designing it right now!

And Jesus Christ himself? I do believe he thought he was the son of God, but anybody can make an innocent mistake. He probably was a good man. A fashion leader, certainly. A little self-absorbed. A tad deluded, just like us. But as an elegant acquaintance recently pointed out, "My husband died of cancer and it took him about five years of terrible pain and agony to finally expire, and Christ was only on the cross for a weekend. What's the big deal?" She may have had a point. Many of my friends spent years slowly and painfully dying of AIDS. Have the limits of suffering been extended in modern times?

Look, I don't care if you had theological beliefs before you joined us. You are certainly allowed to have them. If your faith brought you comfort, I'm all for it. JUST DON'T TRY TO MAKE *ME* DO IT! But now, it's time for us to come up with our own insane doctrines. Our own rigid rules for cockeyed happiness right here on earth while we still have the chance. Cult followers, it's up to you. I need a mortal-sin brigade who can go out there and recruit. Damaged people make the best warriors, so get busy. I'm a fascist about my work habits and I expect you to be, too. Never have a spontaneous moment in your life again. If you're going to have a hangover, it should be scheduled on your calendar months in advance. Rigid enjoyment of planning can get you high. Militant time-management will enable you to ignore how maladjusted you would be if you had the time to notice it in the first place. Discipline is not anal compulsion; it's a lifestyle that breeds power. The only insult I've ever received in my adult life was when someone asked me, "Do you have a hobby?" A HOBBY?! DO I LOOK LIKE A FUCKING DABBLER?!

You'll need a new name, too. Forget who you used to be. "Mr. Hatt" was my initial code name and you, too, will need an alias. Why do you think movie stars' names are made up? To conquer their pasts, that's why! I want you to leave behind your debt and your parents' expectations, and even more important I want a fresh identity to mold into joy and madness. Pick a character's name from one of my movies and make it your own. But select an obscure supporting player whose name is only said fleetingly in the dialogue, like Sandy Sandstone or Vera Venninger. Sometimes just a character's first name is enough. How about Flashlight? Or Doyle, Eater, Flipper, Dribbles, or Butterfly? Adding on the last name of the person who was meanest to you in high school can be the perfect solution to the new "you."

You'll need a uniform. A habit. A "fallen angel" look to intimidate yet attract. Have all your tattoos removed surgically. Yes, it's expensive and, true, it doesn't really work, but we have to start over, clean the slate, open up our bodies to a new lewd light. Be too thin and too poor. Study Karl Lagerfeld's hilarious diet book daily. I know I became the patron saint of chubby girls because of the success of *Hairspray*, but those days are over. Fat is not enough anymore unless you were once thin and gained weight on purpose to confuse authority. This time, we're all going to be lean and mean. If I could go to the gym to get the body of a junkie, I would. Guzzle tap water and only eat candy— but pick the brands with the racist or sexist names, like Black Crows, Mexican Hats, or Jujyfruits, so you feel guilty and won't pig out.

Let your hair grow out from whatever style or length you currently wear so my trained team of alarmingly stylish hairdressers without licenses can give you the signature cut of our cult; longer for boys (unless they are balding, in which case hair should be drawn on) and shorter for girls (bring back the one-sided Sassoon with a W in the back?). A unisex cut from beyond the outer limits of severity that will confound and dominate the fashion timid is what any self-respecting filth follower must demand.

Boys, never let me see a pleat in your pants. Turn your belt around to the right side so the buckle is forty-five degrees off center. Nothing is sexier, the secret sign that your gun is loaded, so to speak. Joe Dallesandro wore his that way in *Trash*, and so did Joe Spencer in *Bike Boy*. Lustful, beautiful juvenile-delinquent boys have been wearing their belts this way for decades of erotic confidence, and I expect you to do the same.

Girls, the bigger your breasts, the higher the necklines. What you *don't* see is always sexier. If you're flat-chested, go topless. Prove your self-confidence and uninterest in the male gaze. Tight pants can be a good look for you and will come in handy when you have to climb over a fence or run from a store detective. Always be dressed in your full cult finest in case you are arrested. There is only one fashion photograph that counts in our world: the perp walk.

But dressing "cult" is a tricky thing. One false move and you can easily look ridiculous. Now every once in a great while "ridiculous" can look amazing, but that is rare. Think of the middle-aged cult Mormon women who grieved their children being taken away from them by the government, wearing Edith Massey's *Pink Flamingos* hairdo and those insane Little Miss Muffet outfits. Now *that* was a great cult look. But it's a tough thing to pull off. I remember moseying into the long-gone Process Church headquarters in New Orleans in the early seventies (627 Ursulines Avenue), and being intrigued by this cult that supposedly worshipped both Jesus and Satan, which seemed oddly democratic at the time. The Process had a certain notoriety for suing the U.S. publishers of Ed Sanders's book *The Family*, and successfully making them remove the chapter that implied Manson had stolen the religion's "fear" belief and used it as his own. I wanted to like the Process kids; they wore all-black clothes and were really cute in a witchy-warlock kind of way, but they had one big fashion blunder. They wore cloaks. Nobody can appear all-knowing wearing a stupid cloak. Like donning a top hat or featuring a thumb ring, it's the look of a fool. Who could fuck anyone who wore a cloak?

We do need a signature look, though. Black is always good. But never *all* black the way male movie stars do it at the Oscars. A black tie with a black shirt and a black suit isn't black tie, it's bad formal. How about we add a subtle hint of devil red to our cult black outfits? Socks that only reveal their shocking hue when you sit down and cross your legs. Or red stitching around the pocket of your jacket. The tight red collar of a deranged priest? Or an all-black uniform accessorized by a satanic red handkerchief you whip out to blow your nose? Better yet, wear black rags. Rags dyed black by the hardworking cult members who will add a touch of their own red blood to show their commitment to the cause.

Both men and women can add to their threatening glamour by the creative use of eye makeup. It doesn't have to be used just for your eyes; try sketching on the stigmata of show-business celebrities who died for your sins. Paint in terrible deep lacerations at the nape of your neck to properly honor the wounds the hustler Pino the Frog inflicted on the holy man—film director

Pier Paolo Pasolini. Diagram on the top of your forehead the horrible scalping Jayne Mansfield went through in that fatal car accident. Draw on the violent incisions actress Capucine must have experienced after jumping out the window and impaling herself on that fence in her successful suicide attempt. Or just imagine the "invisible" stigmata that some saints claim leave no marks at all but cause excruciating pain. Better yet, concentrate on the stigmata wounds that refuse to clot and, in some cases, have a pleasant aroma known as "the odor of sanctity." I *knew* there had to be a name for it. Come on, let's hold hands and smell like pain.

There will be homework. *Lots* of reading. You might as well start now. Here are a few of the titles that are the cornerstones of our new religion. Of course, you've already read *The Bad Popes* by E. R. Chamberlin and *How the Pope Became Infallible* by August Bernhard Hasler, but I expect you to dive into *The Cult of the Virgin Mary* by Michael P. Carroll, *Why Catholics Can't Sing* by Thomas Day, *Encountering Mary* by Sandra L. Zimdars-Swartz, *The Bleeding Mind* by Ian Wilson, and *Mariette in Ecstasy* by Ron Hansen. After you've digested these and discussed the theology in each ad nauseam with your fellow fanatics, we can get serious. Serious about excess spirituality. Serious about reverse dogma.

But we must prepare ourselves physically, too. Our assholes will be clean but we must never wash our hands. Our immune systems will be strengthened by our being dirty. Not filthy. Just mildly grimy. Filthy fingernails have always been a favorite fashion accessory of mine. Especially when you place your hands in the prayer position. Matter of fact, I urge all my followers to forgo nail polish permanently and replace it with expertly applied soot. The nonexistent gods above will ignore our prayers better this way. Germs, at least in small doses, are good for you. Aren't all vaccinations filled with a tiny bit of the diseases they are designed to prevent? I'm always mystified to see grown men scrubbing their hands as if they are about to perform open-heart surgery after urinating in New Jersey Turnpike rest stop bathrooms. Did they piss all over their hands at the urinal? Didn't they already wash their penises that morning in the shower? How does your unit get dirty by aiming a stream of urine into the proper receptacle? These germ freaks will get sick, I guarantee you. They'll be so healthy they'll get old and die of "nothing." Avoid them! Run from the overly clean before they infect you!

Dirty hair is kind of heavenly, too, if you know how to wear it. Matted. In clumps. Stringy. All those negative terms can be turned around if you are carefree and have good cheekbones. David Lochary always recommended cleaning your hair not with some overpriced shampoo, but with cornstarch. He would just pat it all over his bleached hair and then brush it out. I tried it. It kind of worked. Your hair *did* feel thicker. Just be careful if it rains, though. Rainwater and cornstarch equals gravy.

As your leader, I will try to set a good example. William Burroughs once called me "the Pope of Trash" and I've been milking that title for decades. Now it's time to finally live up to it. I always knew visiting the actual Vatican would be a terrible idea for me, but when I had a speaking job in Rome and the sponsor wanted to take me, what could I say? Once inside the anti-vow-of-poverty walls of the Vatican, I figured the only safe place for me would be the gift shop. I lurked near the postcard rack pick-

ing out the most hideously pious cards to mail to business associates, hoping to kill time while the rest of my group toured the
opulently oppressive sites. When it was time to pay for my pur-
chases, I approached the no-nonsense nun behind the counter
and she rang up my sale. When I asked for a receipt, as I always
do for any corporate-related expense like this (Warhol's diaries
taught us well), she sniffed her nose in the air like she had just
seen a leper and snarled, "The Vatican doesn't give receipts!"
"The Vatican doesn't give receipts??!!" I repeated in my mind,
stunned at the simplicity of her knee-jerk response. "I guess
not!" I started fuming as my host gently grabbed me by my el-
bow and began leading me toward the exit. "I guess my cash
will be funneled to anti-abortion and homophobic lobbyists all
over the world!" "But the Vatican doesn't pay taxes," the nun
suddenly tried to explain in a nice voice, totally not getting it. "I
know they don't," I shrieked in my mind, "but *I* do!!" The politics of the Catholic Church never seemed more obviously expressed.

I hated my Catholic high school, so I certainly never went back
to a reunion, although I did get to comment to *The Baltimore
Sun*, on the school's fifty-year anniversary, that the Christian
Brothers and lay faculty there had "discouraged every interest I
ever had." A friend who attended the reunion that year said he
heard me called "faggot" and "pornographer" by some of my
pissed-off fellow classmates who had read my criticism, but I
didn't mind. The only reason to attend any school reunion is to
see how the people whom you had wanted to have sex with then
look today. And I had already looked up those people's addresses
and driven by their homes to stalk them years before.

Decades later, I was contacted by a group of men from my high school who claimed they were sexually abused by one of the Christian Brothers long after I had attended. They wanted me to join their case because, apparently, he'd been doing it for years, but I had to tell them, "Hey, he didn't fuck me!" I was even rejected by the child molesters in my school! Is this supposed to make me feel lucky? Or double-rejected?

I can't predict the future the way some cult leaders pretend they can. But who on earth would *want* to know what was going to happen to them? Isn't that the only reason we get out of bed every day—to find out? Imagine the burden of knowing the exact date you were going to die? Talk about pressure to have fun NOW! I can, however, rearrange your past if you'll let me. Make you *use* whatever pain you may have felt to experience a new level of lunatic anti-piety. I was lucky enough to have worked out most all of my onetime troubling issues with my dad before he died. The ones that lingered, I turned into a career.

Praying does not have to feel so empty. Try starting every day with Divine's prayer from *Mondo Trasho* and say it exactly as I have edited it here.

Oh Mary. Oh Mary.
Oh Mary, our Most Beloved Lady
And it is to you and only you
That I owe my crackpot admiration, my divinity!
BUT I CAN ONLY PRAY SO HARD!
I can but only pray that the Holy Trinity will grant me
The necessary grace to combat the evil forces

That have reared their heads so often in our lives.
Please, Mary! I only ask for what is rightfully mine!
I BESEECH THEE! SHOW ME A SIGN!
GRANT ME MY WISHES!!
So that once again I will be able to believe . . .
To be Divine.

See? It's easy to get in the mood for God even if he isn't there! As Crackers and Cotton say to each other in *Pink Flamingos*, "You are God" and "You are God," and you know what? They are both right.

I will make your sex life better by encouraging your fantasies. Believe in incubi? I do. Bisexual demons in male form who lie upon sleepers in the night and have sexual intercourse with them. No dating. No unsafe sex. No alimony. Just demon sex when you want it! Or how about a succubus? The title of a bad sixties exploitation movie, but what a sexy concept. Women devils who drain semen from the men they seduce in their sleep, collecting energy "often to the point of exhaustion of the victim." Who needs sleeping pills with these babes? Just hit the hay and we'll all score!

Of course, there are some saints we *do* take very seriously. Saint Catherine of Siena is without a doubt the most insane of these and we have no choice but to honor her daily. Reading *Holy Anorexia* by Rudolph M. Bell, the best encyclopedia of deranged saints ever written, we learn that in Catherine's time (the 1300s) she was known as "a person of considerable reputation for outstanding holiness"—in other words, nuts! At the peak of her career she "urged the holy hatred of oneself" and advised others to "build a cell in your mind that you can never escape." She was a "bottom" for God.

Little Miss Catherine the Lunatic supposedly had her first vision at the age of six. Who didn't? When I was six I saw myself as the winner of a full-length mink coat on the Bess Myerson–hosted 1950s TV quiz show *The Big Payoff*, and for weeks wore a filthy piece of material around my shoulders that only *I* knew was the coveted prize. Catherine organized a group of fellow child masochists who flagellated themselves daily. Well, I can understand that, too. I had a Horror House in our garage and I'd charge the neighborhood kids twenty-five cents to enter. After they gave me the money, I'd tell them to wait, and I'd go inside and then yell, "Okay, come in!" The little ticket buyers would grope their way into the darkness and I would squirt them with a fire extinguisher (my dad's company sold them) and then kick them in the leg. They loved it. They even came back for more. I also used to play "school" as a kid with the little girl who lived next door, and I was always the teacher and she was always the student. Every time we played I failed her, yet she *still* eagerly agreed to play every time I asked, fully knowing the results. Failing can be a relief for some. A sexual position. A way of life. A choice. Some kind of happiness that never lets you down.

Saint Catherine was also, like us, thin. Her favorite diet? Drinking "only a little cold water" and "chewing on bitter herbs" and then "spitting out the substance." Well, we can imitate that! But we're not anorexic, for chrissakes. We eat. Six white Necco wafers (the ones that look like Communion hosts) for lunch. And dinner? Well, we usually don't swallow past one p.m., but on special occasions, two red French radishes make a delicious late-night treat.

Saint Catherine was out of her mind, but she tried to do good deeds. Volunteering as a nurse, she was dressing the cancerous breast sores of a woman she was tending to when she "felt repulsed at the horrid odor of the suppuration." Going for a new level of religious excess and "determined to overcome the bodily sensations," Catherine carefully drained the pus "into a ladle" and chugged it all down. For God, I guess! Maybe one of you followers could volunteer somewhere and reenact this new station of the cross and see what happens. But "do" a goiter instead. Goiters are so scary. Every day of my life I worry about growing a goiter. But maybe chugging goiter juice is some sort of miracle cure for baldness? You can never know until you try it. Let me know if it works.

Like all good tales, Catherine's story has a happy ending—at least from her viewpoint. "Her final days were filled with pain, tormenting devils, self-doubts and fear of the church's future." That's where our stories will have to differ. We know no self-doubts, our egos are way too big to die yet, and we laugh a lot. And we never doubt our church's future because we have been praying for years to the biggest saint of all. "The Most Hated Woman in America," as *Life* magazine once called Madalyn Murray O'Hair. And she will definitely answer us.

Madalyn Murray, as she was initially known, tried to defect to Russia in 1960, was rejected, and then opened the New Era Bookshop in downtown Baltimore, locally known as "the Commie bookshop." I was afraid to go inside but fascinated that someone was actually out of the Communist closet in my hometown. I didn't like Ike in grade school, and secretly rooted for Adlai Stevenson, even though I had no idea of the differences in these presidential candidates. I just knew no one in my entire private school claimed to be for Stevenson, so I naturally jumped on board his campaign, at least in my head. In the early sixties, when I was festering in Catholic high school, Madalyn Murray hit pay dirt and, using her son as a test case, had prayer removed from the Baltimore public school system. She then made a federal case out of it and suddenly the whole world made her the Enemy of God, the hag in the housedress who took away the "Our Father" from our Christian children. One of my lay teachers even hinted to our class that he "wouldn't be against someone breaking the windows of her house in protest." I remember being outraged when I heard him say this, and that's when I became Madalyn Murray's fan. "She wouldn't care if you hate her!" I wanted to shout out to my classmates. "She's fighting for our rights!"

Madalyn actually exhibited her hate mail and loved to quote publicly from it. "Someone is going to put a bullet through your fat ass," one read. "You swine, you masculine lesbian bitch!" Madalyn went on to sue anybody and everybody who dared mix church and state, even trying to have "In God We Trust" removed from all U.S. coins. The Baltimore cops especially loathed her, beating her up, yelling, "Get that bitch!" before finally terrorizing her so much that they ran her and her family out of town to Austin, Texas.

According to the fascinating biography *America's Most Hated Woman*, by Ann Rowe Seaman, Madalyn adored infuriating people. She put out bumper stickers reading "Praying Is Begging" (it *is*) and "Jesus Is Lard" (he isn't). She raided a San Diego church and turned over bingo tables, "pushing and shoving people." She called Jesus "the most despicable man in history, including Hitler" and you can imagine how her enemies rose to that bait. When Pope Paul VI died, she commented, "I only wish I could spit on his corpse for the world to see." Manners, for her, were nonexistent. When a pious preacher came to her house and offered to "explain about Jesus, about the blessings that could come back when you did the Lord's work," Madalyn pretended to listen but then reasoned, "Yes, you can tell me about Jesus but first let's go up and fuck. Then after we're fucking you can tell me about Jesus. Or maybe you can tell me about Jesus *when* we're fucking." Later in her career, Madalyn even came onstage in some of her lecture tours riding a broomstick!

The very people whose support Madalyn needed didn't find it any easier to deal with her. When a gay militant sent her some of his writings, Madalyn wrote him back, "I would expect this kind of literature to issue from a misogynist. I am a female head of the American Atheist Society. You are a cocksucker." So much for gay rights. She threw Jews out of her organization, claiming "a Jew could not be an atheist, Judaism was a religion, not a race." "Why don't you go to the gas chamber?" she challenged the very red-diaper babies who could help her. "It's people like you who promote the need for them." Despite claiming "Jesus Christ, it's wonderful to be rich" from all the donations she pocketed from her followers, she was still a really tough boss, calling her staff "flotsam, jetsam, cunt lappers and nigger-fuckers."

She'd sometimes realize she had gone too far and would apologize. "Oh, I'm sorry," she'd beg, before adding with a vengeance, ". . . that you are such an asshole!"

No one was really surprised when Madalyn Murray was eventually murdered in 1995. By a man named Waters. David Waters. No relation of mine, of course. A onetime hood turned disco stud turned gay hustler and wife beater who even set fire to his own mother's wig and then urinated in her face! This former employee of Madalyn's thought she had more money on hand than she did, got the help of two low-life buddies, kidnapped Madalyn, her son, and her granddaughter, kept them hostage in a motel for months, and then strangled them, cut up their bodies, and buried the pieces in a shallow grave. Not her son Bill, the one Madalyn used to take prayer out of the schools. No, he found Jesus in 1977, broke away, and wrote a *Mommie Dearest*–type book about Madalyn entitled *My Life Without God*. It was the other son, John, who was martyred for his mom. The one who lived with Madalyn his entire life and never married, fighting the atheist battle to the end. Robin, too, Madalyn's grandchild, the ultimate loyalist to the cause, who died like a defiant holy woman. How proud Madalyn must have been of her offspring, as she continued "humiliating and infuriating" her captors until Waters finally wrung her neck. They gave up their lives for us, you know. All three of them.

Participation in certain "actions" would be expected of all cult members, and this includes bringing in daily monetary donations. In other words, begging in the streets. I always remember the insane Catholic panhandlers I saw in Rome: the true nutcases, usually female and on their knees, who had gone completely off the deep end, whipping themselves on the streets and wearing cloth bags over their heads with no eye or mouth holes as horrified tourists pretended not to see them. I won't expect you to go as far as that, but I would hope you'd be creative. When we were a young starving film troupe and didn't have enough money for our needed LSD, Mary Vivian Pearce sent away for a UNICEF kit, dressed in straight disguise, and went door-to-door, collecting charity money until she had enough cash to pay for some of our doses. Today, I would recommend making our marks laugh. This seems like the best way to get the employed to give us their hard-earned wages. I have a few examples of witty panhandling that might inspire you. In New York, I once saw a middle-aged hobo type sitting on the street with a tin cup in front of him and a hand-lettered sign reading I USED TO BE QUITE ATTRACTIVE. I noticed his tin cup was flush with bills. Another time, in San Francisco, I spotted another grimy homeless guy with a sign that simply read I NEED $ FOR A HOOKER, which also seemed to be inspiring charity from the local citizens. Go ahead—think like a grifter. You have to chip in here. I need money.

If you're too proud to beg, maybe you could peddle for me a prayer cloth I've designed. Decorated with sketches of dead film gods like Armando Bó (the Argentine Russ Meyer, who made an endless number of movies with his amazing sexpot mistress, Isabel Sarli) and Delmer Daves (the unheralded-in-America director of *Susan Slade*, in which Connie Stevens's character's baby catches fire and Troy Donahue's puts it out), it should be an easy sell. This cloth really works. Touch it to your genitals and then rub it on whatever script or music CD you are trying to get produced and put it in the mailbox. SHAZAM! A deal will happen. I guarantee it.

Or better yet, maybe you could be the first on your block to sell a perfume I'm planning on marketing with my name attached. Don't laugh: the actor Alan Cumming did quite well with his and the scent really *was* called Cumming. Whenever I say my name in Paris, the French laugh because to them it means in English "toilet waters." So my perfume would have to smell like, what? The humorous absence of God mixed with the odor of a piece of 16 mm film getting caught in the projector gate and burning? Maybe we have to be ruder. I was amazed to see in a sex shop a fragrance called Bottom 20 that promised to deliver the smell of an asshole. Isn't America a great country? Where else in the world could there be enough disposable income to make a wonderful product like this available? Maybe we could take the smells of leftover Odorama cards (especially #2 and #9) and mix them with the scent of Rosy Crucifixion Oil, which you used to be able to buy in voodoo shops in Baltimore, and buy out all the Bottom 20 leftovers that didn't sell and mix them together. Eau de Waters—the smell of an obsessed film fanatic.

Like a fraternity that demands hazing, my cult religion would have its own rituals for newcomers. You would have to *prove* your dedication by taking risks. Stealing a Baby Jesus from a crèche at Christmas has always been popular with rebel teenagers, but to me it feels a little old hat. I am a big fan of the living crèche at Christmastime, when adults get in the costumes of Mary and Joseph and the Three Kings, a real baby plays Jesus, and actual farm animals take their place alongside for a Diane-Arbus-photograph-from-hell if there ever was one. Every year when I go out to visit my mom on Christmas Eve, I stop by one near her house and something about it makes me . . . well, horny. I just sit in the car with the windows rolled up and watch the pious neighbors holding their votive candles, but secretly I'm cruising. Does anybody actually "cruise" anymore? I don't have the nerve to actually make eye contact with anyone because I'm afraid I'll get recognized or arrested. Still, the idea of a quickie with a stressed-out Joseph or a sex addict shepherd has an erotic appeal I can't deny.

If you are serious about studying with me, I would ask any potential followers to infiltrate one of these living crèches and get the part of Mary or Joseph. Better yet, dress your daughter as Baby Jesus (no one will check the Christ child's crotch). Right at the height of the event, start suddenly speaking in tongues. It's really fun! I speak in tongues at the drop of a hat. You should try it first at home. Just start hollering out nonsense words and I guarantee your mood will improve. Cinematic speaking in tongues is even more satisfying. Try "Bibbidi-Bobbidi-Boo" in Pig Latin. Yelling "Supercalifragilisticexpialidocious" in the middle of a living crèche will create panic, joy, sexual relief, and cinematic anarchy. In other words: a sacrament.

Sometimes we'll have to get more militant. I have always been inspired by the Catholic radicals commonly referred to in the press as "the Shouting Ladies." Joan Sudwoj and Cynthia Balconi are two Pennsylvania women who have repeatedly burst into Catholic churches and "bellowed out the mysteries of the rosary so vehemently" that the confessions taking place at the time "had to be shouted to be heard." Their acts resulted from "a sign from God who told them to pray often and loudly because the world faced imminent tragedy." Sometimes they splashed holy water on worshippers and disrupted Mass with their loud praying. Sermons couldn't be heard and choirs were drowned out by these fanatics screeching. Because of this "unholy racket" (and God, do I love that term!), armed guards had to be posted to block the doors of the church when the congregation saw the Shouters approaching. Unperturbed, these loudmouths for Mary simply went to another Mass and started bellowing their prayers again, forcing twenty-five worshippers to flee. Suddenly quiet, the Shouting Ladies reportedly moved to Ohio, and I can only hope their silence is temporary and an even louder comeback is in the works.

Let's all go "shouting"! How about pro-life meetings? Just imagine bursting in and splashing popper liquid on all the filthy men who dare tell a woman what to do with her body. Shout out Divine's prayer and watch these fuckers run! Or how about the MPAA?! Let's all burst in when they are trying to give an R rating to a film because it shows the smoking of a cigarette. Not because we believe in smoking. It *does* kill you! That's the only true thing the government ever told you. But because people *do* smoke and why should that give a film a restricted rating? A *new* kind of censorship?? Great! Just what we *don't* need! Start shouting vintage cigarette jingles at the top of your lungs. "Winston tastes good, like a cigarette should!" Get even louder! "You get a lot to like with a Marlboro!" Keep going! You know the chorus. Sing along! "Filter. Flavor. Pack or box!" Bring a portable generator so we can all have microphones! Make these fuckers deaf with our shouting!! BURST THEIR CENSORING EARDRUMS!

Now we can get serious. I will teach you how to levitate. It's a private thing. You really have to concentrate. Pot helps. I'm not talking about a big rise up off the ground; I'm talking two to three inches. It's possible if you believe. Just focus on something that makes you really excited, like the fact that the great writer and outcast alcoholic Jean (*Sleep It Off Lady*) Rhys's own daughter fainted at the sight of her mother coming over to visit because she knew how mean she would be. Or remember great moments of evangelical style. Think of the black preacher Daddy Grace's purple suits, his hideously long clawlike fingernails. See? You went up a little. It's fun, isn't it? Concentrate on the beauty of Dorothy Day, the Catholic left-wing activist who begged, "Don't trivialize me by trying to make me a saint." Wheeeee! You're levitating! If you're lucky you might stay up for three or four seconds!

Okay, you're getting close to being able to perform miracles. Little ones. Pitiful ones. Like curing pimples. Or lowering price tags on designer clothes. But keep these acts a secret. It's a personal power you've reached through spiritual study, but don't expect the stupid little outside world to believe you. Scientologists call it "clear"; we'll call it "cloudy." Once we have identified and embraced our sickness, we'll have strength! And that's when we get dangerous. Identify the spots of guilt on your body and pluck them out like the chicken livers evangelists pretend is the cancer they cure in shills planted in the congregations of their tent revivals. Where are you feeling you're not worthy? In your hair? Behind your ears? In your private areas? Well, cast it out! We're Porn Again and we have no regrets! Repent? Hell, no! I HAVE A SCREAM! NO REMORSE! NO SHAME! ALL LAUGHING ALL THE TIME! CINEMATIC DELIRIUM!

There's only one way we want to die—spontaneous combustion. The unexplained phenomenon of being so guilty and happy, so obsessed, so driven, and so fanatical that you just burst into flames for no apparent reason. On the street. At work. Hopefully, for me, in an airport. And if we work together, it could happen to us all at once when we're out somewhere causing trouble. It's a beautiful death, dramatic, scary, internally cleansing, and all you leave for the rest of the world to see is a really good pair of shoes. I have a lot of books on spontaneous combustion, or "fire from heaven" as it has been called, and all the pictures of the lucky dead are the same. Ashes. Shoes. Ashes. Shoes. So it all boils down to a religious lesson. Be prepared. Always wear stylish shoes. They won't be comfortable. They shouldn't be. It hurts to be this pure.

SOURCES

JOHNNY AND ME

The Baltimore Sun; The Wall Street Journal; The New York Times; The Herald-Dispatch (Huntington, WV); *Milwaukee Journal Sentinel; New York Post; Daily Mirror* (U.K.); *Daily Express* (U.K.)

US Weekly; Time; Billboard; LA Weekly

www.wikipedia.org
www.classictvads.com
http://blogs.indiewire.com/eug/archives/Meserve_Island
www.IMDB.com
www.classicbands.com
http://constantmusic.com

- *Say, Kids! What Time Is It?* by Stephen Davis. Little, Brown, 1982.
- *Cry: The Johnnie Ray Story* by Jonny Whiteside. Barricade Books, 1994.
- *Australian Dictionary of Biography*, vol. 14. Melbourne University Press, 1996.
- *The Case of Mary Bell* by Gitta Sereny. McGraw-Hill Book Company, 1973.

• *Cries Unheard* by Gitta Sereny. Metropolitan Books, 1999.
• *Jackal* by John Follain. Arcade Publishing, 1998.
• *Monster Mash* by Bobby Pickett. Trafford Publishing, 2005.

THE KINDNESS OF ȘTRANGERS

Memoirs by Tennessee Williams. Doubleday, 1975.

LESLIE

New York *Daily News; Los Angeles Times; The Washington Post; The Baltimore Sun; New York Post; Goshen College News* (Goshen, IN); *Press Enterprise* (Riverside, CA); The Associated Press

National Enquirer

www.charliemanson.com

Leslie Van Houten parole hearing transcripts, 1991, 1993, 1996, 1999, 2000, 2002, 2004, 2006, 2007
Charles Watson parole board hearing transcripts, 1990, 1998
Charles Watson psychiatrist report, 1971
Patricia Krenwinkel parole board hearing transcripts, 1990, 1997
Steve Grogan parole board hearing transcripts, 1978, 1979, 1980
Susan Atkins, parole board hearing transcripts, 1993

Court TV
CNN
When Women Kill, HBO documentary, 1983
Most Evil: Cult Leaders, Investigation Discovery series, season 2, episode 1, 2007
The Mind of Manson, NBC, *Today*, 1987
Turning Point: The Manson Women: Inside the Murders, ABC TV, 1994

- *Helter Skelter* by Vincent Bugliosi with Curt Gentry. W. W. Norton & Company, 1974.
- *Helter Skelter* (Twenty-fifth Anniversary Edition) by Vincent Bugliosi with Curt Gentry. W. W. Norton & Company, 1994.
- *Talk About Leslie* (working title) by Connie Turner (unpublished manuscript).
- *Will You Die for Me?* by Charles "Tex" Watson as told to Chaplain Ray. Fleming H. Revell Company, 1978.
- *The Long Prison Journey of Leslie Van Houten* by Karlene Faith. Northeastern University Press, 2001.
- *Albert Speer: His Battle with Truth* by Gitta Sereny. Alfred A. Knopf, 1995.

REI KAWAKUBO

The New York Times; *The Baltimore Sun*; *The Washington Post*

Vogue; *The New Yorker*; *Women's Wear Daily*; *Newsweek*; *DNR*; British *Vogue*; *Washington Blade*

www.blog.charmcityscene.com
www.wikipedia.org

- *Guerrillazine No. 5—Extracts of a Corporate Nightmare*, June 2006.

BALTIMORE HEROES

The Baltimore Sun; *Herald-Journal* (Spartanburg, SC); Baltimore *City Paper*

Baltimore Magazine

http://cityguide.aol.com/baltimore

• *Baltimore Sounds: An Illustrated Encyclopedia of Baltimore Area Pop Musicians, Bands and Recordings 1950–1980* by Joe Vaccarino, MJAM Press, 2004.

BOOKWORM

The New York Times; The Sunday Times (London)

The New Yorker; The New Republic; Time

www.wikipedia.org

• *Denton Welch: The Making of a Writer* by Michael De-la-Noy. Viking, 1984.
• *In Youth Is Pleasure* by Denton Welch. Vision Books, 1950.
• *The Journals of Denton Welch*, edited by Michael De-la-Noy. Penguin, 1987.
• *Denton Welch* by Robert Phillips. Twayne Publishers, 1974.
• *Denton Welch, Writer and Artist* by James Methuen-Campbell. Tartarus Press, 2002.
• *We Need to Talk About Kevin* by Lionel Shriver. Counterpoint, 2003.
• *The Man Who Loved Children* by Christina Stead. Simon & Schuster, 1940.
• *Christina Stead: A Biography* by Hazel Rowley. Henry Holt, 1994.
• *Two Serious Ladies* by Jane Bowles. Alfred A. Knopf, 1943.
• *A Little Original Sin* by Millicent Dillon. Holt, Rinehart and Winston, 1981.
• *Ivy, the Life of I. Compton-Burnett* by Hilary Spurling. Alfred A. Knopf, 1984.
• *Darkness and Day* by Ivy Compton-Burnett. Victor Gollancz, 1951.
• *Ivy Compton-Burnett* by Kathy Justice Gentile. St. Martin's Press, 1991.
• *Ivy Compton-Burnett: A Memoir* by Cicely Greig. Garnerstone Press, 1972.

• *The Life of Ivy Compton-Burnett* by Elizabeth Sprigge. George Braziller, 1973.

LITTLE RICHARD, HAPPY AT LAST

Playboy; *Jet*

• *The Life and Times of Little Richard* by Charles White. Harmony Books, 1984.
• *Father Divine* by Sara Harris. Collier Books, 1971.

OUTSIDER PORN

Los Angeles Times; *The Baltimore Sun*; *The New York Times*; *The Press of Atlantic City*; *Philadelphia Daily News*; *The Plain Dealer* (Cleveland); *Pittsburgh Post-Gazette*; *New York Post*; *The Washington Post*; *San Luis Obispo County Telegram-Tribune*; *The Eagle-Tribune* (Andover, MA); *The Independent on Sunday* (UK)

Details; *Adult Video News*; *Advocate*; *People*; *GQ*; *The National Enquirer*

www.warholstar.org
www.rainbowhistory.org
www.wikipedia.org

• *Meat: True Homosexual Experiences from S.T.H.*, vol. 1, edited by Boyd McDonald. Gay Sunshine Press, 1981.
• *Speeding: The Old Reliable Photos of David Hurles*, written and designed by Rex. Green Candy Press, 2005.
• *The Big Penis Book*, edited by Dian Hanson. Taschen, 2008.
• *Lovemaps* by John Money. Prometheus Books, 1986.
• *The Great Deluge* by Douglas Brinkley. William Morrow, 2006.

- *The Andy Warhol Diaries*, edited by Pat Hackett. Warner Books, 1989.
- *Ich, die Autobiographie* by Helmut Berger. Ullstein, 2000.

ROOMMATES

Los Angeles Times; The Washington Post; The New York Times

Art & Auction; Vanity Fair; British Vogue; Parkett; Frieze; Vogue Hommes International; Time Out New York

- *Cy Twombly: Catalogue Raisonné of the Paintings, Volume 1, 1948–60.* Schirmer/Mosel, 1992.
- *Letter of Resignation* by Cy Twombly. Schirmer/Mosel, 1991.
- *Lee Lozano: Seek the Extremes*, vol. 2, by Sabine Folie and Lee Lozano. Verlag für Moderne Kunst Nürnberg, 2006.
- *Cy Twombly: Photographs, 1951–2007*. Schirmer/Mosel, 2008.
- *Cy Twombly: Das graphische Werk* by Heiner Bastian. Edition Schellmann, 1984.
- *Cy Twombly: "Bacchus."* Gagosian Gallery, 2005.
- *Airports*. Edition Patrick Frey, Zurich, 1990.
- *Fischli/Weiss: Flowers & Questions*. Tate Publishing, 2007.
- *The Art of Richard Tuttle*, edited by Madeleine Grynsztejn. San Francisco Museum of Modern Art/D.A.P., 2005.
- *A Short Life of Trouble* by Marcia Tucker. University of California Press, 2008.
- *The Problem of Reading* by Moyra Davey. A Documents Book, 2003.
- *Long Life Cool White: Photographs and Essays by Moyra Davey*. Yale University Press, 2008.

CULT LEADER

The Wall Street Journal; Daily Mail (UK); The Baltimore Sun; The Independent (UK); USA Today; San Francisco Chronicle; The Seattle Times; The Washington Post

SOURCES

American Atheist Press

www.catholic.com

www.wikipedia.org

- *Simpson's Contemporary Quotations*, compiled by James B. Simpson; foreword by Daniel J. Boorstin. Houghton Mifflin, 1988.
- *The Karl Lagerfeld Diet* by Karl Lagerfeld and Jean-Claude Houdret. PowerHouse Books, 2005.
- *Love Sex Fear Death* by Timothy Wyllie, edited by Adam Parfrey. Feral House, 2009.
- *The Family* by Ed Sanders. E. P. Dutton & Co., 1971.
- *Holy Anorexia* by Rudolph M. Bell. University of Chicago Press, 1965.
- *America's Most Hated Woman* by Ann Rowe Seaman. Continuum International Publishing Group, 2005.
- *My Life Without God* by William J. Murray. Thomas Nelson Publishers, 1982.
- *Daddy Grace* by Marie W. Dallam. New York University Press, 2007.
- *Jean Rhys* by Carole Angier. André Deutsch, 1990.
- *Ablaze! The Mysterious Fires of Spontaneous Human Combustion* by Larry E. Arnold. M. Evans, 1995.

ACKNOWLEDGMENTS

Big thanks to my assistants Susan Allenback and Trish Schweers for their patience, endless research, and help in editing the manuscript of *Role Models* before I turned it in to the publisher. Trish can actually read my handwriting and decipher the rhythm of my alternative morality, while Susan can zero in on an unclear phrase like a seasoned vice cop busting a streetwise hooker.

I also had great literary detectives working for me: Jim Hollenbaugh, Mathew Bainbridge, Scott Huffines, Kristin Miller, Pat Moran, and Jim West, who tracked down sources and missing persons in my quest for the details of subversive lives. The Maryland State Library Resource Center of the Enoch Pratt Free Library was also invaluable in helping me find obscure information concerning local lunatic history in my hometown, Baltimore. Joan Miller at the Wesleyan Cinema Archives is quite adept at locating obscure news articles I've clipped and shipped off to my collection there, and I thank her for being so organized and diligent in her search for the exact right one, which I sometimes only dimly remembered.

Thomas Keith, an editor at New Directions, accidentally gave me the idea for the book by asking me to write the introduction to the reprint of Tennessee Williams's *Memoirs*. Bill Clegg, my literary agent, knew immediately where to go with *Role Models* and set up this book with the publisher I wanted the most in a quick, painless way. Jonathan Galassi, at Farrar, Straus and Giroux, understands my humor and edited the memoirs with a dignified, kind, decisive respect for filth, brevity, and the twisted logic that healthy, happily damaged readers might understand.

Most important, I thank the role models themselves and their friends and families for letting me poke around in their lives as I tried to understand how they survived with such grace and honor.

OCTOBER 19, 2009